INTERPLANETARY SPACECRAFT

INTERPLANETARY SPACECRAFT

General Editor: Bill Yenne

with
Gary Deichsel, Gary Hudson and Joseph A LeBlanc

Bison Books

First published in 1988 by
Bison Books Ltd
176 Old Brompton Road
London SW5
England

ISBN 0 86124 439 7

Printed in Hong Kong

Captioned by Bill Yenne and Timothy Jacobs.
Designed by Bill Yenne

Picture Credits

All Photos courtesy of the National Aeronautics and Space
Administration with the following exceptions:

Catalyst Research: 78 (bottom, both), 79 (bottom, both)
Collection of the author: 9
Gary Deichsel: 98 (bottom, both), 99 (bottom left)
Ford Aerospace & Communications Corporation's Western
  Development Laboratories: 1
Honeywell: 112
Hughes Aircraft: 23 (top right), 25, 72 (top left), 77
Johns Hopkins University-Applied Physics Laboratory: 55
  (top and bottom)
Lockheed Missiles & Space Company: 72 (bottom left)
Lowell Observatory: 21 (bottom right)
McDonnell Douglas: 28–29, 79 (top)
MIT: 58–59, 61 (top left and right)
Morton Thiokol: 22 (bottom), 23 (bottom)
Pacific American: 27 (top), 94 (bottom), 95 (top left and
  right, bottom)
Promeon Division of Medtronic: 76 (bottom right)
Sony: 45 (top right)
Tandy Corporation: 8
US Geological Survey: 97 (bottom)
US Naval Observatory: 125, 128
© Bill Yenne: 4, 26 (bottom), 31 (bottom), 38 (bottom), 48
  (bottom), 49 (bottom), 82–83, 85 (top right), 110
  (bottom), 111 (bottom), 127

Page 1: This artist's conception of Voyager 2's Saturn flyby
clearly shows the spacecraft's large white high gain
antenna, which was built by Ford Aerospace. The antenna
is made of light weight graphite epoxy, and is the means by
which Voyager transmits its spectacular live television
images back to Earth. Voyager will be active throughout
our lifetimes.

Page 2–3: Saturn and its gigantic ring system dominate this
portrayal of the Voyager 1 flyby in 1980. The Sun can be
seen brightly in the distance, a Saturn moon at lower photo
right, and the bright blue speck just to the left of the Sun is
planet Earth, toward which Voyager's high gain antenna
points. Voyagers 1 and 2 are identical spacecraft.

Below: A proposed spacecraft flyby of the planet Pluto and
its moon Charon, with insertion of the spacecraft into orbit
around the Solar system's most distant known planet.

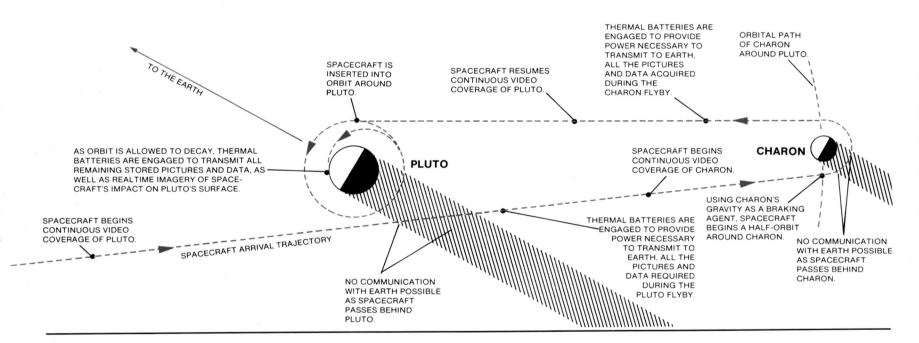

The Panel

Bill Yenne is the San Francisco-based aviation and aerospace
writer who conceived and organized this project and designed this
book. Among his previous works are *The Encyclopedia Of US
Spacecraft*; *Space Shuttle*; *The Astronauts: The First 25 Years Of
Manned Space Flight*; and *The Atlas Of The Solar System*. He has
also written histories of a number of major aerospace companies including Boeing, Lockheed and McDonnell Douglas.

Gary Deichsel is an instrument and electrical designer with the
Chevron Oil Company of California. He was principally responsible
for our discussion of spacecraft trajectory planning.

Gary Hudson is president and chief executive officer of Pacific
American Launch Systems, Incorporated, of Redwood City, California, the designers and builders of the Liberty family of launch
vehicles (*see pages 94–95*). He has also had many years of practical
experience in the field of spacecraft development.

Joseph A LeBlanc is president of American Microsat, a firm
founded to develop both small spacecraft and low-cost infrared
trackers with seekers for use by parks departments, hiking groups,
and for things such as tagging marine coast mammals. American
Microsat is now dedicated to providing all basic overhead services
for small satellites using its Avatar Modular Satellite Systems.
American Microsat has identified all the requirements for a low cost
satellite for use by former Space Shuttle customers whose projects
were bumped from the Shuttle when it was grounded in 1986. The
Avatar design concept, which spans that range effectively, builds on
lower cost components. It is a modular spacecraft that starts with
being one module, 22 inches across and 11 inches long, a little less
than two feet wide, hexagonal, and it will hold everything—power
fixtures, batteries, as well as some payload. Additional propulsion
and three-axis control modules are added when needed.

Mr LeBlanc's background is in spacecraft propulsion systems and
spacecraft systems engineering. He was Lockheed's last Agena en-
gineer—the last man to get any training and assignments on the
Agenas. He left Lockheed at the termination of the last of the Agena
flights in 1983. He is now involved with system engineering studies
of Soviet space systems and also working on Navstar Global
Positioning System Spacecraft and other vehicles. Mr LeBlanc has
engineering degrees from Syracuse University and Stanford University.

In addition to the members of the panel listed above, the general
editor would like to thank **Richard Friedlander** of Medtronic, Inc
(Promeon Division); **Dennis Walstrum** of Morton Thiokol (Elkton
Division) and **Clinton Winchester** of Catalyst Research, for their
special assistance both in supplying material and in reviewing the
manuscript. We'd also like to acknowledge **Emery Wilson** of
Hughes Aircraft, and to extend a special thanks to **Frank O'Donnell**
and **Jeanne Collins** at NASA's Jet Propulsion Laboratory, and **Mike
Gentry** at NASA's Johnson Space Center for their help in supplying
material and information.

TABLE OF CONTENTS

Technical Profiles of Great Interplanetary Spacecraft (edited from NASA data)

INTRODUCTION

by Bill Yenne

nterplanetary spacecraft are just a tiny percentage of the total number of spacecraft that have been launched in the years since Sputnik 1 in 1957, yet they carry a great deal more mystique than their brothers in Earth orbit. Most spacecraft are satellites, meaning that they are intended to orbit the Earth. These spacecraft perform a variety of functions, many of which—such as communications and weather reporting—are an integral part of our daily lives. Others include navigation and military reconnaissance satellites, as well as manned spacecraft and space stations. The early spacecraft launched by the Soviet Union and the United States in the 1950s essentially were designed to demonstrate that it was *possible* to put a satellite into orbit. Gradually, spacecraft began to carry more and more sophisticated scientific experiments and in 1962 they became viable as commercial ventures when Telstar, the first privately owned communications satellite, was launched by NASA for AT&T.

In the 1960s and early 1970s, a number of spacecraft were launched by the Soviet Union and the United States and directed—beyond Earth orbit—to the Moon. Because the Moon is not a planet, these were not technically interplanetary spacecraft, but the designing and planning was much the same and as such, these lunar probes set the stage for the true interplanetary spacecraft that were to follow.

In 1966 and 1967 the exploration of the Earth's nearest neighbor came of age. Four American Surveyor and one Soviet Luna spacecraft accomplished successful soft landings on the Moon, and five American Lunar Orbiters conducted an orbital mapping program that photographed practically the entire Lunar surface. The successes of the Surveyor and Lunar Orbiter programs gave the United States the experience that made it possible for it to send nine manned spacecraft and 27 men to the Moon starting in 1968, and a dozen of these men to the surface itself.

The six manned Apollo spacecraft that landed on the Moon's surface between 1969 and 1972 were something of an anomaly. They showed the potential and the promise for further manned exploration of the Moon, a permanent base there and manned expeditions to other worlds in the Solar System. It was, however, a potential and promise that went unfulfilled. The Soviet Union gave up on its attempts to send men to the Moon, and the United States dismantled its incredible Apollo program and shelved plans that were in progress for a manned mission to Mars in 1981.

Both countries did go forward in building upon the tremendous fund of knowledge that they had accumulated in their unpiloted Lunar probes—knowledge that included the remote control of delicate machinery a quarter of a million miles into space.

Compared to the thousands of Earth-orbiting satellites and the dozens of lunar probes, there have been relatively few successful interplanetary spacecraft. Venus has been visited by a number of spacecraft, including the American Pioneer Venus that conducted extensive radar mapping of the cloud-shrouded planet after it was inserted into Venusian orbit in December 1978, and the Soviet Venera series spacecraft, which have included both orbiters and landers. Mars, our other close neighbor in the Solar System, was observed and mapped by four American Mariner spacecraft between 1965 and 1971, and in 1976 two American Viking spacecraft successfully landed on the surface of the red planet. The landers then went on to return data for several years.

Beyond these probes to our two nearest neighbors in the Solar System, however, the list of planetary encounters is very small indeed. The American Mariner 10 spacecraft, launched in November 1973, was maneuvered into three flybys of the planet Mercury between February 1974 and March 1975, and the excellent photographs that it transmitted back to Earth are the only close-up photographs ever taken of the first planet from the Sun.

Today, the relics of dozens of Earthly expeditions—manned and unmanned—rest quietly in our Moon's gray dust. The 'USA' and 'CCCP' labels can also be found on hardware parked on the surfaces of both Mars and Venus. Only four man-made objects, however,

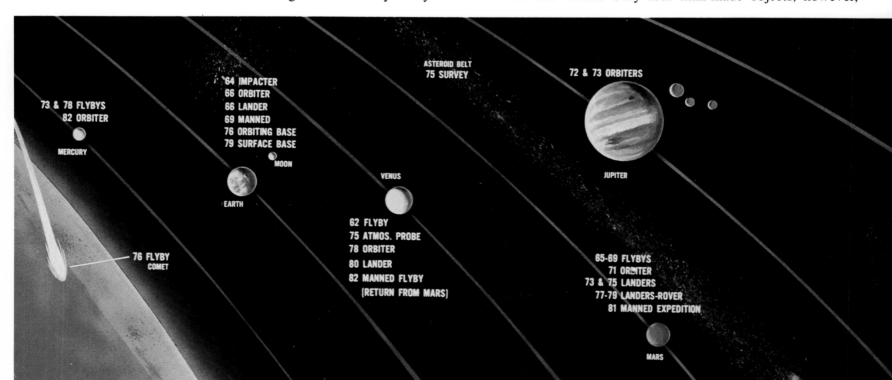

have pierced the darkness beyond the inner Solar System. All were built by NASA's Jet Propulsion Laboratory (JPL) in Pasadena, California and were launched between March 1972 and August 1977. These were Pioneer 10, launched 3 March 1972; Pioneer 11, launched 6 April 1973; Voyager 1, launched 5 September 1977; and Voyager 2, launched ahead of its twin on 20 August 1977. Pioneer 10 passed Jupiter in December 1973, while Pioneer 11 passed Jupiter in December 1974 and Saturn in September 1979 (*see pages 50–51*). The closest views of these, the two largest planets in the Solar System, came with the arrivals of the Voyagers (with Voyager 1 now ahead of its brother), which passed Jupiter in March and July 1979, and Saturn in November 1980 and August 1981 (*see pages 86–93*).

Voyager 1 had its trajectory altered in order to fly past Saturn's moon, Titan, so it was directed north of the ecliptic plane of the planets and hence out of the 'populated' part of the Solar System. Voyager 2, on the other hand, was maintained in a trajectory that allowed it to conduct mankind's first robot reconnaissance of the planets Uranus (January 1986) and Neptune (September 1989). Thus, four expeditions launched in the 1970s went to Jupiter, three of them went to Saturn, then one to Uranus and Neptune, yet *none* to Pluto.

The American Galileo Jupiter observer project, which was scheduled for launch in 1986 before the grounding of the Space Shuttle system, is the only expedition currently planned which will travel to any of the five planets of the outer Solar System in the twentieth century.

Although Voyager 2 will continue to fulfill its destiny twelve years after launch with its 1989 rendezvous with Neptune, the idea of planetary exploration has lost momentum back home on Earth. Because of the postponement of Galileo, the United States will launch no planetary probe of any kind during the 1980s; the Soviets will launch far fewer than they did during the 1970s, with these restricted to the Venera Venus probes and a projected mission to the Martian moon Phobos.

In the late 1960s NASA laid out a far-reaching program of planetary exploration that not only called for a manned mission to Mars in 1981, but also a manned flyby of Venus in 1982 and an unmanned grand tour of all the outer planets, and Jupiter and Saturn orbiters by the mid-1980s (*see illustration, pages 6–7*). Of these grandiose plans, only Voyager 2's spectacular visits to Jupiter, Saturn and Uranus have come close to fulfilling the dream of the old grand tour scheme.

Since that brief 1973-77 window in mankind's history, the active exploration of the outer Solar System has gone into retrenchment. Certainly the high cost of mounting these missions has been a deterrent, but in the ensuing years the spirit of exploration that made the Pioneers and Voyagers a reality has not diminished. Technology has continued to evolve. It should be remembered that in the early to mid-1970s when these spacecraft were being developed, such now commonplace items as hand-held calculators, digital wristwatches

and home satellite dishes were virtually unheard of. When the Voyagers were launched in 1977 the home computer revolution had not yet occurred; today's desk-top models can be as sophisticated as the huge main-frame computers that helped designers develop the Voyagers.

The enduring spirit of exploration and the accessibility of the Voyager technology inspired us to develop this book. Because it is our objective to examine the hands-on development of an interplanetary spacecraft, we will parallel our design and development program with a full description of the Voyager spacecraft project simply because it probably was the most advanced interplanetary spacecraft ever built (*see pages 86–91*). We will also consider many of the details of the Mariner, Pioneer and Viking projects as well. Whereas these programs were once on the leading edge of technology, much of this sophistication has now become mainstream. Today, therefore, it is now possible to build simple interplanetary spacecraft for a fraction of the previous cost. It would certainly be counterproductive to undertake a project of this scope without a close study of other spacecraft, their design, their deployment into the deepest reaches of the Solar System, so we have included technical profiles of these spacecraft as well.

At left: **This was the 1969 projection by NASA of its exploration of the Solar System through 1982.** *Above:* **The Voyager 1 liftoff in September 1977. Voyager 1 transmitted spectacular images of Jupiter in March 1979, and of Saturn in November 1980, and will continue to transmit data as it goes beyond the outer fringes of the known Solar System.**

SOLAR SYSTEM EXPLORATION PLAN

NEPTUNE

URANUS

PLUTO

GRAND TOUR
OUTER PLANETS

77 FLYBY (J-S-P)
79 FLYBY (J-U-N)

SATURN

A. Project Overview

The objective of this book is to provide a detailed look into the development processes and inner workings of interplanetary spacecraft, by taking you, the reader, through the initial steps required to build one.

Our spacecraft will be a hypothetical interplanetary observer designed to travel into the outer Solar System and to transmit photographic images back to Earth (*see pages 114–120*). We've selected Pluto as our objective in this hypothetical study because it is the outermost planet (and hence the biggest challenge), and because it is not the subject of any existing planetary exploration project, and as such, it is an enigma.

Spoiled by the spectacular Viking photographs of Mars and the splendid Voyager imagery of Jupiter, Saturn, Uranus and their moons, one feels cheated by the complete lack of photographs of Pluto and its moon Charon. We know the Galilean moons of Jupiter in relative detail and we have even seen maps of Uranus' awesome Titania, but there is no one on Earth who has the faintest idea what Pluto looks like. We don't know whether its surface is icy or gaseous—we don't even know its exact size, or what color it is!

The immediate reaction when one is faced with the need for photographs is simply to go out and take them. In this case, however, the idea at first seems impossible but upon consideration one questions that conclusion. Much of the advanced technology born in the American space program in the 1960s and 1970s has become commonplace in the 1980s. Ironically, much of this technology was originally developed in connection with far-reaching and, at the time, highly speculative projects aimed at exploring our Solar System—and beyond. This book explains how this same technology could now be applied to its *original purpose*—the exploration of interplanetary space—far more easily than a decade ago and at a fraction of the original cost.

Our hypothetical spacecraft could use a common backyard satellite dish for communications (*see pages 36–39*), radio-controlled gas jets for directional orientation (*see page 29*), and would carry an off-the-shelf video camera (*see pages 42–46, 114–125*) that would take low-light photos of Pluto and transmit them back to Earth where they could be received by NASA's Deep Space Network (DSN). Because there would be no need for the video camera to utilize the moving parts of a tape drive, there would be a good chance it could survive up to ten years in the frigid (-459.67° F) environment of deep space.

The four major components of any spacecraft project are (a) the spacecraft itself (*see Part One*), (b) the launch system (*see Part Two*), (c) the trajectory program (*see Part Three*), and finally (d) communications (*see Part Four*). The proper planning of each of these components is vital to the successful completion of the project. These components are previewed briefly on pages 10 through 13.

*Above:*Scientists of 20 years ago would be utterly astonished at the plethora of sophisticated electronics that are available to the average consumer today. Much of this technology originally developed as a spinoff of space exploration systems—see the text, this page. *At right:* Hypothetical spacecraft date back to Jules Verne's writings before the turn of the century, but in the November 1946 issue of *Air Trails Pictorial*, astrophysics writer Willy Ley described how a manned moonship might be built with *existing* components! Like Leonardo da Vinci's airplanes 500 years before, the only problem was power—or in this case, thrust. This was overcome by using a series of ever more powerful stages, a procedure that Werner von Braun had developed in 1944, but which was not actually used until the late 1940s, and not used to put a craft into space until the late 1950s.

In his 1946 illustration, artist Frank Tinsley shows here a hypothetical spaceship, based on the World War II-era, German V-2 design, and incorporating many fully tested devices and principles. The hull is essentially a cylindrical, stressed skin structure, 80 feet long and 10 feet in outside diameter. It is double walled, with very efficient insulation. The extreme nose contains a series of glass fiber parachutes to be used for vertical stabilization in atmospheric landings, with actual deceleration effected by the main jet. Below the chute hold is space for recording cameras, cosmic ray detectors, and other instruments. Beneath this is the upper deck of the pressurized control cabin.

Next is a compartment packed with mechanisms; autopilot, gyrostabilizer, air and temperature control plant, radio and radar installations, etc. An airlock gives access to the outside through a two-piece door, the lower part of which serves as a platform when open. Below the crew space, the fuel and oxidizer tanks occupy more than a third of the ship's length, and beneath them is the rocket engine, with its pumps and plumbing. Worm-gear driven tubular legs in the fins permit levelling the ship for takeoff.

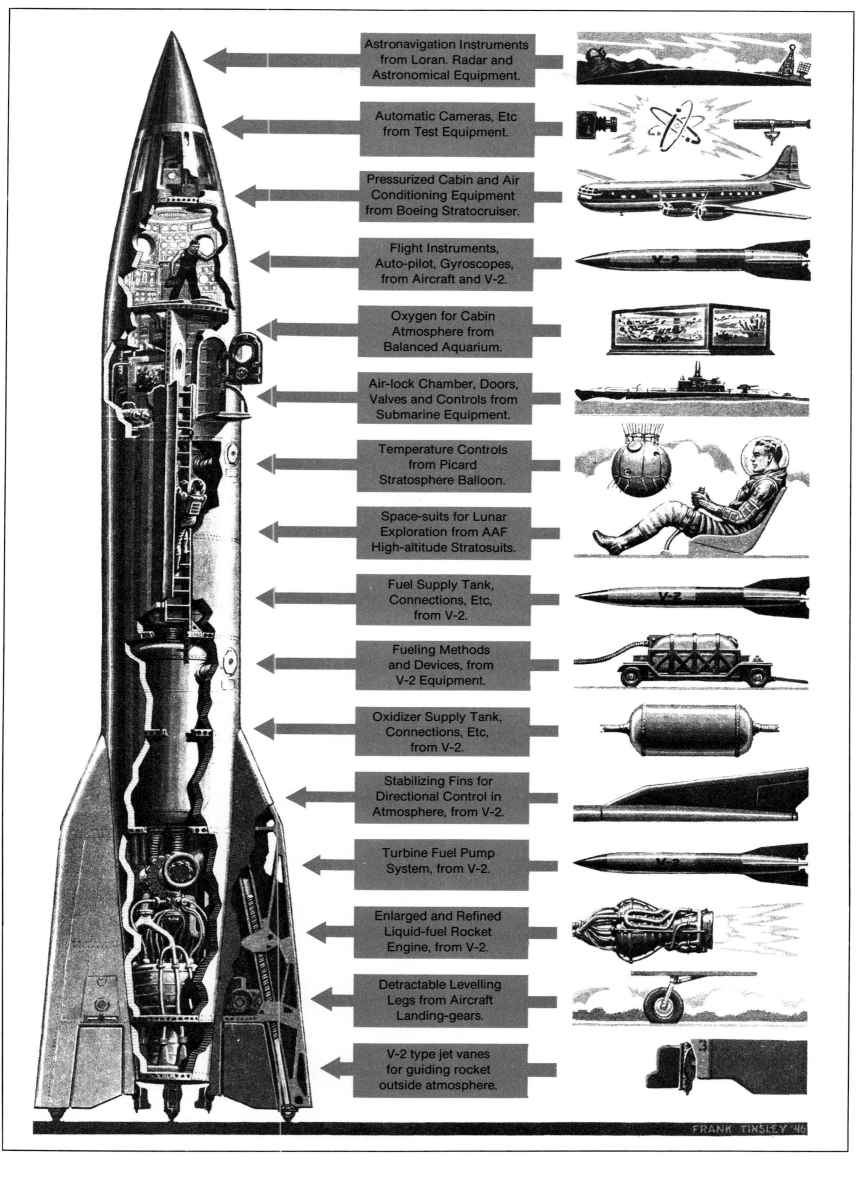

Astronavigation Instruments from Loran. Radar and Astronomical Equipment.

Automatic Cameras, Etc from Test Equipment.

Pressurized Cabin and Air Conditioning Equipment from Boeing Stratocruiser.

Flight Instruments, Auto-pilot, Gyroscopes, from Aircraft and V-2.

Oxygen for Cabin Atmosphere from Balanced Aquarium.

Air-lock Chamber, Doors, Valves and Controls from Submarine Equipment.

Temperature Controls from Picard Stratosphere Balloon.

Space-suits for Lunar Exploration from AAF High-altitude Stratosuits.

Fuel Supply Tank, Connections, Etc, from V-2.

Fueling Methods and Devices, from V-2 Equipment.

Oxidizer Supply Tank, Connections, Etc, from V-2.

Stabilizing Fins for Directional Control in Atmosphere, from V-2.

Turbine Fuel Pump System, from V-2.

Enlarged and Refined Liquid-fuel Rocket Engine, from V-2.

Detractable Levelling Legs from Aircraft Landing-gears.

V-2 type jet vanes for guiding rocket outside atmosphere.

FRANK TINSLEY '46

The Spacecraft
(see Part One, pages 16–85)

In the design of a spacecraft one must take into account both the missions that one wants it to accomplish, and the duration of the flight. As we've noted, the simpler the mission, the simpler the spacecraft. The early spacecraft launched by the Soviet Union and the United States were intended for short duration and orbits within a couple of hundred miles of the Earth's surface. As space launches became routine it was theoretically possible to replace a failed Earth-orbit satellite in a couple of days if a second one was available for launch. It takes less than an hour to place a spacecraft into Earth orbit and even a round trip to the Moon can be accomplished in about a week. Interplanetary missions, on the other hand, cover distances of billions of miles over years of time. The Vikings took just under a year to reach Mars, while Voyager 2 took four years to reach Saturn and twelve to reach Neptune.

When planning a spacecraft, one must therefore consider it as a precious and irreplaceable piece of hardware. If an automobile broke down after eight years, we could replace it. If an interplanetary spacecraft broke down after eight years on a nine year mission to Pluto, it would be at least 10 years before we could get another spacecraft into position, and a total of 18 years would have been spent on the effort to get back to the point of the failure.

It is for this reason that a great deal of care must go into the design, construction and testing of a spacecraft. NASA's interplanetary spacecraft were designed with myriad back-up systems. *Redundancy* became a watchword. If one system failed, another identical system would have to be present to take its place because there are no repairmen 100 million miles into interplanetary space. The idea of redundancy was even behind the idea of launching *two* identical Voyagers. The second spacecraft was in itself a redundancy.

Luckily, in these cases, both spacecraft functioned as planned and Earthly observers were treated to double the data. But had a single spacecraft been employed, Murphy's Law would almost certainly have intervened—to the detriment of the entire mission.

The development cost for two spacecraft is roughly 150 percent the cost of one and as such is recommended. As with any type of product, the unit cost declines rather sharply as the number of units increases. The cost of three would, for example, *probably* not exceed *double* the cost of one, provided all three were identical and produced simultaneously. An additional spacecraft should also be produced for use in testing.

Testing is an essential part of the preflight development of a spacecraft and can consume as much time as building the craft itself. It may take two or three years to build a spacecraft and it can easily take a year to test. The first tests should be directed toward confirming that the components will function (a) in the frigid vacuum of space and (b) over the nine to ten year duration of the mission. In the case of the pacemaker-type batteries which we suggest be used as a principal power source, the manufacturer has already undertaken some rather rigorous endurance testing (*see page 76*).

Additional tests should include acoustic vibration tests, to determine whether the spacecraft and its components will withstand the noise and violent vibrations that it will experience during launch. The Lockheed Missiles & Space Company in Sunnyvale, California maintains a huge accoustical facility for this type of testing.

This book will also discuss a package of rather basic photographic and scientific experiments (*pages 42–63*), along with a revolutionary system of landing probes which could be considered as an option. The latter would add to the overall cost and weight, but they would also add tremendously to the value of the spacecraft once it reached the vicinity of another celestial body.

A final general consideration in the design of a spacecraft is the cost/weight ratio. It may be possible to buy a number of the required electronic components 'off-the-shelf.' However, by custom-building a single board of chips (*see page 31*) we might be able to reduce the overall weight of the electronics by half. Throughout the design of a spacecraft the cost of individual components must be carefully measured against their launch weight (*see pages 22–26, 82 and references thereon*). Even a few ounces may later be offset by saving thousands of pounds of thrust when it comes to the launch (*see page 94*).

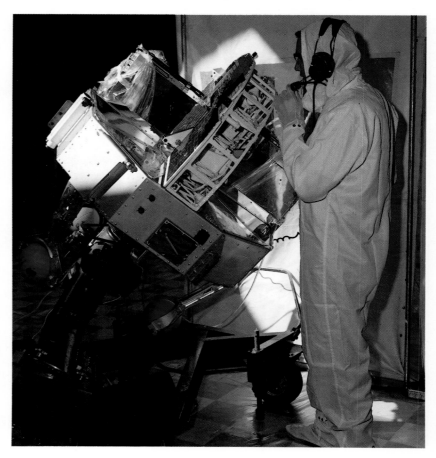

Above: The NOAA 7 environmental satellite in preparation. Note the 'clean suit' worn by the technician to protect the satellite's sensitive systems. *Below:* OSO 2, built to conduct solar observations, with a similarly suited technician. *At right:* Viking Mars lander number 1 before being sealed in its capsule, and *above right*, after being sealed in its capsule. See also the photos on pages 69 and 71. The sterile capsule prevented contamination of Mars by Earth bacteria, and eliminated false 'life readings' which could be caused by same.

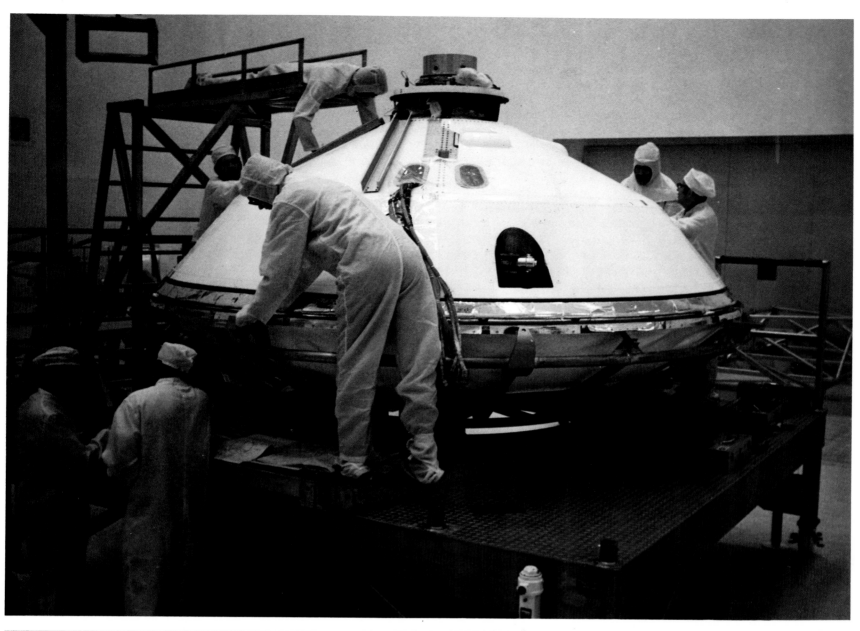

The Launch (see Part Two, Pages 94–97)

Launching a spacecraft is perhaps the most critical few minutes of the entire project. Designing and building a spacecraft may take two or more years. The spacecraft may take five years or more to reach its objective in space. It takes less than an hour to fire up a launch vehicle or booster rocket and place a spacecraft beyond the Earth's atmosphere. Those minutes, however, contain the greatest potential hazard for the project and for the spacecraft itself.

The construction of the spacecraft is marked by delicacy; the launch phase of the project is marked by brute force—the brute force necessary to escape the Earth's atmosphere and put our spacecraft on its way into interplanetary space.

Although a spacecraft *could* literally be built in someone's garage, a launch vehicle might stand taller than a ten-story building and would require a flat open area of several square miles for its launch.

Because of the wide selection of launch vehicles now on the market, the cost of designing and developing a launch vehicle for a single launch probably would not be worth it. Therefore, we will focus our attention on the development of a spacecraft and select an existing launch system. Specifically, we will be discussing the project with the launch vehicles of Pacific American Launch Systems of Redwood City, California in mind (*see also Page 21*).

Below: The Apollo/Saturn 5 space vehicle lifts off on 18 May 1969, carrying the Apollo 10 astronauts to a lunar orbital mission. The Saturn 5 was the most powerful launch vehicle ever (see the table on the facing page). A manned planetary mission would require a much larger rocket, but a small (120 pounds) payload could be launched to the far corners of the Solar System with a rocket a third as tall as the 363-foot Saturn 5. (See Part 2 of text.)

The Trajectory (see Part Three, pages 98–113)

In its simplest terms, planning a trajectory means aiming a spacecraft at a target. In the Solar System, however, the Earth is a *moving platform* from which we are aiming at a *moving target* tens or hundreds of millions of miles away. The simplicity is further qualified by a concern with a delicate projectile that will be traveling thousands of miles per hour for several years. A tiny miscalculation could put our spacecraft hundreds of thousands of miles off course.

Other considerations in planning a trajectory might include the gravitational effects of other planets. For example, the route to Pluto may cross the path of Jupiter or perhaps Saturn. In planning the trajectories for their Voyager spacecraft, NASA's engineers cleverly used the massive gravitational force of these grand bodies as a slingshot to give the spacecraft an extra push into deeper and more distant space.

Communications (see Part Four, Pages 114–125)

Anyone who has ever operated a radio-controlled model knows that such a model can be operated only within the range of the transmitter. Beyond that range, the model simply cannot be controlled. The principle of communicating with—and controlling—our spacecraft is basically little different than controlling a model airplane but the distances are phenomenally greater. Pluto is nearly four billion miles away and radio signals can take more than five hours to reach a spacecraft in the vicinity of that planet.

B. Manned Interplanetary Spacecraft

The complexities of *manned* space flight are enormous. Only two countries—the United States and the Soviet Union—have developed the means of sending a manned craft into Earth orbit and only one spacecraft has ever been developed which successfully transported human beings *beyond* Earth orbit. Nine of these—the American Apollo series spacecraft—took their three-man crews to the Moon and back, a round-trip distance of about a half million miles.

Flown between 1968 and 1972, the Apollo program missions proved that it was technically feasible for human beings to travel beyond Earth orbit, but they also demonstrated that such an effort is extremely costly. Where an unmanned spacecraft might cost a million dollars, a manned spacecraft would several billions to develop—not to mention the cost of the hardware and manpower necessary for crew training. To take this a step further, the dollar cost of a manned mission *beyond* Earth orbit would be exponentially greater. The Apollo program cost $25.4 billion in 1967, which in turn translates to about $75 billion in 1987 dollars, vastly more than any individual or corporation could afford for a purely scientific project. Apollo succeeded in sending nine spacecraft to the vicinity of the moon and six of them to the lunar surface. The cost of a *single manned interplanetary* mission, however, could cost *ten times* what Apollo did.

For example, take the scale of launching a manned interplanetary mission in terms of the size of the launch vehicle required. The Saturn 5 which was designed for the Apollo program was the largest launch vehicle ever put into service in history. The table below puts this into perspective:

Launch Vehicle	Application	Total Thrust, all stages (in millions of pounds)
Titan 3	2-man Earth orbit mission (Gemini)	0.60
Delta	typical Earth satellite missions	1.00
Saturn 1B	3-man Earth orbit missions (Apollo)	1.60
Titan 3/Centaur	Voyager and Viking unmanned interplanetary probes	3.00
Space Shuttle	2 to 8-person Earth orbit mission with heavy payloads	6.70
Saturn 5	Apollo 3-man Lunar missions	9.00
Liberty 1C	Current hypothetical Interplanetary project	0.06

It is also useful to compare the weights of manned and unmanned spacecraft. Typical Earth orbit weather and communications satellites generally weigh between 1500 and 2500 pounds, while interplanetary spacecraft weigh less. Pioneers 10 and 11 weighed 570 pounds and the Voyagers weighed about 1800 pounds. The Viking spacecraft with both their orbiting *and landing* modules weighed about 7500 pounds.

Manned spacecraft, meanwhile, required a great deal of extra weight for life support. The Apollo 11 Command/Service Module component (nicknamed *Columbia*) weighed 63,493 pounds and the Apollo 11 Landing Module, *Eagle*, added an additional 33,205 pounds, for a total of nearly 50 tons including fuel weight. (The Space Shuttle Orbiters weigh between 148,000 and 153,000 pounds *without* fuel or payload.)

A major factor in the consideration of any manned mission is *time*, because people have to breathe and eat even while the spacecraft is just traveling through space. The Apollo lunar missions, the only manned space flight beyond Earth orbit, required six days simply for the roundtrip, while a manned mission to Mars—one of the two nearest planets—would require a minimum of a year or two, simply for *travel* time, not to mention the surface time. The Apollo Lunar missions spent no more than three days on the moon, but one would expect to spend at least a couple of weeks on a planet such as Mars if one were spending a year just to get there. (The manned Mars landing mission that NASA once had scheduled for 1981 envisioned a surface stay of 30 days).

A human being could probably be supported for a short duration Earth orbit mission within a two-ton spacecraft, but an interplanetary mission probably would require a spacecraft far heavier than Apollo and a launch vehicle much larger than a Saturn 5. For an interplanetary mission, a human being or a crew of them would require not only a large payload of food, water and oxygen, but a spacecraft large enough to provide adequate living and exercise space.

Beyond the enormity in terms of both cost and weight, there are a myriad of physiological and psychological questions that are yet to be answered. No human being has attempted to spend two years in space, much less the twenty years that current technology would require for a round trip to Pluto. The Soviet Union has had several cosmonauts staffing its space stations for periods exceeding 150 days, but serious, and frequently unexpected, physiological and psychological difficulties have been encountered. The Soviets are today seriously looking at ways to overcome all of the obstacles that would make a two-year manned Mars mission possible, but it will be many years before manned space flight, even to the nearest planets, will be practical.

In summary, we don't mean to imply that manned interplanetary space travel is impossible. It is, however, so costly with current technology that it would require a seriously mobilized effort combining the resources of an entire nation or even a group of nations. As such, it is beyond the scope of this book.

Above: **This 1969 artist's conception shows the immense size of the spacecraft which was envisioned to carry US astronauts to Mars and back again in 1981. Landing would have involved a landing module similar to, but larger than, the Apollo Command Module (on top).**

13

Mariner 3 and Mariner 4

The launch vehicle for each spacecraft was an Atlas-Agena D, which was a 360,000-pound-thrust Atlas D first stage with a 15,500-pound-thrust Agena D second stage (the first NASA use of Agena D). Their height was 104 feet.

These Mariners had an octagonal magnesium main body, 50 inches across. A high-gain dish was mounted atop the main structure along with low-gain antenna on top of an aluminum tube. Four solar panels extended from top side of the octagon, with solar pressure vanes, each seven square feet of aluminized mylar sheet, attached to end of each solar panel. The spacecraft itself was 9.5 feet high, 22.6 feet across, and weighed 575 pounds.

The project objectives were to perform two planetary experiments during Mars fly-by (the aiming zone centered 8600 miles from surface) and six interplanetary experiments along the spacecraft's trajectory. The mission was also intended to provide engineering experience in spacecraft operation during long-duration flight away from the Sun. The project was designed for a flight distance of 350 million miles to reach Mars (about eight and one-half months flight time) and a communication distance of 150 million miles at the time of planetary encounter.

The spacecraft payload included a single camera to take up to 21 still photos during flyby along with playback capability for real-time transmission in digital form to Earth which was expected to take 8.3 hours per photo. A second planetary experiment, occulation studies of Martian atmospheric pressure, was to be based on spacecraft transmissions as it passed behind the planet. Interplanetary experiments included a solar plasma probe, ionization chamber, solid-state radiation detector (with three Geiger-Mueller tubes), helium vector magnetometer, cosmic ray telescope and two cosmic dust detectors. The spacecraft attitude control system employed 12 nitrogen gas jets, three gyros, sun sensors and a Canopus Star Tracker, plus the solar pressure vanes. A hydrazine-fueled engine with 51 pounds of thrust was carried for up to two midcourse corrections. The central computer and sequencer were provided to control mission sequences. A combination of painted and polished surfaces, thermal shields, insulation and louvers were employed for temperature control. Power was supplied by 28,224 solar cells and silver-zinc batteries.

Mariner 3 was successfully placed in parking orbit following launch from Cape Kennedy on 5 November 1964. Earth escape trajectory was achieved by a second Agena burn but the spacecraft did not reach the planned speed of 25,661 mph and subsequently failed to extend its solar panels, and to acquire the Sun and Canopus. Project officials concluded that Mariner 3's *fiberglass* shroud did not completely jettison, as scheduled five and one-half minutes after launch. Tests indicated that the fiberglass shroud's inner layer separated under combined stresses of aerodynamic heating and rapid pressure drop at altitude. Transmissions ceased nine hours after launch and the spacecraft was in solar orbit.

Equipped with a *magnesium* shroud, Mariner 4 was successfully launched from Cape Kennedy on 28 November 1964 and injected into a Mars trajectory with a 'miss distance' of 151,000 miles. The spacecraft acquired Canopus on November 30, after first locking on several wrong stars. The midcourse maneuver was successfully carried out December 5. By firing the engine for 20.06 seconds, the trajectory was altered so that Mariner 4 would pass behind Mars and within 5400 miles of planet. A second correction was not required. On 7 December, Canopus lock was lost, but was reacquired on 17 December. A programmed switch from cavity amplifier to TWT amplifier on 13 December increased the spacecraft's transmitter power level, and telemetry rate was reduced to eight and one-third bits per second on 3 January 1965. On 10 January the spacecraft was traveling 8624 mph relative to Earth and 70,099 mph relative to the Sun, and had traveled a total of 74.5 million miles. Travel distance to Mars was 325 million miles and the planet was 134 million miles from Earth during Mariner 4's flyby, which occurred on 14 July 1965.

Figure 1: Schematic drawing of the Mariner 3/4 Spacecraft Configuration.

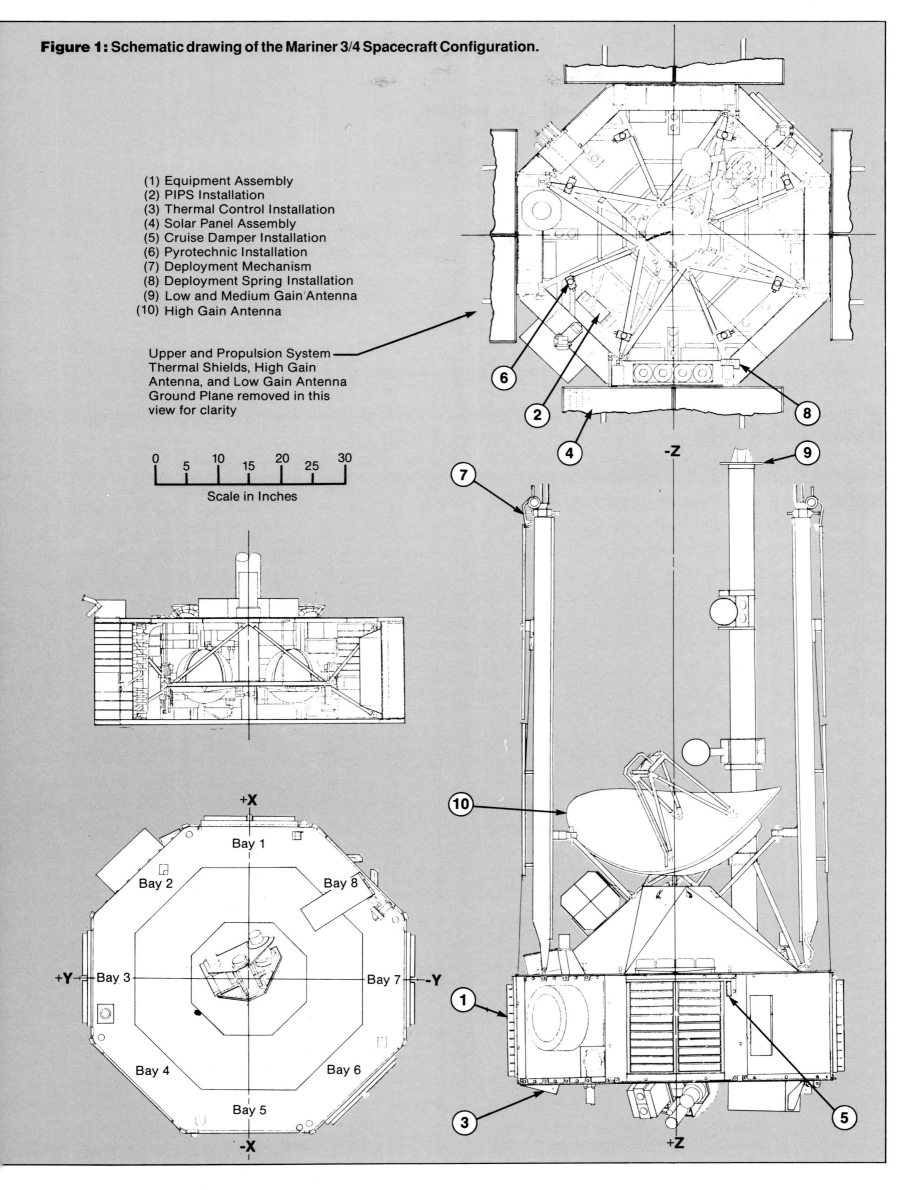

(1) Equipment Assembly
(2) PIPS Installation
(3) Thermal Control Installation
(4) Solar Panel Assembly
(5) Cruise Damper Installation
(6) Pyrotechnic Installation
(7) Deployment Mechanism
(8) Deployment Spring Installation
(9) Low and Medium Gain Antenna
(10) High Gain Antenna

Upper and Propulsion System Thermal Shields, High Gain Antenna, and Low Gain Antenna Ground Plane removed in this view for clarity

Scale in Inches

15

PART ONE

THE SPACECRAFT

A. Overall Design

Objectives and Launch Requirements

The objective in our hypothetical case study is to build a spacecraft that will travel to Pluto, photograph the planet and transmit these photos to Earth via digital telemetry (television) (*see pages 42–46 and 114–120*).

For this, one needs an upper stage rocket motor to propel the craft (*see pages 22–30*), a computer to control the craft's subsystems (*see page 31*), an antenna for transmissions to and from Earth (*see pages 36–38*), the camera and other scientific subsystems (*see pages 42–63*) and finally, the electrical source to power the computer, the transmissions and other subsystems (*see pages 70–80*). They must not only be able to survive for up to 10 years in the hostile, frigid vacuum of interplanetary space, but to function flawlessly when called upon. At the same time, they must be small and light enough to meet the requirements of the launch vehicle.

By using the Liberty C configuration—the largest launch vehicle built by Pacific American Launch Systems—one could plan a Pluto flyby (*see pages 98–111*) with a 100-120 pound spacecraft. The size is also dictated by the 55 inch interior diameter of the Liberty 1C. The 100-120 pounds include only the weight of the spacecraft and not the fuel it would carry. In this case, there would be an 800 pound propellant stage attached to the spacecraft (*see pages 22–29*). Those 800 pounds include the hardware as well as the propellant (fuel plus oxydizer). This would result in a *total weight budget* of 920 pounds (*see tables, pages 26, 30, 32, 46, and 82*).

The propellant typically weighs about 720 pounds, or 90 percent of the total. The weight of the propellant is, of course, relative to the amount of work that the spacecraft motor must do. A trajectory that would take the spacecraft to Pluto by way of Jupiter would save both propellant and time. However, that also has a disadvantage. The design of the spacecraft itself would have to be significantly different if one went to Pluto by way of Jupiter rather than to Pluto directly because the radiation problem at Jupiter is extremely severe. All four of the spacecraft (Pioneers 10 and 11, and Voyagers 1 and 2) that have been to Jupiter have suffered radiation degradation effects. They were designed specifically for the levels they were expected to encounter and they survived because they were completely shielded and thus were prepared. The Jupiter encounter was the principle structural and shielding requirement in the whole of those programs, dominating everything else—including the thermal shielding, the G loading, and the launch. Surviving Jovian radiation was the dominant factor for all the weight calculations. Nature imposes a radiation penalty for doing almost anything around Jupiter (*see pages 32 and 102–109*).

To transmit and receive intelligible radio signals at that distance, a large diameter antenna designed with adequate radiation hardening to deal with Jovian radiation is needed. If one didn't have to deal with the radiation, one could build a large, flexible lightweight antenna.

The Pioneer and Voyager antennas were solid one-piece castings, but the size of the launch vehicle permitted a sufficient diameter. In the case of our hypothetical spacecraft (the size of the Liberty 1C), it might be necessary to use a folded antenna that deploys to the necessary minimum of nine feet after it is in space. There are two types of folding antenna which might be considered: the *umbrella* type and the *rib-wrap* type (*see pages 36–38*). The former unfolds like its namesake, while the latter is spring-loaded and unfurls from a fixed axle when released. It is the most complicated. A rib-wrap antenna light enough for use in our spacecraft probably would not function in the Jovian environment because it couldn't be shielded properly. The antenna that NASA used in building the Galileo spacecraft is rib-wrapped for storage, and is very heavy. Because the antenna has to transmit from Jupiter at a high data rate, it must also survive the Jovian radiation. One of the things that makes survival possible is that Galileo is not going in very close to Jupiter itself. The project is more interested in Jupiter's moons. It won't get as close to Jupiter as an interplanetary probe such as ours would need to go for the gravity slingshot effect.

If one goes by way of Jupiter, the antenna that would be required must weigh at least 100-150 pounds itself, in order to survive the launch structurally, be big enough to collect transmitted data, and to *survive the radiation*. To get to Jupiter or to get to Pluto by way of Jupiter, a spacecraft first would have to survive a passage, essentially through hell.

It is possible—as Pioneer and Voyager proved—but it dominates spacecraft design. The weight factor would be more than double if the craft went by way of Jupiter, rather than going directly to Pluto. If a spacecraft were to go directly to Pluto it could probably be built at 120 pounds, whereas the minimum for Jupiter would be 300-350 pounds. By using radiation-hardened materials, the craft could be a little lighter, but the cost would be tremendous because the technology is very expensive, and largely classified.

This avenue is therefore not considered because one of the functions of this book is to demonstrate how such a mission could be flown using off-the-shelf components.

continued on page 21

At right: **Jupiter, the gate guardian of the outer Solar System. Like a traveller in the same Roman mythology from which this awesome monster derives its name, any spacecraft wishing to venture past Jupiter must first survive the withering blast of its radiation. Also like a mythic hero, such spacecraft's survival depends upon the strength of its 'armor'—in this case, actual shielding, as well as redundant backup systems.**

Technical Profiles of Great Interplanetary Spacecraft

Mariner 5

Launched by an Atlas-Agena D, Mariner 5 was actually the modified Mariner 4 backup spacecraft. Its main body was a magnesium octagon 50 inches across and 20 inches high. Four solar panels deployed from top, high-gain ellipse antenna mounted on superstructure atop body and 88-inch tube on top supported low-gain omnidirectional antenna and helium magnetometer. In flight the spacecraft was 18 feet across solar panels, 9.5 feet high, weighing 540 pounds.

It was intended to pass within 2000 miles of Venus to provide data on the structure of that planet's atmosphere, and its radiation and magnetic field environment. Mariner 5 also was designed to return data on the interplanetary environment before and after planetary encounter.

Planetary experiments included S-band occulation based on spacecraft telemetry signals and UV photometry of upper atmosphere atomic hydrogen and oxygen radiation using three

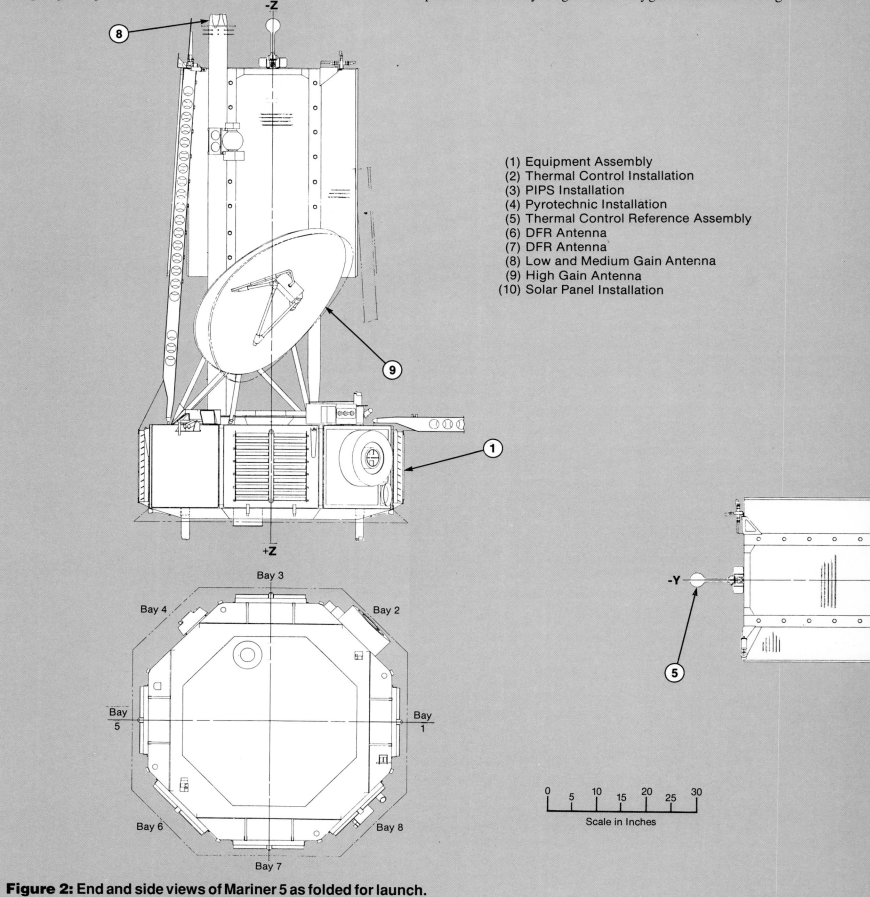

(1) Equipment Assembly
(2) Thermal Control Installation
(3) PIPS Installation
(4) Pyrotechnic Installation
(5) Thermal Control Reference Assembly
(6) DFR Antenna
(7) DFR Antenna
(8) Low and Medium Gain Antenna
(9) High Gain Antenna
(10) Solar Panel Installation

Scale in Inches

Figure 2: End and side views of Mariner 5 as folded for launch.

photomultiplier tubes. Dual frequency (423.3 and 49.8 MHz) propagation, trapped radiation, magnetic field, solar plasma and celestial mechanics experiments were intended to provide data throughout flight. The data automation system handled data from five experiments. The communication system employed dual transmitter-single receiver, telemetry and command subsystems, tape recorder and high and low gain antennas. Six and one-half-watt cavity amplified and 33 and one-third bit per second rate were employed early in mission, 10.5-watt TWT and 8 and one–third bit rate later on. A monopropellant (anhydrous hydrazine) engine with 50.7-pound-thrust was carried for one or two mid-course corrections. Attitude control and navigation was provided by a redundant nitrogen gas jet system with input from three gyros, Canopus Star Tracker, two primary sun sensors, secondary sun sensors, earth sensor, planet sensor and Venus terminator sen-

sor; 17,640 solar cells and silver-zinc batteries supplied 370 watts near earth to 555 watts at Venus. Spacecraft systems were programmed by central computer and sequencer. Temperature control was maintained by combination of thermal louvers, deployable sunshade, insulation, paint pattern, polished metal surfaces and reference units mounted on three solar panels.

Mariner 5 was launched 14 June 1967 from Cape Kennedy, placed in parking orbit and then injected into interplanetary trajectory. Sun and Canopus acquisition accomplished without incident. Midcourse maneuver was carried out with 17.66-second burn 19 June, reducing Venus miss distance to approximately 2500 miles. Telemetry bit rate was lowered 24 July to 8-1/3 bits per second. Mariner 5 encountered Venus on 19 October 1967, passing at a distance of 2429 miles.

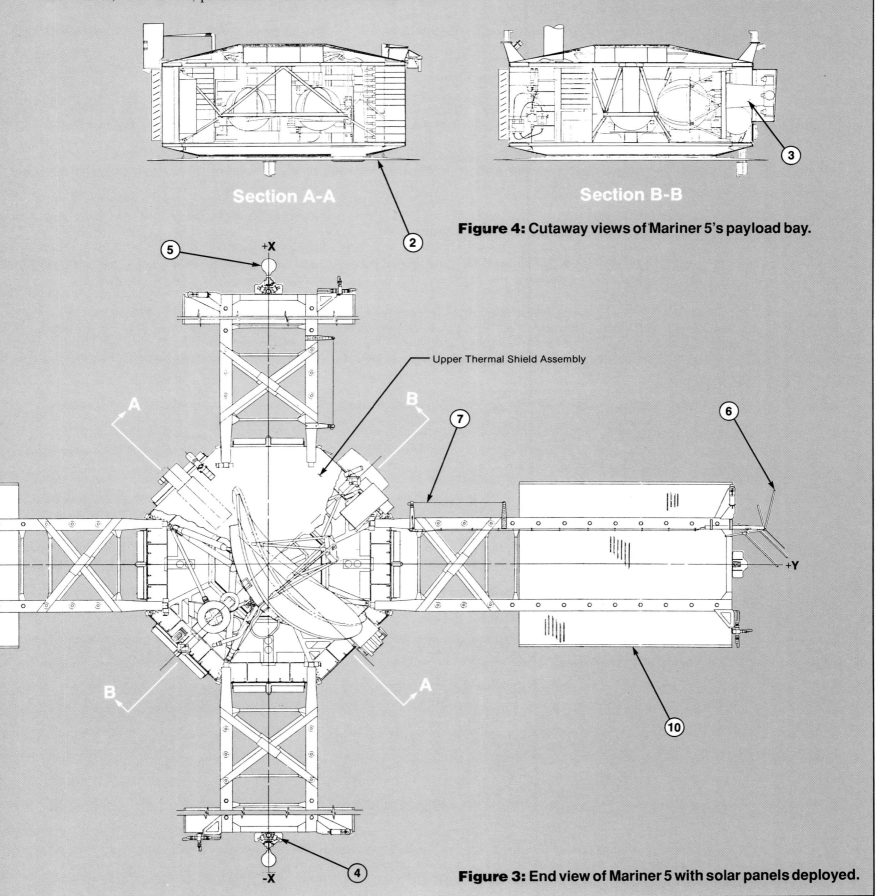

Section A-A

Section B-B

Figure 4: Cutaway views of Mariner 5's payload bay.

Upper Thermal Shield Assembly

Figure 3: End view of Mariner 5 with solar panels deployed.

Mission Planning

Having determined the final objective and the weight that can be launched toward that objective, the next step is to make the choices in subsystems, timing and trajectory that will make it possible to send 120 pounds of spacecraft to a flyby of Pluto. Reviewing the mission plan allows one to discover unforeseen problems and possibilities. Ninety percent of the cost in an interplanetary spacecraft is associated with the two day's worth of work at the time of the planetary encounter (*see pages 114–120*). Pluto is someplace that has not been visited—and probably won't be for a long time. Unless we were able to discover Planet X, there is really nothing beyond Pluto to visit. A hypothetical plan may include a Pluto flyby, followed by a swing around the moon Charon, and a hope to come back around and go into orbit around Pluto. If this were accomplished, one could allow this orbit to gradually decay, until impact. Theoretically, the last image could be one that was transmitted in real time a few feet from the surface. It is even possible that it might survive impact and continue transmitting from the surface. The sensors that Pioneer Venus released into the Venusian atmosphere were not supposed to survive a landing on the surface, but one did! Beyond the flyby, each one of these steps would be a bonus (*see page 111*).

The spacecraft discussed here is not a complicated craft at all. It is well within easily accessible technology—both in terms of structure and communications—to produce spacecraft in a variety of configurations to conduct flybys to Saturn, Jupiter or even Pluto. To turn it from simply a flyby spacecraft to an orbital probe would not be a big step, but it would make the spacecraft more complicated. It also *would* involve a communications problem because one must continually reorient the antenna to continue transmitting data to Earth (*see pages 36–38*).

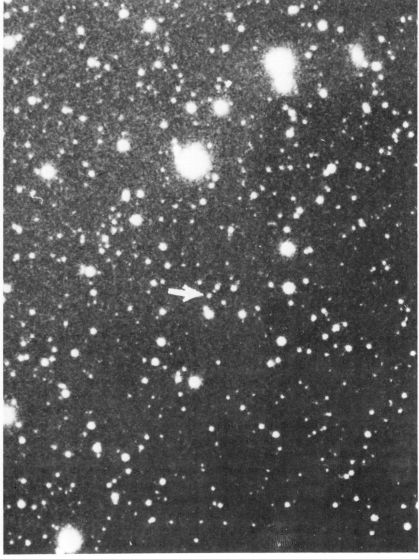

At left: Pluto and its moon, Charon, in an artist's conception. Three *billion* miles away, the Sun is nothing more than a bright star. *Above:* As viewed from Earth, even with a large telescope, Pluto is nothing but an indistinct speck of indeterminate size. Once thought to be 3658 miles in diameter, it is now estimated to be 1375 miles across, and even that is still only a guess!

B. ENGINE (Upper Stage)

Overview and Configuration

A spacecraft's motor is often referred to as the Upper Stage of the overall system. The lower stages are the launch vehicle (*see pages 94–95*), while the final—upper—stage *can* be an integral part of a spacecraft. The lower stage motor(s)—the launch vehicle—provide the enormous power necessary to push the spacecraft out of the Earth's atmosphere, and the upper stage motor sends the spacecraft off to its duty station, whether that be in Earth orbit or a flight past another planet. Often in orbital spacecraft, the upper stage is separated after motor operation in order to keep the spacecraft orbital weight down, reducing the amount of fuel necessary to keep the spacecraft in orbit.

The total loaded weight of the Morton Thiokol Star 27 *solid fuel* rocket motor, for example, is 796.3 pounds, with an empty weight of 60.6 pounds. It delivers an average of 6070 pounds of thrust for 33.46 seconds of burn time, with a peak maximum of 6440 pounds. The thrust is relatively constant within those parameters, so the average 'action time' (36.2 seconds) thrust would be about 5900 pounds with 60.0 pounds of empty weight, while the gravitational

force would be 36.1 Gs. This is a bit more than one would normally want because of burnout acceleration, so it might be worthwhile to consider *two small* solid rocket boosters rather than a single Star 27.

For example, the Morton Thiokol Star 13 solid rocket motor, which was used in the Anchored Interplanetary Monitoring Platform (AIMP) spacecraft program, delivers 830 pounds of thrust over 22 seconds of burn time, and has a total loaded weight of 78.63 pounds. The Star 13D solid rocket motor, which was used to inject Hughes Syncom communications satellites into geosynchronous orbit, delivers an average thrust of 776 pounds over 22.25 seconds of action time and has a total loaded weight of 77.63 pounds (*see Figure 5*).

Other possibilities might include the Thiokol Star 24, which has a total loaded weight of 481 pounds and an average burn time thrust of 4170 pounds for 29.6 seconds; or the spherical Star 20, which weighs only 270.5 pounds fully loaded while delivering an average burn time thrust of 5800 pounds for 10.6 seconds.

The diameters for these motors range from 13.5 inches for the Star 13 series to 27.3 inches for the Star 27. Lengths, including nozzle assemblies, range from 21.226 inches for the Star 13 to 48.725 inches for the Star 27. All of these would fit into the parameters of the Liberty 1C interior diameter limitation of 55 inches. A pair of Star

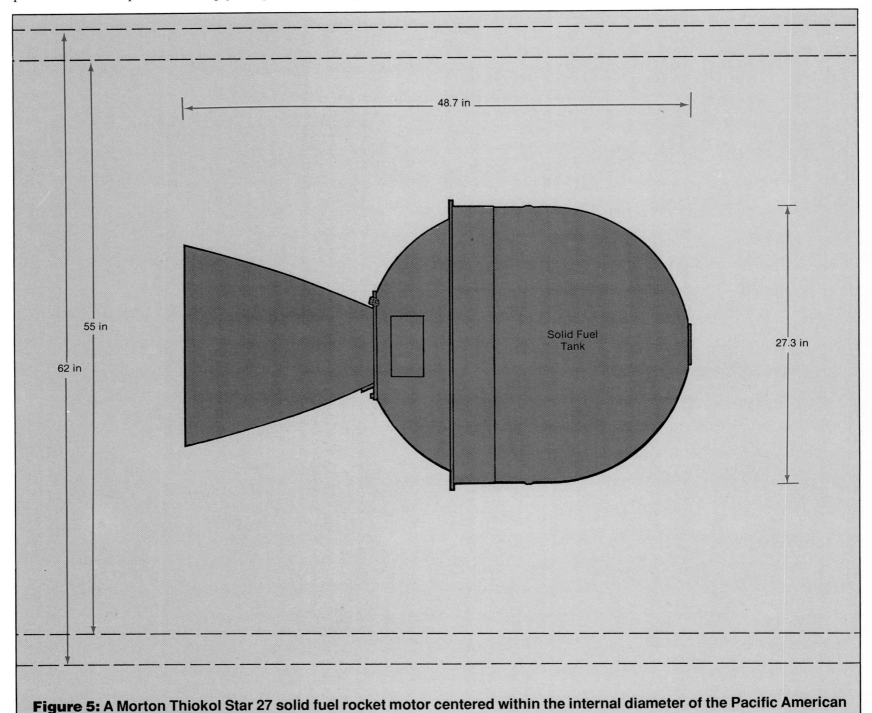

Figure 5: A Morton Thiokol Star 27 solid fuel rocket motor centered within the internal diameter of the Pacific American Liberty 1C launch vehicle.

24s could, for example, be positioned *side by side*—with four inches of clearance between them—in a 53 inch space (*see Figure 6*). This, however, would not be considered a good operational option, because it would play havoc on spacecraft mass moments of inertia during motor operation.

By comparison, the solid rocket used in the Voyager spacecraft weighed 350 pounds empty, carried 2340 pounds of propellant and delivered 15,300 pounds of thrust during a 43 second burn. It had a 39 inch tank diameter, with the nozzle fairing being 62 inches across (*see Figure 9*).

Solid fuel rocket motors have the inherent limitation of unstoppable burning until the fuel is exhausted. They operate only to a predetermined profile and cannot be adjusted. *Liquid* fuel rocket motors, on the other hand, may be started and stopped and can be throttled, or adjusted, during operation. Of course, this flexibility necessitates the added complexity of remote control valves. They would not necessarily come off the shelf with a pre-loaded tank like solid fuel motors, so two tanks would have to be constructed, one for the fuel and one for the oxydizer.*

continued on page 26

---

*Rocket motors, by definition, require self-contained oxygen, unlike conventional jet motors, or internal combustion motors, which take their oxygen from the air. This is why rocket motors are the only fuel-burning motors that can function in the airless void of space. Liquid fuel rocket motors carry fuel and oxidizer in separate tanks, while the 'solid fuel' in solid fuel rocket boosters is actually a *propellant* mixture containing both fuel and oxydizer.

Above: **A Thiokol Star series solid fuel rocket motor at work! A 72-inch Star 48 boosts a Hughes HS 376 communications satellite out of the Space Shuttle payload bay. All rocket fuel must contain its own oxygen for combustion purposes in the airless void of space.**

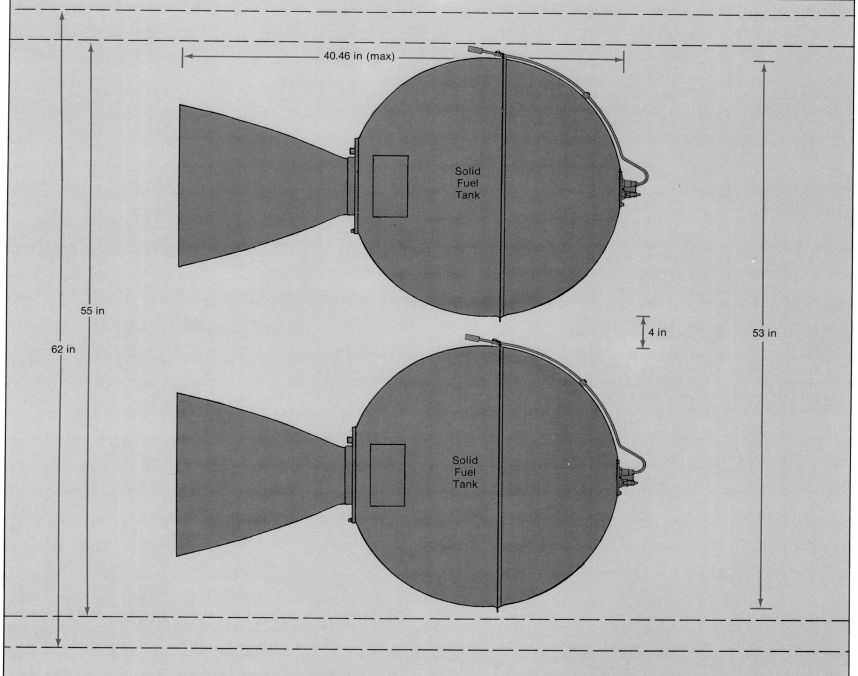

Figure 6: A pair of Morton Thiokol Star 24 solid fuel rocket motors centered within the internal diameter of the Pacific American Liberty 1C launch vehicle.

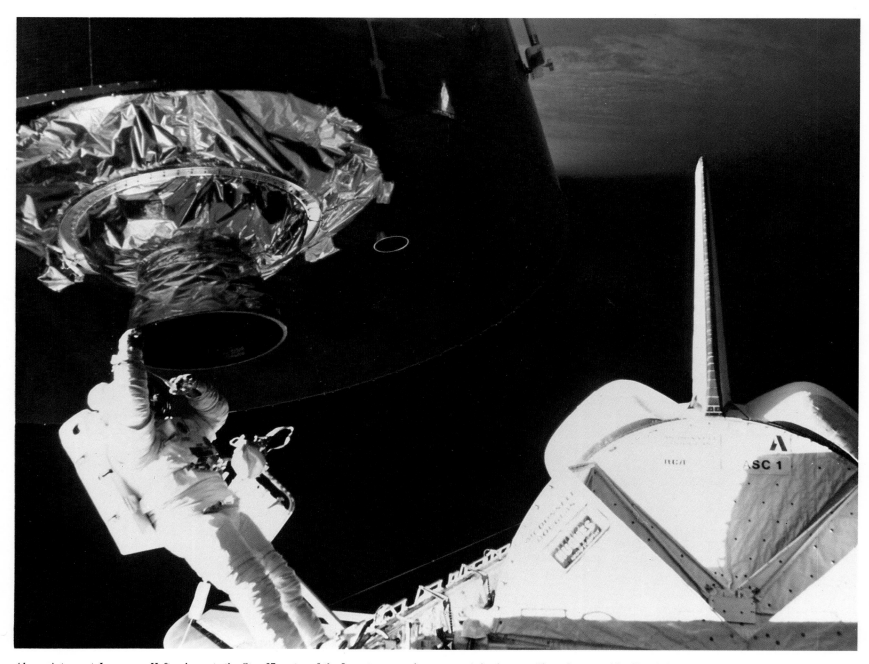

Above: Astronaut James van Hoften inspects the Star 37 motor of the Leasat communications satellite which was recovered during Space Shuttle mission 51-I in August of 1985. *Below:* Preparing Intelsat 1 for its 6 April 1965 launch, technicians work on the spacecraft's X-258 solid propellant motor, rated at 5700 pounds of thrust. *At right:* The SBS 4 business communications satellite spins out of its Shuttle-borne cradle on 30 August 1984. Clearly visible is the Thiokol Star 48 rocket motor with which the satellite was shortly thereafter maneuvered into proper orbital position. This 72-inch motor contains 4405 pounds of propellant and generates 16,860 foot-pounds of thrust.

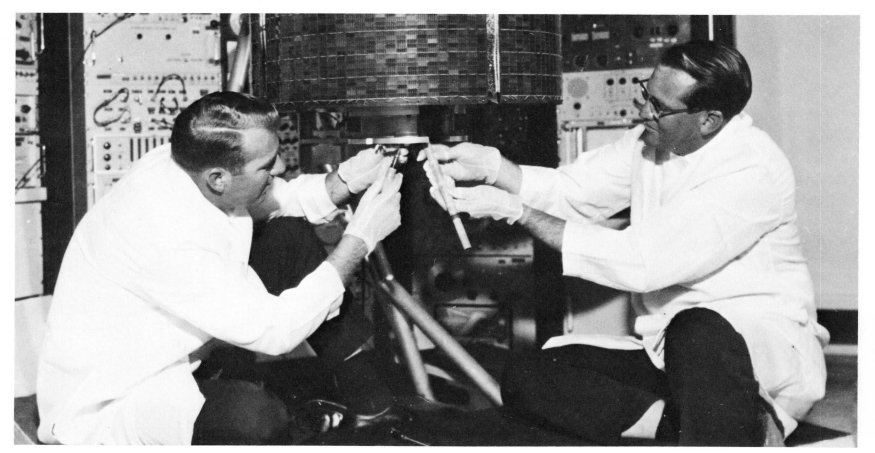

continued from page 23

A good choice of liquid fuel rockets might be something on the order of the small attitude control thrusters that were used on the Gemini and Apollo manned spacecraft in the 1960s. They are fairly compact and weigh something on the order of 15 pounds. Some of these still exist in the secondhand market and hence, they could be purchased off the shelf relatively cheaply, tested and refurbished.

Propellant here, of course, refers to both the fuel and the oxidizer. The fuel in this case is hydrazine (N_2H_4), while the oxidizer is nitrogen tetroxide (N_2O_4). The fuel and oxidizer tanks would be spheres constructed of aluminum and would weigh roughly 14 of the 80 pounds that has been budgeted for the motor hardware (*see page 22*). Knowing this, we can undertake an exercise in designing stages. If the average density of this propellant is about 72.5 pounds per cubic foot, then one would need 10 cubic feet of tank volume, or two 5 cubic foot spheres because each propellant is essentially identical in volume and this amounts to two 26 inch diameter tanks (*see Figure 7*).

The motor runs at about 100 psi (pounds per square inch), so that the tanks should have a tolerance of 150 psi for a safety factor. They would have a diameter of 26 inches, with a wall thickness of .003 inch (1mm), which is very thin. That would take some custom machining, would be about 2000 square inches, and would weigh 6.6 pounds. With fixtures the weight would go to eight pounds, or 16 pounds for the two tanks (*see Figures 7 and 8*).

If one takes the residual weight (the weight of the propellant that doesn't burn) and figures one percent of 720 pounds, it leaves 7.2 pounds. We then must compute the weight of the bracketry needed to hold all this together. One must use a light barrel section, or a network of struts. The weight difference between struts and a barrel section would be almost insignificant. It is likely to be made of aluminum, titanium or perhaps glass filament. This structure would hold the spheres about four inches apart, to allow a little bit of clearance. A barrel section running from the center of one sphere to the center of the other would be 30 inches x 26 inches, .05 of an inch thick, and it would weigh 12 pounds. It would be fastened or bolted rather than welded. It *might* be welded depending on how the plumbing between the spheres was configured, but welding may be rather tricky on something this thin.

Weight Budget		**920.0 lb**
Propellant		720.0 lb
Propellant stage hardware		
Rocket motor	15.0 lb	
Fuel tank	6.6 lb	
Oxydizer tank	6.6 lb	
Fixtures and fittings	2.8 lb	
Residuals (unburned propellant)	7.2 lb	
Bracketry	12.0 lb	
Subtotal:		50.2 lb
Running Total (*continued on page 30*):		**770.2 lb**

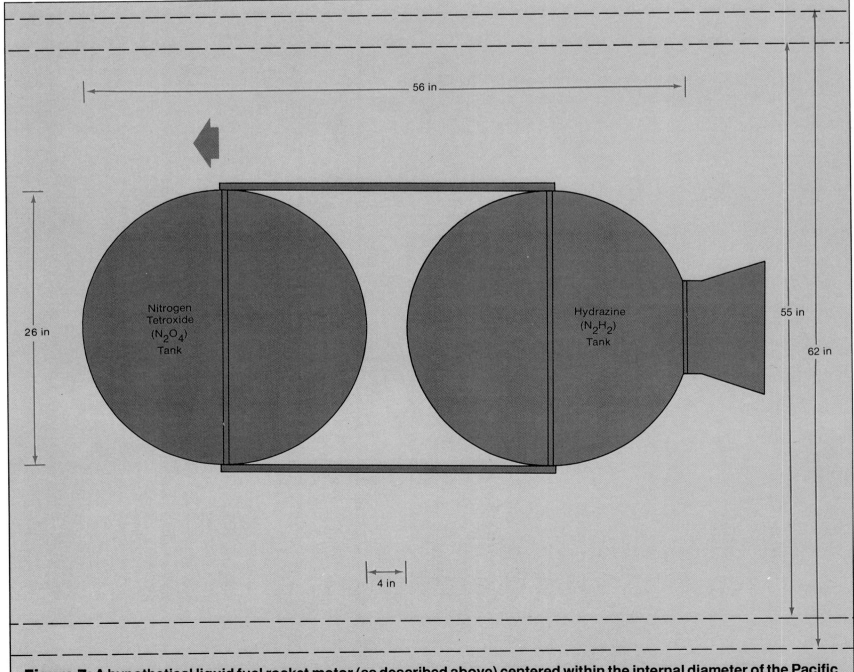

Figure 7: A hypothetical liquid fuel rocket motor (as described above) centered within the internal diameter of the Pacific American Liberty 1C launch vehicle.

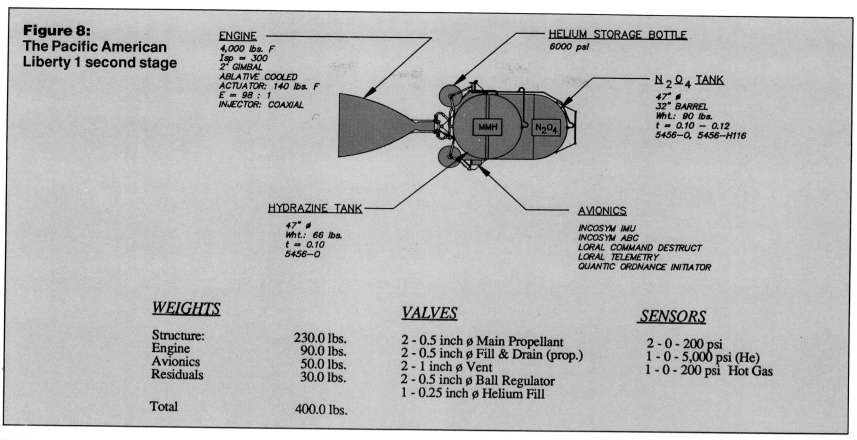

Figure 8:
The Pacific American
Liberty 1 second stage

ENGINE
4,000 lbs. F
Isp = 300
2° GIMBAL
ABLATIVE COOLED
ACTUATOR: 140 lbs. F
E = 98 : 1
INJECTOR: COAXIAL

HELIUM STORAGE BOTTLE
6000 psi

N_2O_4 TANK
47" ø
32" BARREL
Wht: 90 lbs.
t = 0.10 − 0.12
5456-0, 5456-H116

MMH N_2O_4

HYDRAZINE TANK
47" ø
Wht.: 66 lbs.
t = 0.10
5456-0

AVIONICS
INCOSYM IMU
INCOSYM ABC
LORAL COMMAND DESTRUCT
LORAL TELEMETRY
QUANTIC ORDNANCE INITIATOR

WEIGHTS

Structure:	230.0 lbs.
Engine	90.0 lbs.
Avionics	50.0 lbs.
Residuals	30.0 lbs.
Total	400.0 lbs.

VALVES

2 - 0.5 inch ø Main Propellant
2 - 0.5 inch ø Fill & Drain (prop.)
2 - 1 inch ø Vent
2 - 0.5 inch ø Ball Regulator
1 - 0.25 inch ø Helium Fill

SENSORS

2 - 0 - 200 psi
1 - 0 - 5,000 psi (He)
1 - 0 - 200 psi Hot Gas

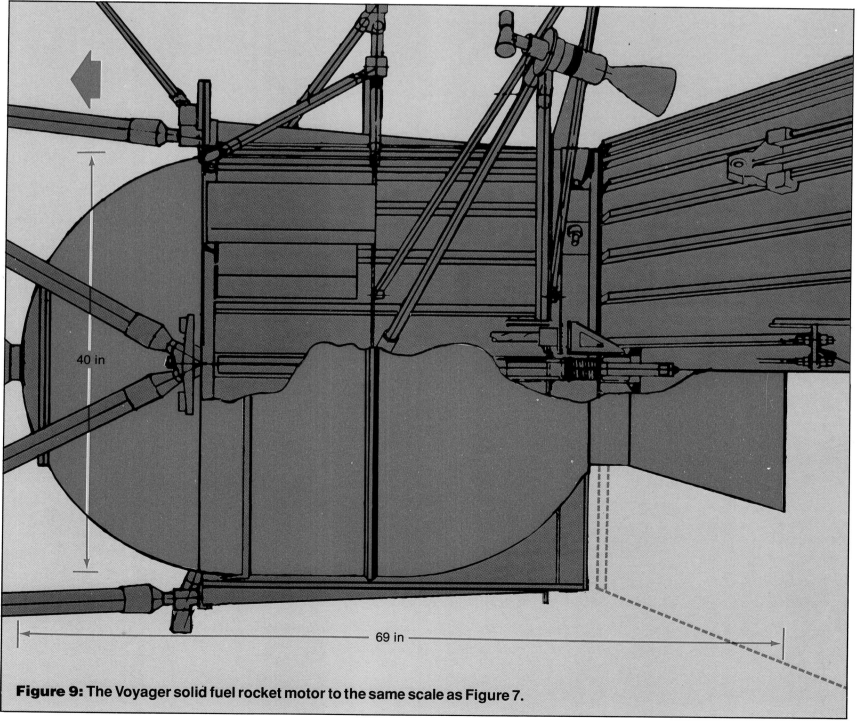

40 in

69 in

Figure 9: The Voyager solid fuel rocket motor to the same scale as Figure 7.

Attitude Control Thrusters

While the main spacecraft motor would provide the major thrust necessary for sending an interplanetary spacecraft on its way, smaller, simpler thrusters would be required for attitude control and for steering the spacecraft. Steering an airplane or a boat involves the use of flaps and rudders within the flow of air or water. In space, which is devoid of such fluids, directional control is strictly dependent upon Sir Issac Newton's Third Law of Motion that 'every action has an equal and opposite reaction.' Hence, spacecraft carry thrusters which, if fired to the right, will direct the spacecraft to the left, and vice-versa. They may be small rocket motors directed to the four points of the compass (plus up and down) or they might be as simple as little gas jets, which are equally effective in answering the parameters of Newton's law (*see Figure 11, page 30*).

For a small interplanetary spacecraft such as ours, gas jets would definitely be the choice for reason of both simplicity and weight. We must now choose a gas. Helium is the second lightest of all elements and the lightest of nonflammable gases. Its molecular structure is so tiny and inert, however, that no material can completely contain it. A helium balloon, for example, will lose half its volume in about a day. While it is commonly used in thrusters of Earth orbiting spacecraft (*see Figure 10, below*), there is no material on Earth that would both fit our weight requirements and completely contain the helium over the several years of a deep space mission.

Pure nitrogen wouldn't leak, but it would require a 10 inch diameter, highly pressurized hot gas tank located somewhere within the spacecraft. Thus, hydrazine may be considered the optimum choice because it is already present as part of the propellant mix and because it could be stored at relatively low pressure. One could physically couple the engine to the base of the hydrazine tank without any gimbeling.

It is in turn necessary to add some cold gas to pressurize these tanks. There is not very much in the way of tank volume (10 cubic feet at 150 psi), so one could be somewhat arbitrary and say that the

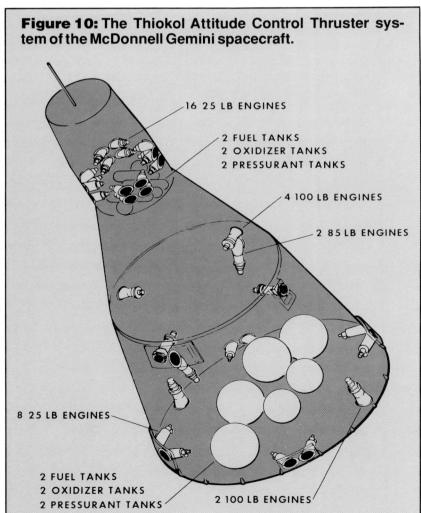

Figure 10: The Thiokol Attitude Control Thruster system of the McDonnell Gemini spacecraft.

16 25 LB ENGINES

2 FUEL TANKS
2 OXIDIZER TANKS
2 PRESSURANT TANKS

4 100 LB ENGINES

2 85 LB ENGINES

8 25 LB ENGINES

2 FUEL TANKS
2 OXIDIZER TANKS
2 PRESSURANT TANKS

2 100 LB ENGINES

The entire attitude thruster system of the Gemini manned spacecraft of 1965–66 is illustrated *above*. The photo *at left*, an astronaut's view of the spectacular Gemini 6 and Gemini 7 rendezvous, shows the external ports of the thrusters as they appeared in real life.

gas system weighs 5 pounds. The gas in the Liberty 1C upper stage itself is pressurized at 4500 pounds and weighs about 10 pounds, so the gas to pressurize these should only weigh about 0.6 pounds, and could be included in a small bottle anywhere in the structure.

A cold gas system may have all the impulse needed to let the spacecraft conduct a flyby. If one were going to do an orbit around Jupiter or one of its moons, then indeed one would need to use hydrazine, but on a simple baseline mission of going to Pluto one might want to stick with cold gas because one wouldn't have to worry about it freezing. Unlike a cold gas, hydrazine needs to be heated and warmed during the trip, so some thermal protection (and electrical power) must be used. No heating would be required except whatever was needed for the valve. For eight years we would coast and then one day before our encounter we'd turn the heater on and hope it worked (*see pages 31, 80 and 114*)!

When we speak of cold gas, we're actually speaking of nitrogen. One pound of nitrogen will give us 20 feet per second of Delta V change (*see Figure 50, page 100*). One pound of helium would give us about 48 feet per second, and one pound of hydrazine would give us about 75 feet per second.

If one were planning a Pluto orbital mission (*see page 111*), one would not purposely expend all of the hydrazine in the propellant stage during escape from Earth atmosphere. One would want to preserve some that could be used later.

Optional Enhancements and Engine Summary

With a five pound cold gas system and a miscellaneous 15 pounds for plumbing, bolts and brackets, the total weight of the motor installation would increase to 70 pounds. With a target of 80 pounds for the propellant stage less the propellant, we have roughly a 10 pound margin, which is handy. That margin could be utilized to increase the weight of the tanks by 9.8 pounds, double their thickness and make them easier to machine. The tooling costs would be less and the tanks would be easier to build.

Another possibility is increasing the size to carry more hydrazine to use later. If that were done, one might add a bladder pressurization system—installing a flexible polymar bladder. On one side is the gas and on the other side is the liquid. There are no bubbles and no free-floating propellant. The gas behind the bladder always holds the liquid from linkup to the sump so that it drains neatly straight from there into the engine (*see Figure 8, page 27*). This would be very useful for restarting the engine and for maneuvering the

spacecraft subsequent to the final burn of the engine. It might then be useful to stretch the tank to add a little bit more hydrazine, thus changing the propellant mixture ratio so some hydrazine is left for attitude control. That would involve channeling it through a different valve, but that is a relatively minor matter.

By comparison, the propulsion subsystem of the Voyager spacecraft consisted of a solid propellant rocket motor for final Jupiter transfer trajectory velocity and a hydrazine system which fuels 16 thrusters on the mission module and eight reaction engines on the propulsion module (*see pages 86–91*).

The single hydrazine supply of each Voyager is contained with a 28 inch diameter spherical titanium Teflon-covered rubber bladder. The tank, located in the central cavity of the mission module's 10-sided basic structure, contains 231 pounds of hydrazine at launch and is pressurized at 420 psi. As the propellant is consumed, the helium pressure decreases to a minimum of about 130 psi.

All 24 hydrazine thrusters use a catalyst which spontaneously initiates and sustains rapid decomposition of the hydrazine. The 16 thrusters on the mission module each deliver 0.2 pounds of thrust. Four are used to execute trajectory correction maneuvers while the others (in two redundant six-thruster branches) are used to stabilize the spacecraft on its three axes. Only one branch of attitude control thrusters is needed at any time.

Mounted on outriggers from the propulsion module are four 100 pound thrust engines which, during solid motor burn, provide thrust-vector control on the pitch and yaw axes. Four five pound thrust engines provide roll control.

Weight Budget (*Continued from page 26*)		**920.0 lb**
Propellant		720.0 lb
Propellant stage hardware		
Rocket motor	15.0 lb	
Fuel tank	6.6 lb	
Oxydizer tank	6.6 lb	
Fixtures and fittings	2.8 lb	
Residuals (unburned propellant)	7.2 lb	
Bracketry	12.0 lb	
Subtotal:		50.2 lb
Attitude control subsystem		
Cold gas system	5.0 lb	
Fixtures, fittings and bracketry	15.0 lb	
Subtotal:		20.0 lb
Propellant stage, optional enhancements		9.8 lb
Running Total (*Continued on page 32*)		**800.0 lb**

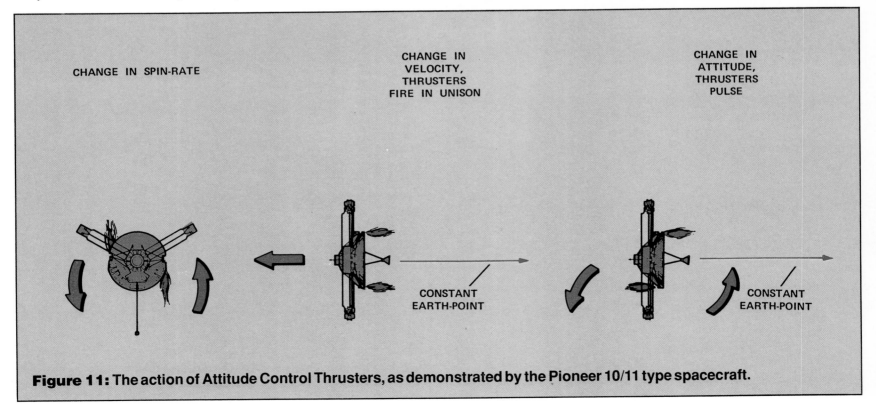

CHANGE IN SPIN-RATE

CHANGE IN VELOCITY, THRUSTERS FIRE IN UNISON

CHANGE IN ATTITUDE, THRUSTERS PULSE

CONSTANT EARTH-POINT

CONSTANT EARTH-POINT

Figure 11: The action of Attitude Control Thrusters, as demonstrated by the Pioneer 10/11 type spacecraft.

C. ONBOARD COMPUTER

Overview

There is probably no area in spacecraft design where greater strides have been made since the early 1970s than in the area of computer engineering. In fact, because of the proliferation of high quality, low cost computer hardware, this vital element of spacecraft design is probably one of the most easily accomplished with off-the-shelf components. A system could be constructed using an Apple or IBM PC that could not only perform all of the necessary onboard tasks, but which would be relatively lightweight.

As an example, and without implying an endorsement, let us look at an IBM XT Personal Computer. The basic system has 256KB of standard memory, which is entirely adequate for the requirements of our hypothetical planetary flyby mission, and could be expanded to the requirements of a planetary orbital mission. Without such unnecessary components as keyboard and video display terminal, the IBM XT (like the more advanced IBM PS-2 computers introduced in 1987) weighs 25 pounds and measures 6x6x20 inches. This size and weight include a substantial metal case that could be removed and the computer system itself incorporated into the spacecraft 'bus,' or main body. An Apple Macintosh, on the other hand, weighs about 16.5 pounds for a weight savings of one third over the IBM systems mentioned.

These dimensions, however, would give us a good idea of the final size of that bus, because the computer system would be the major component within it. Using the inside diameter of the Liberty 1C, the bus *could* have a maximum diameter of 55 inches. This is, however, much larger than is necessary and would add tremendously to the overall weight. The diameter of 26 inches that was calculated for the liquid propellant tanks on page 26 could also be used for the bus. If two IBM XTs were selected as the primary and back-up computers, they could be bolted together back to back and form a unit somewhat smaller than 20x16x12 inches, which would fit easily into a cylindrical bus 26 inches in diameter and 16 inches long. This configuration would bring us up to a weight of roughly 40 pounds for the computers and casing for two. (Roughly 10 pounds could be saved by boxing them together.) Our computation requirements could probably be addressed in a four pound, six inch cube, but there are concerns present in the proper packaging which are discussed on page 16 and page 32. The remaining spaces would allow plenty of room for all the other necessary hardware, such as transformers, batteries, switches, wiring, gas lines, etc (*see Figure 12, below*).

Function

The function of the computers (there are two computers, for reasons of redundancy) would be to serve as the 'brain' of the spacecraft. All subsystems would be controlled either by the computers' onboard memory (such as in the case of routine functions) or by ground control speaking to the subsystems through the computer. The trajectory and entire mission plan would be programmed into the memory of both computers. Both would monitor the progress of the mission and either would be available to take over any task at any time.

The mission would be managed by a ground-based computer during launch (*see page 94*), but the onboard computer would take over management of the spacecraft from launch control as soon as it had been put into space. The first task would be to direct the thrusters to aim the spacecraft on the course of its intended trajectory (*see pages 98–100*). During this critical phase, it would process commands sent from mission control back on Earth, as well as utilizing its own pre-programmed memory of the trajectory and mission plan. Once the spacecraft's attitude control system had been put into position, the computer would fire the main rocket motor, and the plunge into interplanetary space would be underway.

Within one minute, mission velocity would be achieved, the motor would be shut down and eight to 10 years of routine would begin. During this period the spacecraft would be in a state of semi-hibernation. There would be very little for the computers to do other than to monitor one another periodically. The primary computer would be programmed, for example, to 'wake up' every 24 or 48 hours and to run through a periodic check of the other subsystems (including the back-up computer), collate this data, and transmit it back to Earth.

It would also calculate the spacecraft's position relative to the Sun and fixed stars that it could view through the CCD camera (*see pages 42–46*). This latter information would be used to make midcourse corrections to the trajectory, if necessary. In planning interplanetary missions, NASA always puts midcourse corrections (*see page 110*) on the schedule, and uses navigational data transmitted back to Earth in determining the nature of each of these corrections. In some cases, the trajectory is so well executed that planned corrections are unnecessary and simply are not made as scheduled.

As with all the spacecraft subsystems, 90 percent of the computer's workload will come during the 48 hours of the planetary encounter (*see page 114*). Because the spacecraft will be four billion

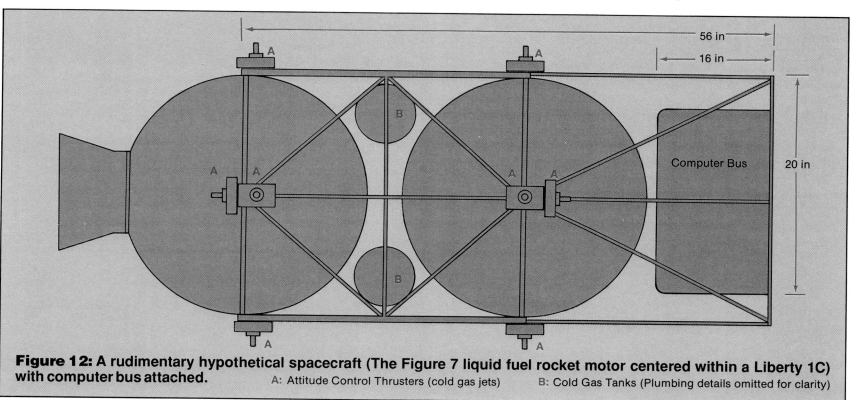

Figure 12: A rudimentary hypothetical spacecraft (The Figure 7 liquid fuel rocket motor centered within a Liberty 1C) with computer bus attached. A: Attitude Control Thrusters (cold gas jets) B: Cold Gas Tanks (Plumbing details omitted for clarity)

miles from Earth and telemetry time will be roughly five hours, the mission will depend heavily on the computer's memory. It will have to be programmed with precise instructions for maneuvering, aiming the camera and activating the thermal batteries (*see page 78*) required to provide the burst of electrical power needed to transmit the pictures.

During the days leading up to the encounter, it will be possible to fine-tune the trajectory from Earth and to aim the camera in the general direction of the planet. But the period of closest encounter will be shorter than the length of time that it takes for instructions to travel from ground control to the spacecraft, so the computer must be capable of 'thinking on its feet.'

By comparison the computer command subsystems (CCS) aboard Voyager include two independent plated wire memories, each with a capacity of 4096 words. Half of each memory stores reusable fixed routines which will not change during the mission. The second half is reprogrammable by updates from the ground, which is worth considering as part of any spacecraft computer design (*see page 86*).

Most commands to other spacecraft subsystems are issued from the CCS memory, which, at any given time, is loaded with the sequences appropriate to the mission phase. The CCS also can decode commands from the ground and pass them along to other spacecraft subsystems.

Under control of an accurate onboard clock, the CCS counts hours, minutes or seconds until some preprogrammed interval has elapsed and then it branches into the subroutines stored in memory, which results in commands to other subsystems. A sequencing event can be a single command or routine which includes many commands (*eg*, manipulating the tape recorder during a playback sequence).

The CCS can issue commands singly from one of its two processors or in a parallel or tandem state from both processors. An example of CCS dual control is the execution of trajectory correction maneuvers (*see page 110*). TCM thrusters are started with a tandem command (both processors must send consistent commands to a single output unit) and stopped with a parallel command (either processor working through different output units will stop the burn).

Voyager's CCS can survive any single internal fault. Each functional unit has a duplicate elsewhere in the subsystem.

Radiation Hardening

A major concern in choosing a computer (and building the case to enclose it) is radiation. Over 10 years, solar radiation could destroy the computer if it isn't 'rad hard' or properly shielded. If a trajectory that takes the spacecraft near Jupiter were selected, this would make the concern even more critical as we discussed in graphic terms on page 16.

The irony here is that modern silicon chip computers are very sensitive to radiation, whereas old tube-type hardware, and even 1960s-vintage transistors, would survive high doses. A major problem with such hardware is weight. This is why we have budgeted roughly 40 pounds for computers when four pounds would provide our computing needs. We would have to either heavily shield a modern computer or build a larger, heavier, more primitive one.

One might prevail upon some interested electronics company to build the tiny, tube-based computer that is required. A spacecraft isn't like a launch vehicle, where the computer must respond very quickly (eight or 10 times a second) to do all the vehicle steering as it ascends. In deep space a computer could respond very leisurely and still do the job.

The biggest problem in using a tube-type computer is power, because they use a great deal. An old-fashioned computer might require 20 watts, whereas if one uses contemporary technology, it might take one or two watts to run the entire computer. That is a trade off that has to be made.

Weight Budget (Continued from page 30)		920.0 lb
Propellant		720.0 lb
Propellant stage hardware		
Rocket motor	15.0 lb	
Fuel tank	6.6 lb	
Oxydizer tank	6.6 lb	
Fixtures and fittings	2.8 lb	
Residuals (unburned propellant)	7.2 lb	
Bracketry	12.0 lb	
Subtotal:		50.2 lb
Attitude control subsystem		
Cold gas system	5.0 lb	
Fixtures, fittings and bracketry	15.0 lb	
Subtotal:		20.0 lb
Propellant stage, optional enhancements		9.8 lb
Computer, casing and wiring		40.0 lb
Running Total (Continued on page 46)		**840.0 lb**

Below: **An artist's conception of the Galileo Jupiter probe smashing into the turbulent and highly radioactive Jovian atmosphere sometime in the mid-1990s. The as-yet unflown Galileo orbiter and planetary probe are both well-hardened against the planet's ferocious radiation. Gigantic Jupiter (*at right*) could be used as a fuel-saving 'whip-pivot' toward the outer planets, but its destructive radioactivity must be taken into account.**

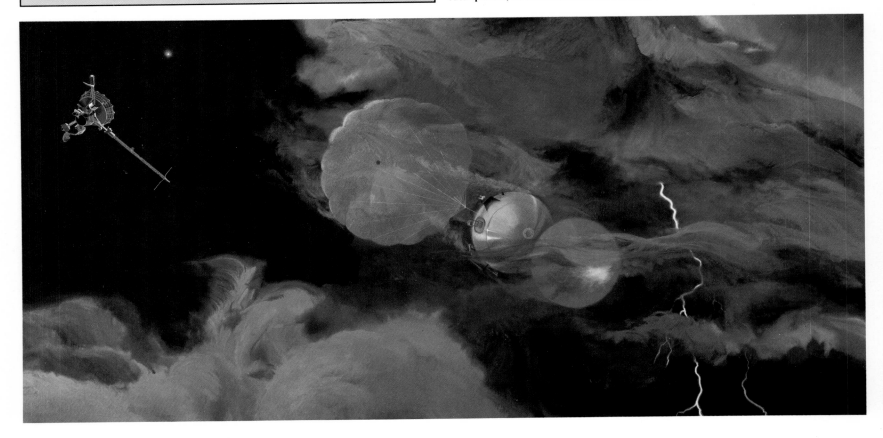

Technical Profiles of Great Interplanetary Spacecraft

Mariner 6 and Mariner 7

Both spacecraft were launched by an Atlas-Centaur with the Mariner 6 launch being its first use for interplanetary missions. This included a 395,000-lb-thrust Atlas first stage (including two 670-pound-thrust vernier engines for roll directional control) and a 30,000-pound-thrust Centaur second stage. Both stages were inertially guided and their overall height was 123 feet.

Mariner 6 and 7 spacecraft were identical. Their base structure was a 37-pound octagonal forged-magnesium frame, 54.5 inches diagonally and 18 inches deep, containing eight subsystem compartments that also provided structural strengthening. Four solar panels 84 inches long and 35.5 inches wide were attached to the top; each panel had 20.7 square feet of solar cells (83 square feet total, each spacecraft). When deployed, they spanned 19 feet. Attitude control jets were mounted at panel tips. A low-gain omnidirectional antenna was mounted atop a four-inch-diameter aluminum tube, which served as a waveguide and extended 88 inches from the top of the base. A cone-shaped thermal control flux monitor was also mounted at top of mast. Their total height was 11 feet from top of low-gain antennas mast to bottom of lower experiment-mount scan platform. Each weighed 910 pounds.

Primary mission objectives for both Mariner 6 and 7 Mars flybys were the scientific study of the surface and search for extraterrestrial life, to develop technologies for future Mars missions, and also to further demonstrate engineering concepts and techniques required for long-duration flight away from the sun. Flight duration and distance for Mariner 6 was to be 156 days and 226 million miles; for Mariner 7, 133 days and 193 million miles; communication distance to Earth during planetary encounters of each spacecraft to be, respectively, 59.5 million miles (about 5.5 light-minutes) and 61.8 million miles.

Both Pioneer 6 and Pioneer 7 carried two television cameras: Camera A, for medium-resolution (wide-angle) approach pictures, equipped with red, green and blue filters to delineate corrected-color differences of the planetary atmosphere and surface; Camera B, for high-resolution (narrow-angle) pictures, programmed to overlap specific areas within regions studied by Camera A, equipped with a yellow filter to reduce the effects of planetary atmospheric haze, and with a modified Schmidt Cassegrain telescope to be used for approach pictures. Camera A was similar to the camera flown on Mariner 4, but with a wide-angle lens to cover an area 12 to 15 times larger than for Mariner 4 yet with the same two-mile resolution quality. Camera B's optical resolution was 10 times sharper than Camera A and designed to cover an area 100 times larger on the Martian surface. Cameras operated alternately, each taking one picture every 42.25 seconds within the experiment range of 6000 to 2000 miles. Improved vidicon tubes with 704-line resolution were used to store and transmit images. The cameras were mounted on a scan platform which was movable, on Earth command, 215° clockwise and 64° conically. They were capable of focus adjustments to account for surface altitude variations up to 8.3 miles

Other experiment packages, which, together with cameras, were mounted on motor-driven, two-degree-of-freedom scan platform below the octagonal base, included the following: infrared radiometer (IRR) to perform thermal mapping of areas covered by TV experiments; two detectors in each instrument to provide 30 readings (one every 63 seconds); one detector to operate in the range near 300° K, the other around 140° K. IRRs were on both spacecraft to scan the Martian surface from late morning to late evening, yielding cooling rates and indices of surface compositions, especially valuable from the 'dark' side of Mars not seen by Earth. Chemical constituents of upper atmosphere (60 to 600 miles) were to be identified and measured, as well backup density and temperature data to be provided, by an ultraviolet

spectrometer operating in the range from 1000 to 4300 angstroms in three second sweeps (the first attempt to use this technique to identify Martian atmospheric gases).

Lower atmosphere and surface compositions were to be measured by an infrared spectrometer (IRS), to scan in the 1.9 to 14.3 microns wavelength range with one reading every 10 seconds. Celestial mechanics experiments were performed also, using radio signals during flight, at encounter, and the flight behind and beyond Mars; objectives included determining the mass of Mars, Earth-Mars distance at encounter, and the Earth-Moon mass ratio. Occultation experiment utilized S-band radio signals from the spacecraft, to obtain precise measurements of the radius of Mars, the reflection of radio signals from the planet's surface, and the electron density of its atmosphere.

Primary contents (*see Figures, these pages*) of the eight compartments in base of each spacecraft were: (1) power conversion equipment; (2) midcourse correction propulsion system; (3) central computer and sequencer and attitude control subsystem; (4) telemetry and command subsystem; (5) tape recorders; (6) radio receiver and transmitter; (7) science instrument electronics and data automation subsystem; (8) power booster regulators and nickel cadmium battery, which supplemented the primary power source—17,472 solar cells (4368 per panel) providing nominal 800 watts near Earth, decreasing to 449 watts at Mars distance.

Temperature control was maintained by a combination of thermal louvers, deployable sunshade, aluminized teflon insulation, paint patterns, and polished metal surfaces. Thermal control flux monitor experiment on both spacecraft was to provide measurements of the sun's intensity during the trip to Mars and beyond. Attitude control provided by redundant, six-jet nitrogen-gas thrusters with input from three gyros, Canopus Star Tracker located on upper ring structure of the base, and two primary sun sensors mounted on pedestals atop the base; four secondary sensors attached to lower ring adapter. Data automation subsystem controlled and synchronized five scientific experiments, and digitalized data prior to transmission to Earth.

Mariner 6 was launched 25 February 1969 from Cape Kennedy in a direct ascent single-burn ballistic trajectory with an initial heliocentric injection velocity of 25,700 mph. About 30 minutes after launch, the spacecraft was rotated from random attitude, to acquire the Sun. About four hours out, the vehicle was again rotated to lock on Canopus, and space-stabilized with solar panels perpendicular to the sun for the remainder of the flight. A midcourse trajectory correction was made on 29 February, while the spacecraft was 750,000 miles out. Mariner 6 was ahead of Mars at launch but, affected by solar gravity, slowed to 17,633 mph relative to Mars so that Mars passed the spacecraft—slightly ahead of it at encounter. Mariner 6 crossed the orbit of Mars within 2120 miles, 31 July 1969, on its equatorial flyby, and subsequently flew behind the planet for about 25 minutes.

Mariner 7 was launched 27 March 1969 from Cape Kennedy in a direct ascent single-burn ballistic trajectory with an initial heliocentric injection velocity of 25,700 mph. About 30 minutes after launch, the spacecraft was rotated from random attitude, to acquire the sun. About four hours out, the vehicle was again rotated to lock on Canopus, and space-stabilized. A midcourse trajectory correction was made on 8 April, while Mariner 7 was 2.5 million miles out. Mariner 7 was ahead of Mars at launch but, affected by solar gravity, it slowed to 16,063 miles per hour relative to Mars, so that Mars passed the spacecraft and was slightly ahead of it at encounter. Mariner 7 crossed the orbit of Mars within 2190 miles, 5 August 1969, on its trajectory over the region from the equator to the South polar cap, and subsequently flew behind the planet for over 20 minutes. There were the same three encounter phases for Mariner 7 as for its earlier twin. Far-encounter for Mariner 7 began about encounter minus 72 (E-72) hours, and resulted in 93 far-approach analog pictures with Camera B; during near-encounter, 33 pictures were taken with both cameras for a total of 126 for Mariner 7.

When the Mars flyby mission phase ended, both spacecraft continued to transmit, their 20 watt outputs being used in continuing celestial mechanics experiments. When they passed behind the sun, tests were made of the theory of electromagnetic radiation bending when in the vicinity of the large solar gravitational fields. Television experiments transmitted nine times the number of proposed far-encounter TV pictures, 20 percent more near-encounter pictures; a total of 1100 analog and digital pictures.

(1) Spacecraft Structure Assembly
(2) Adapter Assembly
(3) V-Band Payload Separation Assembly
(4) Electronic Packaging Assembly
(5) Scan Science Installation
(6) Attitude Control Installation
(7) Thermal Control Installation
(8) Low and Medium Gain Antenna Installation
(9) High Gain Antenna Installation
(10) Solar Panel Installation

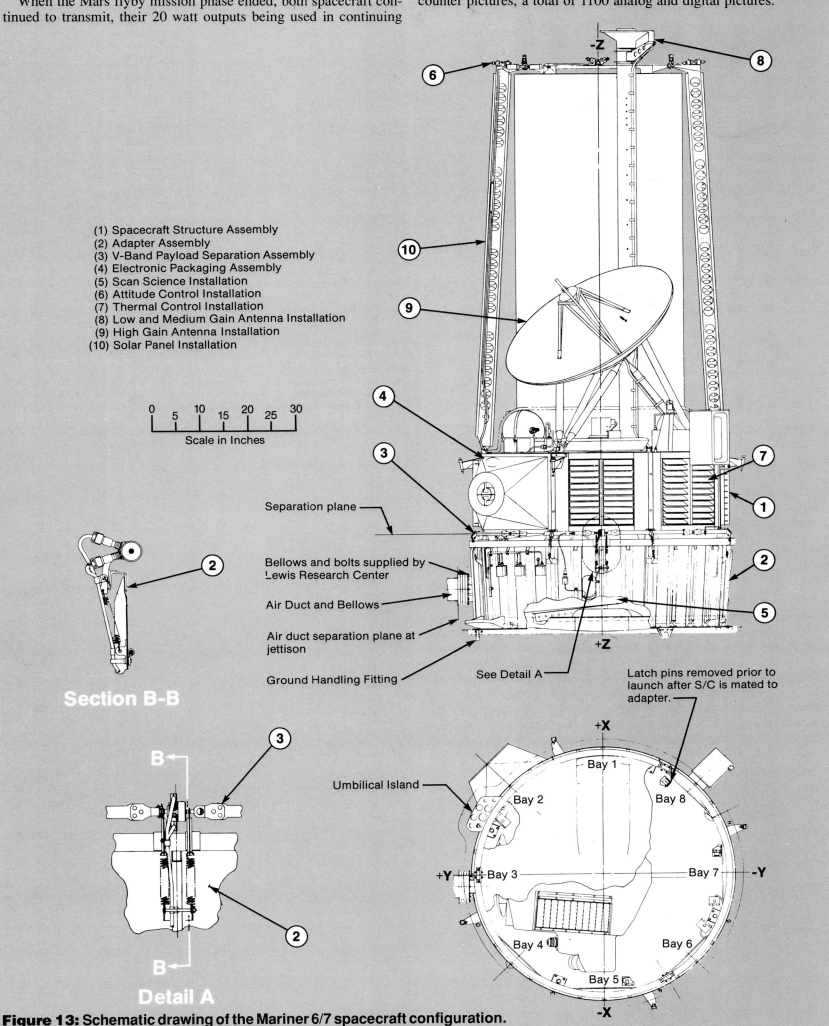

Figure 13: Schematic drawing of the Mariner 6/7 spacecraft configuration.

D. THE ANTENNA

Overview

The large dish antennas used on Pioneer, Voyager and other spacecraft were unusual pieces of hardware when they were designed, but today such dishes sprout from rooftops everywhere, and the communications link between one's living room and satellites thousands of miles away in space is taken for granted.

A wide range of satellite dish hardware is available on the market which could handle the band-width requirements for the uplink and downlink transmissions to and from an interplanetary spacecraft; the problem is size (*see pages 16, 50–51, 86–91 and 114*).

While the antenna used on Viking for a mission to Mars had a 57.9 inch diameter, NASA's own communications studies prior to Pioneer 10 showed that an outer Solar System mission must carry a dish at least 108 inches across. NASA didn't choose 108 inches arbitrarily; it was a real number for real reasons. If you want to talk to a spacecraft using the existing or foreseeable DSN as far away as Pluto (which Pioneer 10 has now passed), then 108 inches is the minimum size needed to cut through all the background noise, and be able to hear Earth against any interference that might occur. One could go bigger, but since Pioneer used 108 inches successfully and since the data requirements here aren't as high as for that mission, that size buys everything one needs to get to Pluto.

Voyager, meanwhile, had an antenna with a 144 inch diameter. The inside diameter of the shroud atop Voyager's Titan 3/Centaur launch vehicle was 159 inches, but the equivalent inside diameter on the Liberty 1C launch vehicle is only 55 inches.

This discrepancy will, unfortunately, rule out a fixed antenna unless one can be found that is smaller than 55 inches but still capable of handling the transmission requirements. A fixed antenna would be ideal because one would not have to worry about moving parts necessary to deploy a folded antenna in outer space. It is axiomatic that the potential for malfunction increases proportionally with the number of moving parts, so the simpler the folding antenna is, the better.

As we've noted on page 16, there are two types of folding antenna which might be considered: the *umbrella* type and the *rib-wrap* type. The former unfolds like its namesake, while the latter is spring-loaded and unfurls from a fixed axis when released. It is the most complicated.

An example of the umbrella type of antenna is the Toki TA 550 that is marketed to campers and recreational vehicle owners. It weighs 45 pounds complete, but over half of that is accounted for by the portable aluminum stand. It is designed to fold from 10 inches to 66 inches and is therefore too small to fit our hypothetical requirements, *but* if such an antenna were scaled *twice up*, it would fold from 20 inches to 132 inches. This would make it small enough to fit within our spacecraft when folded, yet give it a diameter of comfortably more than nine feet.

Below: **The Voyager spacecraft, showing its 144-inch transmitting antenna at the top of the spacecraft. This antenna enabled the identical Voyagers 1 and 2 to transmit astonishingly clear pictures back to Earth despite such heavy radioactive interference as that of Jupiter. The Voyager missions were the same in all but their respective outer Solar System soirees.** *At right:* **Pioneer 11, with its fixed nine-foot aluminum high-gain dish antenna, is about to be inserted into the shroud of the Centaur upper stage prior to launch.**

A rib-wrap antenna could be made with a very large diameter. For the ATS-6 communications satellite launched in 1974, Lockheed developed a rib-wrap antenna that folded out to a 30 foot diameter and there have been proposals to use them with up to a 300 foot diameter.

The positioning of the antenna is extremely important. It must transmit *to* and receive transmissions *from* Earth, so it must be aimed backward on the trailing edge of the spacecraft. Because the nozzle of the rocket motor must also point in this direction, these two subsystems must be integrated in such a way that the nozzle fires through the center of the antenna so that the rocket blast will not damage the structure of the antenna (*see Figure 14, below*).

One final consideration in the selection of an antenna is aerodynamics. Because there is no air in space, aerodynamics would be irrelevant unless and until a decision is made to penetrate the atmosphere of a planet. The atmosphere of Pluto—if it exists—is probably much thinner than that of the Earth, but there must be some account taken of the effect this atmosphere might have toward breaking the antenna off the aft of the spacecraft during atmospheric entry were that to be attempted (*see page 111*).

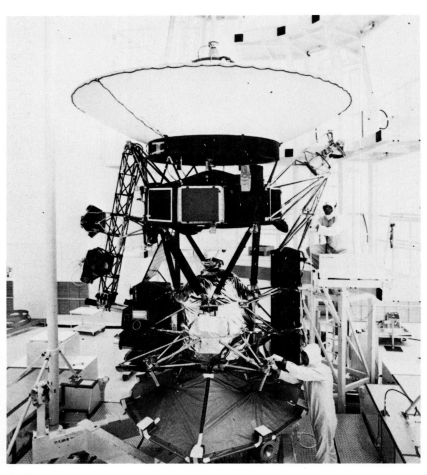

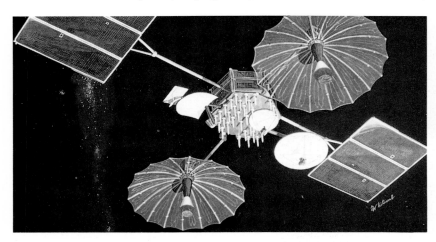

At left: A Tracking and Data Relay Satellite System satellite, showing its two rib-wrap style antennae. Rib-wrapping allows compact storage for very large antennae, with the main drawback being the rib-wrap system's complexity, as compared to the relatively simpler umbrella-type antenna (see below). *At right:* The as-yet unflown Galileo Jupiter-probe spacecraft here shows its rib-wrap antenna unfurled atop the spacecraft body. *Above:* The Voyager test model, showing its 144-inch fixed dish antenna.

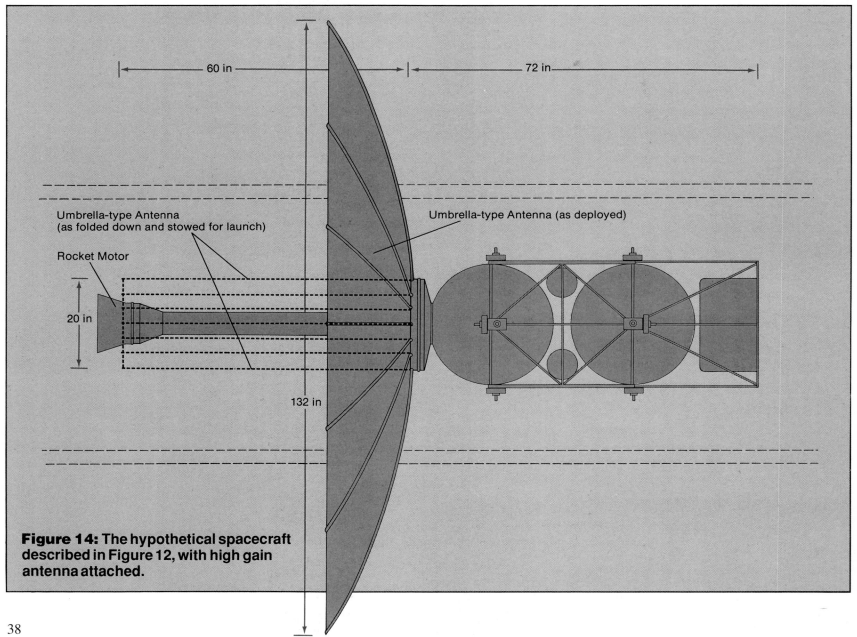

60 in

72 in

Umbrella-type Antenna (as folded down and stowed for launch)

Umbrella-type Antenna (as deployed)

Rocket Motor

20 in

132 in

Figure 14: The hypothetical spacecraft described in Figure 12, with high gain antenna attached.

Mariner 8 and Mariner 9

Each spacecraft was launched by an Atlas-Centaur. The Atlas first stage propulsion included two 171,000-pound-thrust vernier engines. The Atlas guidance was provided by pre-programmed pitch rates through booster engine cutoff, then switched to Centaur inertial guidance for sustainer phase. The Centaur upper stage developed 30,000 pounds thrust from two 15,000 pound-thrust liquid hydrogen and liquid oxygen-fed engines. The Atlas weighed 283,577 pounds; Centaur, 37,657. Total vehicle height was 113 feet.

The basic structure of both Mariner 8 and Mariner 9 was a 40 pound, eight-sided forged magnesium framework (54.5 inches diagonally, 18 inches deep) with eight electronic compartments. Four solar panels, each 84.5 inches long, 35.5 inches wide, were attached by outrigger structures to the top of the octagon. Each panel had a solar cell area of about 20.7 square feet. With solar panels deployed, the spacecraft had a 'wingspan' of 22 feet, 7.5 inches. Height of the spacecraft from the bottom of the scan platform to the top of the low-gain antenna and rocket nozzle was 7.5 feet.

Two sets of attitude control jets, consisting of six jets each for three-axis stabilization, were mounted at the tips of the four solar panels. Two spherical propellant tanks for the liquid-fueled rocket engine were mounted side by side atop the octagonal structure. The two-position high-gain antenna was attached to the spacecraft by a super-structure atop the octagon. Its aluminum honeycomb dish reflector was circular, 40 inches in diameter, and parabolic in cross-section. The low-gain omnidirectional antenna was mounted at the top of a circular aluminum tube four inches in diameter and extending vertically 57 inches from the top of the octagonal structure. A horn-shaped medium-gain antenna was mounted on a solar panel outrigger. The Canopus Star Tracker assembly was located on the upper ring structure of the octagon for a clear field of view between two solar panels. The cruise sun sensor and sun gate were attached to a solar panel outrigger.

Mariner's propulsion system (for small trajectory corrections, deceleration into Mars orbit and trim maneuvers) was capable of at least five starts and produced a continuous thrust of 300 pounds. Hypergolic propellants were monomethyl hydrazine and nitrogen tetroxide. Timing, sequencing and computations for other subsystems aboard the spacecraft were performed by the vehicle's central computer and sequencer and gave the spacecraft the capability to operate through its basic mission without ground commands—with the exception of spacecraft maneuvers. Critical events were backed up by ground command capability.

Two-way communications were provided by a radio link between Earth tracking stations and a dual transmitter-single receiver system aboard the spacecraft. The on-board communications system included a telemetry subsystem, command subsystem, data storage subsystem and hi-, low- and medium-gain antennas.

The primary spacecraft power source was an arrangement of 14,742 photovoltaic solar cells mounted on four panels which faced the sun during most of the flight to Mars and during orbital operations. Nominal power capability of the panels was about 800 watts at maximum voltage for cruise conditions, decreasing to about 500 watts at Mars. Maximum power demand during orbital operations was about 400 watts. Science instruments were mounted on a scan platform which can be rotated about two axes to point the instrument toward Mars during the spacecraft's approach to the planet and while in orbit. Thermal control on the top and bottom of Mariner's basic octagon was provided by multi-layered aluminized Teflon, while temperature control of six of the electronics compartments was provided by polished metal louvers actuated by coiled bimetallic strips. The strips acted as spiral-wound springs that expand and contract as they heat and cool. The science platform and its array of instruments at the bottom of the octagon was also covered by a thermal blanket. Launch weight, including about 1000 pounds of fuel and oxidizer, was 2200 pounds.

The spacecraft payload consisted of subsystems responsible for gathering, formatting, and transmitting data to the Earth during periods of scientific observation. These included: the TV subsystem, consisting of two cameras and an electronics package, (with one camera configured to take wide-angle, low-resolution pictures and the other to take narrow-angle, high-resolution pictures); an Ebert-Fasti type ultraviolet spectrometer to measure incident

ultraviolet radiation emitted by gases in the Martian upper atmosphere; an infrared radiometer to measure infrared heat radiation from the Martian surface; an infrared interferometer spectrometer to make a series of interferograms of the planet surface, deep space and warm blackbody sources; a data automation subsystem for sampling, digitizing, formatting and output processing of all data from the science experiments; a data storage subsystem to record the high-resolution 132.3 kilobits/sec video data stream from the data automation subsystem, store it until an opportune phase of the mission, and then play back through the flight telemetry subsystem which gathers data from many sources and outputs a single composite telemetry signal to the radio system for transmission to Earth. Mariner 9 was launched from Kennedy Space Center, Florida on 30 May 1971. The spacecraft was inserted into orbit around Mars on 13 November 1971, after a 167 day flight. Upon encounter, a massive dust storm obscured virtually the entire planet. The storm's gradual clearing allowed the spacecraft to begin its scientific mission, and by 6 February 1971, the dust had settled in all areas of the planet except the north polar regions. By that time, Mariner 9 had mapped more than one-third of the planet's surface. Despite the delay, the spacecraft was expected to achieve virtually all its initial objectives. Project scientists were pleased with the volume of data that was returned from the spacecraft. Mariner 9 combined the original mission objectives of Mariner 8, which failed shortly after launch on 8 May 1971.

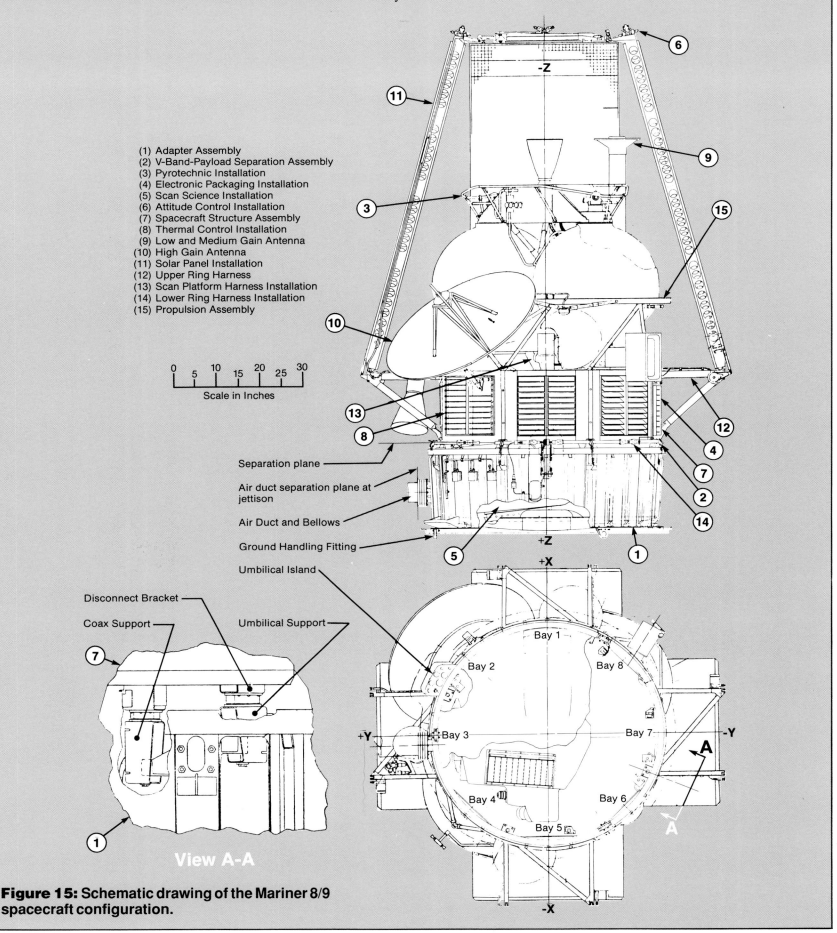

(1) Adapter Assembly
(2) V-Band-Payload Separation Assembly
(3) Pyrotechnic Installation
(4) Electronic Packaging Installation
(5) Scan Science Installation
(6) Attitude Control Installation
(7) Spacecraft Structure Assembly
(8) Thermal Control Installation
(9) Low and Medium Gain Antenna
(10) High Gain Antenna
(11) Solar Panel Installation
(12) Upper Ring Harness
(13) Scan Platform Harness Installation
(14) Lower Ring Harness Installation
(15) Propulsion Assembly

Scale in Inches

Separation plane
Air duct separation plane at jettison
Air Duct and Bellows
Ground Handling Fitting
Umbilical Island
Disconnect Bracket
Coax Support
Umbilical Support

View A-A

Figure 15: Schematic drawing of the Mariner 8/9 spacecraft configuration.

E. SCIENTIFIC SUBSYSTEMS

The Camera

The purpose for this hypothetical low budget interplanetary expedition is to get pictures, so the camera is probably the central piece of hardware in the entire project. The rocket motor sends the spacecraft to its planetary encounter and the antenna subsystem transmits the data, but the camera gets the pictures!

The Voyager spacecraft imaging system was designed with two television cameras that were used for a broad range of picture-taking tasks that were officially designated as the Imaging Science Investigation. The specific science objectives included reconnaissance of Jupiter, Saturn and their moon systems, including high-resolution photography of atmospheric motions, colors and unusual features (such as Jupiter's Great Red Spot and similar smaller 'spots'), vertical structure of the atmospheres of the planets, comparative and detailed geology of satellites, satellite size and rotation, and detailed studies of the rings of Saturn.

Two television-type cameras were mounted on the Voyager spacecraft's scan platform: a 200mm focal-length, wide-angle camera sensitive to 4000 to 6200 Angstroms of light and a 1500mm focal-length, narrow-angle (telephoto) camera with a 300-Angstrom to 600-Angstrom range (*see pages 86–91*).

So close did Voyager come to its targets, that the discs of Jupiter and Saturn exceeded the field of view of the narrow-angle camera about 20 days before closest approach. At that time, resolution was about 250 miles. For several days before and after closest approach, Voyager scientists had several simultaneous imaging opportunities:

- ◆ Photography at high resolution of planets whose angular diameters are many times larger than the field of view.
- ◆ Close encounters with the major satellites. For example, all four Galilean satellites (Jupiter's largest) were photographed at resolution better than 2.5 miles.
- ◆ More distant photography of several additional satellites.
- ◆ High-resolution photography of Saturn's rings.

To exploit such a variety of opportunities, it was necessary for the spacecraft to return large quantities of imaging data so the

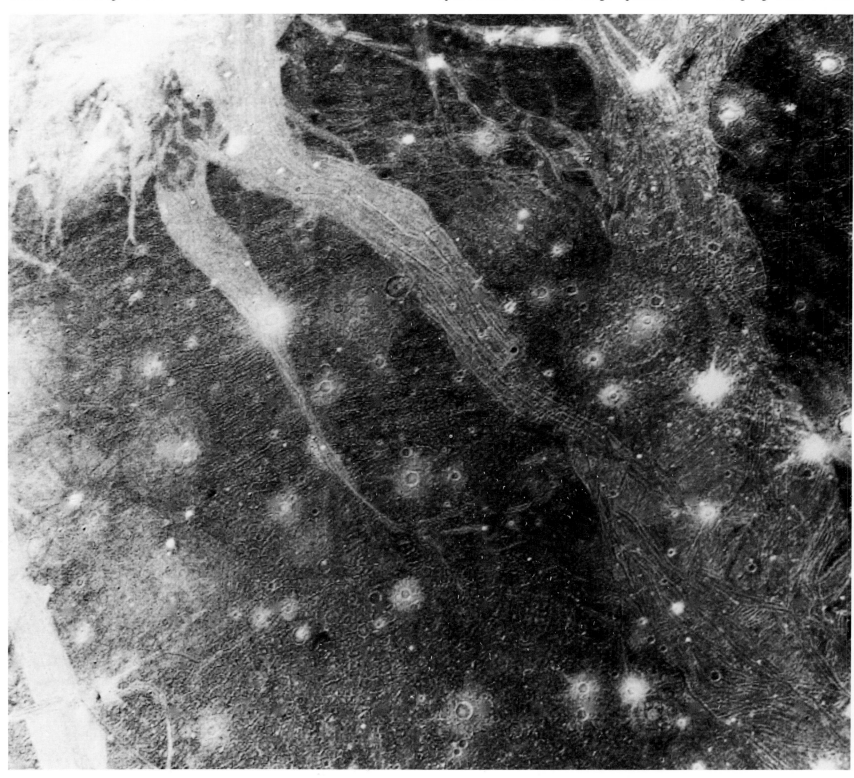

spacecraft's subsystems were designed to return imaging data over a wide range of telemetry rates in real time. Data was also recorded on board the spacecraft for later playback to Earth—during eclipse by Jupiter, for instance.

Each camera was equipped with a filter wheel whose eight individual filters have a variety of uses. The wide-angle camera filter wheel contains one clear filter, one each in violet, blue, green and orange wavelengths, a 7-Angstrom sodium D filter for special observations near the Jovian moon Io and other satellites, and two 100-Angstrom filters at the wavelength of methane absorption for study of the distribution of methane in the atmospheres of Jupiter, Saturn, Titan and Uranus. The narrow-angle camera's filter wheel carries two clear filters, two green and one each of violet, blue, orange and ultraviolet.

Voyager was also the first imaging system with narrow-band capability to directly observe distribution of atomic and molecular species. The 7-Angstrom sodium D filter is the narrowest band width filter ever flown with this kind of camera.

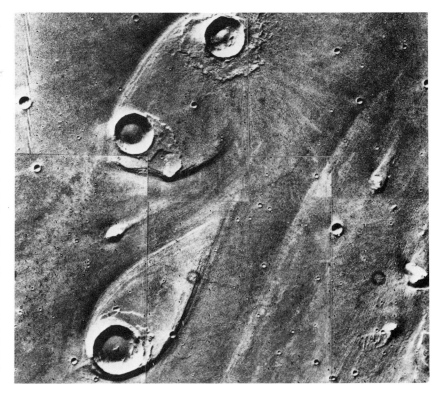

Below left: Voyager 2 took this high resolution picture of Ganymede, one of Jupiter's 'Galilean' moons. The photo was taken from a range of 195,000 miles, and shows features down to 3.1 miles across. For comparison, the broadest band of grooved terrain shown here is 62.1 miles wide. *Above right:* A mosaic of pictures taken by the Viking 1 Orbiter. Shown here is part of Mars' Chryse Planitia region as seen by the Viking 1 cameras from a range of 992 miles. *Below:* This photo of Mars' Valles Marineris was also taken by Viking 1.

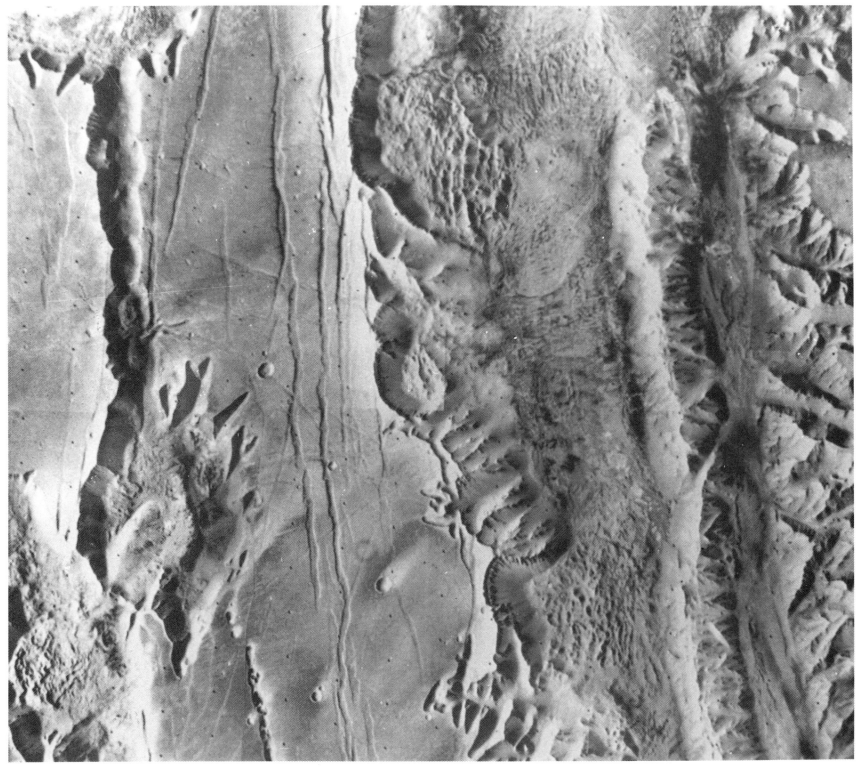

Because the Voyager spacecraft passed the planets and satellites at high velocities and had to take pictures in dimmer light than the Mariner missions to the inner planets, image smear conditions were more severe than on previous flights of Mariner and Pioneer spacecraft. To overcome these problems, the camera's preamplifiers were redesigned to lower the system's electronic 'background noise' and to incorporate a high gain state. Both changes are meant to provide high quality images with minimum 'smear.' (These problems may be obviated by the current state of the art in digital electronics.)

During the several months before closest approach, the narrow-angle cameras photographed Jupiter and Saturn regularly and often to provide information on cloud motions. These pictures were taken on a schedule which permitted scientists to make motion pictures in which the planet's rotation had been 'frozen' so that only the cloud motions were apparent. Resolution during the period ranged from about 100 miles to about 250 miles. Once the planet was close enough and began to appear larger than the narrow-angle camera's field of view, the wide- angle camera began its work. The narrow-angle camera then repeatedly photographed portions of the planets that warranted special scientific interest. Both cameras were shuttered simultaneously during these periods so the JPL scientists could relate small scale motions to larger patterns.

Because of the speed of the planetary flybys, the cameras were unable to concentrate on a single target for hours at a time. For ex-ample, as the spacecraft raced past each of the moons, they presented an ever-changing appearance to the cameras. The planets' clouds were in constant motion. Therefore, observational sequences were structured to provide repeated images at differing intervals for each target.

The two cameras in Voyager's imaging system weigh a total of 84 pounds and use 41.7 watts of power, including 8.6 watts for instrument and scan platform supplementary heaters.

Voyager's two television cameras, ultraviolet spectrometer (*see page 62*), photopolarimeter (*see page 56*) and infrared spectrometer and radiometer (*see page 54*) are mounted on a scan platform which can be rotated about two axes for precise pointing at Jupiter, Saturn and their satellites during the planetary phases of the flight. The platform is located at the end of the science boom, and has a total gimballed weight of 236 pounds.

Controlled by the attitude and articulation control subsystem (AACS), the platform allows multiple pointing directions of the instruments. Driver circuits for the scan actuators—one for each axis—are located in the AACS computer. The platform's two axes of rotation are the azimuth angle motion about an axis displaced seven degrees from the spacecraft roll axis (perpendicular to the boom centerline), and the elevation angled motion about an axis perpendicular to the azimuth axis and rotating with the azimuth axis. Angular range is 360 degrees in azimuth and 210 degrees in elevation.

A large number of lightweight professional video cameras suitable for our purposes are available on the general market. There are certainly more available today than there were in the mid-1970s and this has been made possible because of advancements in the aerospace hardware field.

Because no tape drive is necessary, a full feature hand-held camera such as one might be familiar with from home use would not be used. A fixed surveillance-type camera would, however, be ideal. It would have all the components needed, without the added weight and complexity of many moving parts. It should be a color camera (of course!) and have solid state components. Preferably it should be designed with CCD (Charge Coupled Device) chips which are the state of the art in video technology.

Sony Corporation, a world leader in this industry, describes it thusly: 'Unlike pickup tubes, Sony's CCD chips will not 'burn in' or 'bloom' when shooting extremely bright objects so you can shoot the Sun without causing damage. Unlike tubes, CCDs resist lag and comet-tails ('image smear') when shooting moving objects against a dark background. Unlike tubes, CCD chips are free from geometric distortion. Images are reproduced with 100 percent linearity. Unlike tubes, CCDs resist shock, are immune from magnetic interference, and provide excellent sensitivity in low light.'

In the area of Sony CCD color surveillance cameras, the DXC-102 (*right*) with its f1.4 lens is certainly a contender. It weighs only

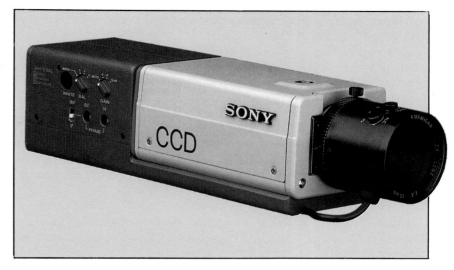

In terms of compactness, light weight and non-distortion of image, a video camera such as the Sony CCD DXC-102 (*above*) could be adapted for a low-cost interplanetary spacecraft. This camera's Charge Coupled Device chips are superior to tube technology in all but the area of resisting intense radiation—it would have to be well shielded. *Below:* This Voyager 2 photo of intensely radioactive Jupiter (with its innermost moon, the volcanic Io shown with remarkable clarity in the foreground) was taken by one of that spacecraft's two television cameras from a distance of eight million miles. Voyager's two cameras weigh a total of 42 pounds. The resolution of individual features in this photo is down to 125 miles.

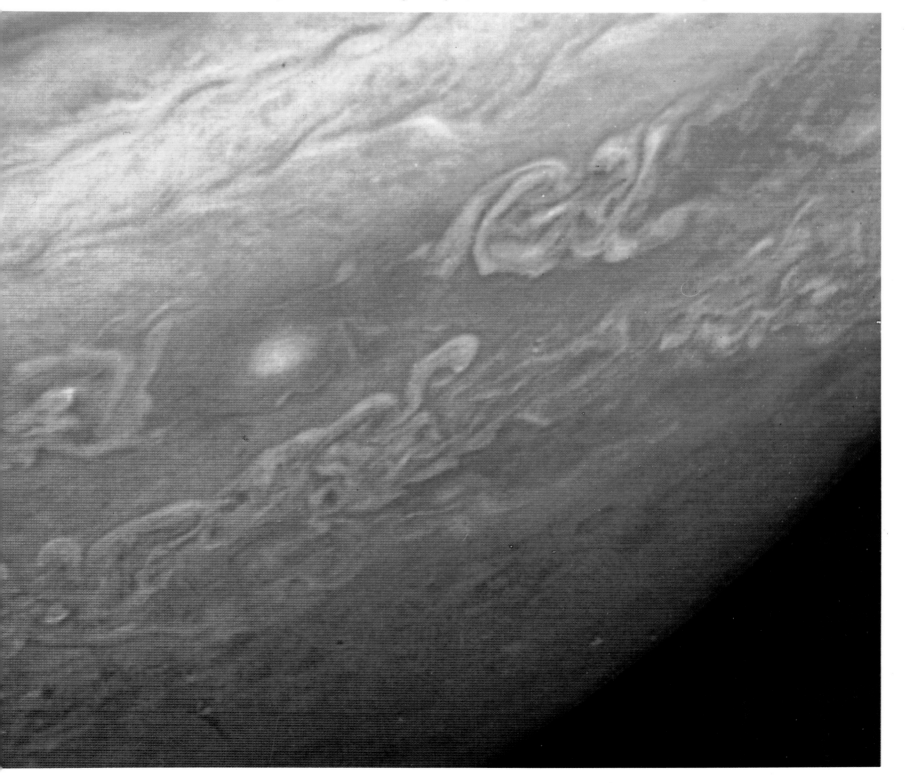

1.75 pounds and measures two and five-eighths inches by two and three-eighths inches by eight inches, so two could easily be accommodated within the size and weight limitations of our hypothetical spacecraft. The DXC-102 is advertised as having 'excellent low-light performance down to 30 lux,' which would be extremely useful in the environment four billion miles from the Sun (*see photo, page 84–85*).

Technically, it has a low power consumption (six watts) and very high resolution (320 lines). It is also designed with no magnetic deflection or convergence circuit, so that it will withstand intense magnetic fields. The latter would, of course, be quite useful in the environs of the larger planets.

An issue to address, however, is heating. The DXC-102 requires temperatures of 23 to 104° F to operate, much warmer than the near absolute zero of outer space, so a heating blanket would have to be integrated into the camera platform (*see page 48–49, 80*) and this entire subsystem would have to be monitored frequently throughout the mission.

Weight Budget (*Continued from page 32*)		**920.0 lb**
Propellant		720.0 lb
Propellant stage hardware		
Rocket motor	15.0 lb	
Fuel tank	6.6 lb	
Oxydizer tank	6.6 lb	
Fixtures and fittings	2.8 lb	
Residuals (unburned propellant)	7.2 lb	
Bracketry	12.0 lb	
Subtotal:		50.2 lb
Attitude control subsystem		
Cold gas system	5.0 lb	
Fixtures, fittings and bracketry	15.0 lb	
Subtotal:		20.0 lb
Propellant stage, optional enhancements		9.8 lb
Computer, casing and wiring		40.0 lb
Antenna		
TA 550 scaled twice up (less stand)		45.0 lb
Camera system		
Two Sony DXC-102s		3.5 lb
Platform		5.0 lb
Running Total (*Concludes on page 82*)		**873.5 lb**

Spectrometer

Second in interest only to the real life imagery obtained by the camera would be spectroscopy. Because little is known about the chemical composition of Pluto or its atmosphere, any spectroscopic information returned by an exploring spacecraft would constitute a major scientific breakthrough.

Spectroscope is, however, just a fancy word for a multi-spectral camera, a camera looking at a subject through a series of filters. This could be accommodated easily—within limits—with filter bins on the CCD array, using a fish group scanner, which is just a row of charge-coupled sensors. These could be a charge-coupled array with 1000 or 2000 cells in it. The motion of the spacecraft or the object carrying the camera would make up the image, the strip. Another option would be to use a full array that takes an instantaneous picture. There could be four of them, each with a different filter on them and these could be sensitive up to a micron (one millionth of a meter), to the infrared. If there were a big square array one would probably need a wheel between the array and the actual optical element. We already have whatever optical elements are necessary in the camera, so it's simply a matter of arranging for the image to pass through the filter wheel.

Even linear arrays with individual filters might work perfectly well. The other possibility is to have multiple feeds from the optical element so that we have four feeds—one each at 0.5 micron, 0.7

The Pioneer Imaging Photopolarimeter

The entire complex of scientific instruments carried onboard The Pioneer 10 and 11 spacecraft was needed to provide the first close-up investigations of Jupiter and Saturn and their environments. The imaging photopolarimeter (IPP) returned the data from which the colored images of the cloud covers of Jupiter and Saturn, and of the magnificent rings of Saturn, were constructed to reveal details never before seen.

The IPP consisted basically of a positionable optics-detector assembly and an electronic equipment housing, supported on a central mounting frame. Special optical materials were selected to retain their transparency even after being subjected to radiation effects from trapped energetic protons and electrons in the radiation belts of Jupiter and Saturn.

The optical system shown diagrammatically in Figure 16 consisted of a one-inch diameter Maksutov-type telescope, a calcite Wollaston prism polarization analyzer, multilayer filters to separate red and blue components of the reflected light from Jupiter and Saturn, relay optics, and two dual-channel multiplier detectors, each designed to sense two polarization components in one of two colors (a total of four channels). The field of view of the instrument could be varied by use of three apertures on a carrier that also carried polarization processing elements (depolarizer and half-wave retardation plate) and an internal calibration lamp.

Analog signals from the detectors were digitized, buffered in the spacecraft's data storage unit, and transmitted together with instrument status information in either of two telemetry formats.

After a command into the data-taking mode had been received, the electronic logic processor automatically provided all internal commands required to sequence a complete measurement operation with the IPP and then return the instrument to standby. Additional commands were available to adjust power supply voltages, thereby controlling the gain of the instrument, to alter sampling rates, to inhibit functions, to change the direction in which the telescope stepped, and so on.

The field of view of 0.028 degrees square was employed in the imaging mode of the IPP. This field of view was moved in steps with every roll of the spacecraft, unless inhibited by command. Step direction could be selected by command. A six-bit telemetry format provided 64 shades of gray for imaging. In that mode only two of the four detector channels were used, and the light was depolarized before detection. Sampling took place on the dark sky, and the resultant output was used to compensate for zero-level shifts and background caused by the radiation belt environment. Detector output was measured, alternating colors, each 0.015 degrees of spacecraft roll, or 0.03 degrees if the low sampling rate had been commanded. The spacecraft buffer stored imaging data collected over 14 degrees of each roll or 28 degrees in the low sampling rate.

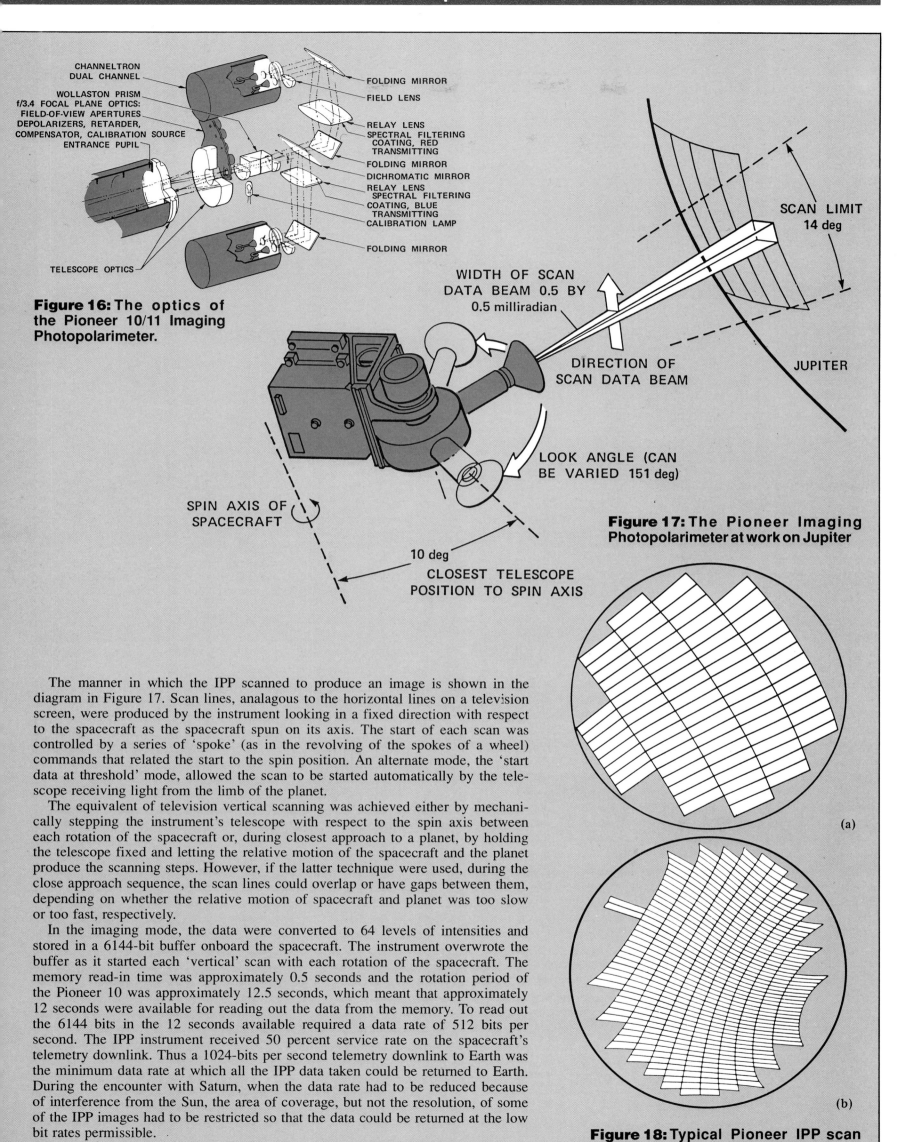

CHANNELTRON
DUAL CHANNEL

WOLLASTON PRISM
f/3.4 FOCAL PLANE OPTICS:
FIELD-OF-VIEW APERTURES
DEPOLARIZERS, RETARDER,
COMPENSATOR, CALIBRATION SOURCE
ENTRANCE PUPIL

TELESCOPE OPTICS

FOLDING MIRROR
FIELD LENS

RELAY LENS
SPECTRAL FILTERING
COATING, RED
TRANSMITTING
FOLDING MIRROR
DICHROMATIC MIRROR
RELAY LENS
SPECTRAL FILTERING
COATING, BLUE
TRANSMITTING
CALIBRATION LAMP

FOLDING MIRROR

Figure 16: The optics of the Pioneer 10/11 Imaging Photopolarimeter.

WIDTH OF SCAN
DATA BEAM 0.5 BY
0.5 milliradian

DIRECTION OF
SCAN DATA BEAM

SCAN LIMIT
14 deg

JUPITER

LOOK ANGLE (CAN
BE VARIED 151 deg)

SPIN AXIS OF
SPACECRAFT

10 deg
CLOSEST TELESCOPE
POSITION TO SPIN AXIS

Figure 17: The Pioneer Imaging Photopolarimeter at work on Jupiter

(a)

(b)

Figure 18: Typical Pioneer IPP scan maps of Jupiter.

The manner in which the IPP scanned to produce an image is shown in the diagram in Figure 17. Scan lines, analogous to the horizontal lines on a television screen, were produced by the instrument looking in a fixed direction with respect to the spacecraft as the spacecraft spun on its axis. The start of each scan was controlled by a series of 'spoke' (as in the revolving of the spokes of a wheel) commands that related the start to the spin position. An alternate mode, the 'start data at threshold' mode, allowed the scan to be started automatically by the telescope receiving light from the limb of the planet.

The equivalent of television vertical scanning was achieved either by mechanically stepping the instrument's telescope with respect to the spin axis between each rotation of the spacecraft or, during closest approach to a planet, by holding the telescope fixed and letting the relative motion of the spacecraft and the planet produce the scanning steps. However, if the latter technique were used, during the close approach sequence, the scan lines could overlap or have gaps between them, depending on whether the relative motion of spacecraft and planet was too slow or too fast, respectively.

In the imaging mode, the data were converted to 64 levels of intensities and stored in a 6144-bit buffer onboard the spacecraft. The instrument overwrote the buffer as it started each 'vertical' scan with each rotation of the spacecraft. The memory read-in time was approximately 0.5 seconds and the rotation period of the Pioneer 10 was approximately 12.5 seconds, which meant that approximately 12 seconds were available for reading out the data from the memory. To read out the 6144 bits in the 12 seconds available required a data rate of 512 bits per second. The IPP instrument received 50 percent service rate on the spacecraft's telemetry downlink. Thus a 1024-bits per second telemetry downlink to Earth was the minimum data rate at which all the IPP data taken could be returned to Earth. During the encounter with Saturn, when the data rate had to be reduced because of interference from the Sun, the area of coverage, but not the resolution, of some of the IPP images had to be restricted so that the data could be returned at the low bit rates permissible.

—*NASA's Jet Propulsion Laboratory*

micron, 0.6 micron and 1.0 micron, or the various colors of the spectrum light in which one is interested. The image is then simultaneously split four ways between all these rays and the computer takes in the data at high speed, stores it and then retransmits it. The spectroscopic as well as real life video imagery would be gathered, transmitted digitally and then sorted out back on Earth.

A key watchword in developing a filter spectroscopy system would be *simplicity*. The fewer moving parts the better, and the inclusion of filter strips or filter wheels would definitely require moving parts. This in turn would require careful integration and a great deal of testing.

Comparable NASA spectroscopy systems are discussed in the section covering interplanetary scientific experiments, which follow *on pages 52–63.*

Camera Platform Integration

Whereas Voyager's camera platform was positioned at the end of a deployable 'arm,' it would be simpler, in terms of the number of moving parts in a hypothetical spacecraft, if it were put into a turret. This would be located at the forward end of the spacecraft and designed so that the camera could be oriented to point in any direction to the front of the spacecraft.

The spacecraft would be spin stabilized. That is, it would be constantly rotating as it travels through space. This would mean that the camera platform, or turret, would have to be *despun*. This would call for a separate segment connected to the spacecraft bus like a phonograph turntable. It would rotate against the rotation of the spacecraft so that it would have the appearance of not moving at all.

At right: **The Intelsat 4F-5 communications satellite during pre-launch checkout. The satellite was spin stabilized, and its antennae were despun; it handled 12 television (and 6000 voice and data) channels. *At far right:* A spinning Hughes HS 376 emerges from a pallet in a Space Shuttle's payload bay. This spin stabilized spacecraft has a fold-down antenna/signal reflector that, when unfolded, is despun for reception and transmission.**

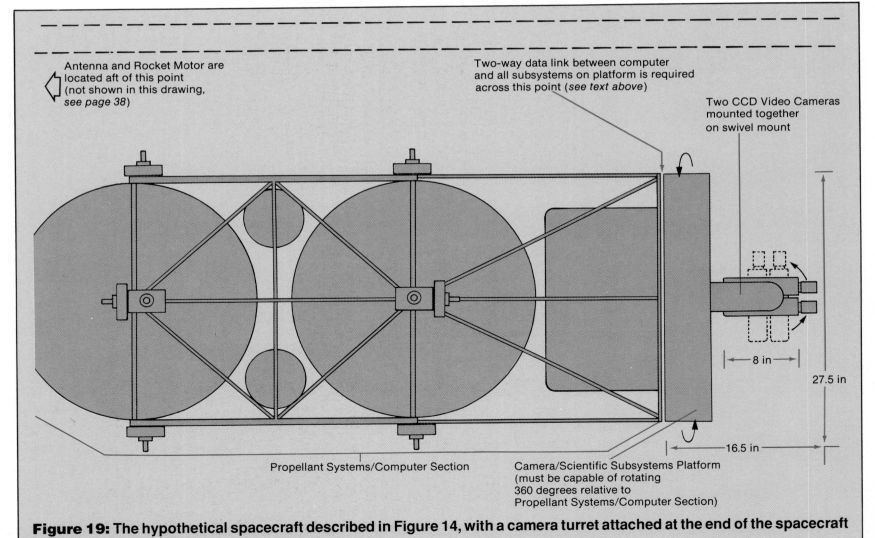

Figure 19: The hypothetical spacecraft described in Figure 14, with a camera turret attached at the end of the spacecraft bus.

The Hughes HS 376 communications satellite, for example, has an antenna that is despun against the rotation speed of the satellite itself (*see photo at left*).

The rotation process would be facilitated not with a central shaft like a propeller, but rather with electric motors which power little teflon wheels on the edges, like a phonograph turntable.

There is a problem inherent in having two major parts of the spacecraft rotating against one another. It will be necessary to connect the camera to the computer, the electrical power source and the antenna. But it is impossible to *hard wire* two objects rotating against one another because the wire would break.

A possible solution to this problem would be to incorporate the spacecraft bus that contains the computer and power source as *part* of the camera turret and rotate it *with* the camera and *against* the rest of the spacecraft. These systems would still have to be linked to the antenna and the motor in the aft part of the spacecraft, but this interface would be *much* simpler than, for instance, one between the computer and the camera platform.

This link could be achieved by a *fiber optic* link through the centerpoint of the circle of rotation. A beam, or beams, of light would carry the necessary communication between sensors on either side of the centerpoint. To limit the amount of electricity that would be transmitted optically, there would be independent battery arrays located on both sides of the optic link.

As the aft section spins and provides the stabilization of the spacecraft, we get a fiber optic signal to the antenna from all the video and there is no problem with data rate. When the spacecraft is ready for its high-power transmission during planetary encounter, there will be no power transmitting across the joint.

There are many firms that build fiber optic links. Marine companies, for example, make them for rotating underwater joints. What one has is essentially two spacecraft that are flying in formation, both of which have independent electrical sources. There would be a whole power distribution system in each part. On one side are the computer, optical elements and other science systems, while on the other side are the transmitter and receiver—the antenna dish—and tanks and motor. The link between the two would be optical.

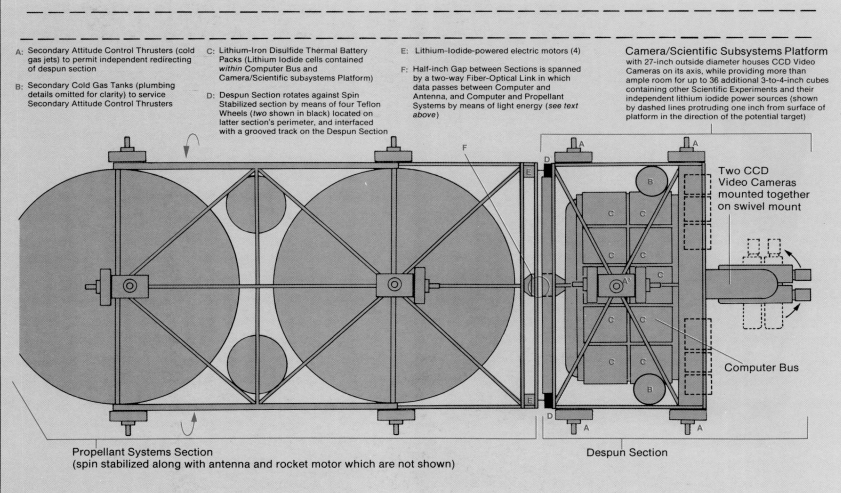

A: Secondary Attitude Control Thrusters (cold gas jets) to permit independent redirecting of despun section

B: Secondary Cold Gas Tanks (plumbing details omitted for clarity) to service Secondary Attitude Control Thrusters

C: Lithium-Iron Disulfide Thermal Battery Packs (Lithium Iodide cells contained *within* Computer Bus and Camera/Scientific subsystems Platform)

D: Despun Section rotates against Spin Stabilized section by means of four Teflon Wheels (*two* shown in black) located on latter section's perimeter, and interfaced with a grooved track on the Despun Section

E: Lithium-Iodide-powered electric motors (4)

F: Half-inch Gap between Sections is spanned by a two-way Fiber-Optical Link in which data passes between Computer and Antenna, and Computer and Propellant Systems by means of light energy (*see text above*)

Camera/Scientific Subsystems Platform with 27-inch outside diameter houses CCD Video Cameras on its axis, while providing more than ample room for up to 36 additional 3-to-4-inch cubes containing other Scientific Experiments and their independent lithium iodide power sources (shown by dashed lines protruding one inch from surface of platform in the direction of the potential target)

Two CCD Video Cameras mounted together on swivel mount

Computer Bus

Propellant Systems Section
(spin stabilized along with antenna and rocket motor which are not shown)

Despun Section

Figure 20: The hypothetical spacecraft illustrated in Figure 19, but with the entire bus and camera platform swivelling as a single unit (*note fiber optic connection*).

Technical Profiles of Great Interplanetary Spacecraft

Pioneer 10 and Pioneer 11

The launch vehicles for both spacecraft were Atlas-Centaur rockets with a TE-M-364-4 third stage weighing 2510 pounds and developing 14,800 pounds thrust, boosting the spacecraft to 31,122 miles per hour top speed.

Pioneer 10 was successfully launched 3 March 1972, from Kennedy Space Center, Florida. It entered the asteroid belt 15 July 1972 and emerged unscathed 15 February 1973, after a seven-month transit. It passed within 81,000 miles of Jupiter on 3 December 1973 and passed the outer edge of the known Solar System in 1987, the first manmade object to do so (*see Figure 58, page 107*).

Pioneer 11 was successfully launched 6 April 1973, from Kennedy Space Center, Florida. It crossed the Moon's orbit 11 hours after. It entered the asteroid belt 18 August 1973, and emerged 18 March 1974. Travelling at a speed of 39,700 mph, the fastest speed yet attained by a manmade object, Pioneer 11 passed within 26,680 miles of Jupiter on 3 December 1974 and within 21,000 miles of Saturn's rings on 1 September 1979.

The Pioneer 10 and 11 project objectives were to investigate Jupiter and its environment, the asteroid belt, the interplanetary medium as far out as Saturn's orbit, two billion miles from the Sun, then to escape the Solar System.

Eleven instruments and the spacecraft radio were carried by both Pioneers, which were used to conduct two experiments (celestial mechanics and S-band occultation). The instruments included a meteoroid detector, an asteroid/meteoroid detector, a plasma analyzer, a helium vector magnometer, a charged-particle detector, a cosmic-ray telescope, a geiger-tube telescope, a trapped-radiation telescope, an ultraviolet photometer, an infrared radiometer and an imaging photo-polarimeter. The plasma analyzer, cosmic ray telescope, asteroid/meteoroid telescopes, meteoroid sensors and the magnetometer sensors are mounted outside the instrument compartment. A flux-gate magnetometer experiment was carried only by Pioneer 11 (*see pages 52–63*).

The spacecraft equipment compartment was a 14 inch deep, flat box, the top and bottom of which were regular hexagons 28 inches on a side. One side joined to a smaller box also 14 inches deep whose top and bottom were irregular hexagons. The smaller box contained 37 pounds of onboard experiments. Attached to the hexagonal front face of the equipment compartment was a nine foot diameter, 18 inch deep antenna. High-gain antenna feed and medium-gain antenna horn were mounted at the focal point of the antenna dish on three struts projecting about four feet forward of the rim of the dish. The low-gain antenna extended about two and one-half feet behind the equipment compartment.

Two three-rod trusses, 120 degrees apart, projected from two sides of the equipment compartment to deploy the radioisotope thermoelectric generator (RTG) power sources about 10 feet from the center of the spacecraft. A third boom, 120 degrees from each of the other two, projected from the experiment compartment and positions the magnetometer sensor 21.5 feet from the spacecraft center. At the rim of the antenna dish was a sun sensor. A star sensor looked through an opening in the equipment compartment and was protected from sunlight by a hood. Both compartments had aluminum frames with bottoms and side walls of aluminum honeycomb. The dish antenna was made of aluminum honeycomb sandwich. Rigid external tubular trusswork supported the dish antenna, three pairs of thrusters located near the rim of the dish, boom mounts, and launch vehicle attachment ring. The spacecraft was spin-stabilized at 4.8 rpm. Total weight of the Pioneer at launch was 570 pounds, including 66 pounds of scientific instruments. RTGs provided 120 watts of power to the spacecraft and its experiments.

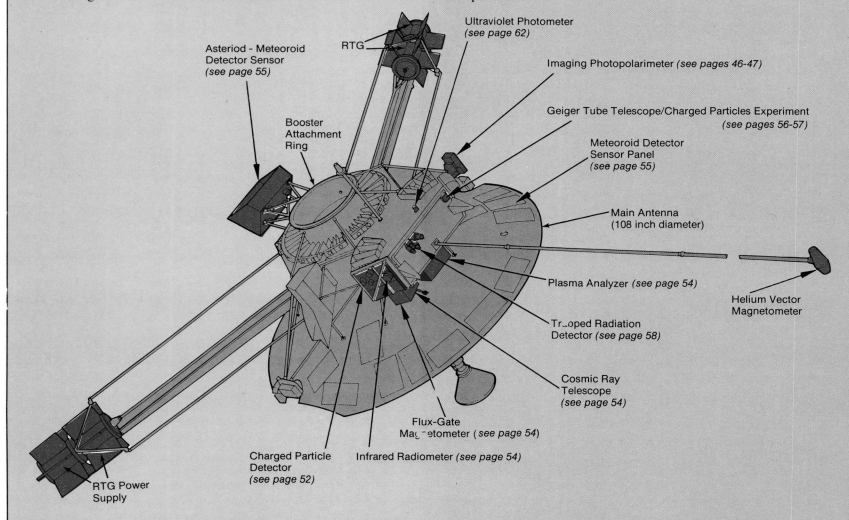

Figure 21: A three-quarter view of the Pioneer 10/11 spacecraft configuration.

Other Scientific Subsystems

I n addition to a video camera and a spectroscopy subsystem, additional instruments might be interesting to explore. A magnetometer measuring the intensity of Pluto's magnetic fields and a charged particle experiment would be useful. They would tell the spacecraft's ground controllers about the environment that the spacecraft has been exposed to and to provide data for use in navigation during the final week of approach to planetary encounter.

These scientific experiments could be located either in the bus or on the camera platform. Most would be self-contained in boxes roughly the same size as the CCD camera, or smaller. They could even have a self-contained power source. Their only necessary connection to the spacecraft would be a data link to the computer.

These subsystems could be solicited from a number of sources including university astrophysics departments, amateur astronomy organizations, industrial firms, or even hobbyists.

For informational purposes, we have listed here NASA descriptions of a number of experiments (including spectroscopy) that were included in their outer Solar System interplanetary spacecraft.

Celestial Mechanics Experiment
Pioneer 10/11 (1972/73)

Deep space tracking of the Pioneer spacecraft determined their velocities along the Earth-spacecraft line to within a fraction of a millimeter per second. This information was obtained once per minute during tracking periods.

The two-way Doppler (*see Glossary*) tracking data, augmented by optical and radar position data about the planets, were used to determine the planetary masses from their perturbations on the path of the spacecraft. Computer calculations, based on the spacecraft's trajectory and known planetary and satellite orbital characteristics, provided a fivefold reduction, for example, in the uncertainty of Jupiter's mass. Masses of the four large satellites of Jupiter (Io, Europa, Ganymede, and Callisto) were determined to an accuracy of better than one percent. The experiment also determined the polar flattening of the planets to great precision (0.5 mile for Jupiter).

The gravitational fields of the planets were determined and their response to a relatively rapid rotation was used to construct new models for the planetary interiors. The equations of state for hydrogen, helium, and rocks under high pressures were used for the models.

Thus, this celestial mechanics experiment made use of the spacecraft itself as a sensitive instrument affected by the gravitational fields of Jupiter, Saturn, and the large satellites of the two planets.

Charged Particle Detector (see photo on page 58)
Pioneer 10/11 (1972/73)

The charged particle detector had four measuring systems: two particle telescopes that operated in interplanetary space and two that measured the trapped electrons and protons inside the radiation belts of Jupiter and Saturn.

During the interplanetary phase of the mission, before and after encounter with Jupiter and Saturn, this experiment sought to identify the chemical elements hydrogen, helium, lithium, beryllium, boron, carbon, nitrogen, and oxygen, and to separate hydrogen, deuterium, helium-3, and helium-4 in an attempt to differentiate between particles emanating from the Sun and those from the galaxy. The instrument was also used to determine how streams of high-energy particles from the Sun travel through interplanetary space.

The main telescope of seven solid-state detectors measured the composition of cosmic rays from 1 to 500 MeV, and a three-element, low-energy telescope measured 0.4- to 10-MeV protons and helium nuclei.

Two new types of sensors were developed to cope with the extremely high intensities of trapped particles in the Jovian magnetosphere. A solid-state electron current detector, operating below -40° C (-40° F), detected those electrons above 3.3 million electron volts (MeV) that generate the decimetric radio waves emitted by Jupiter and similar electrons in the radiation environment of Saturn. A trapped proton detector contained a foil of thorium, the atoms of which underwent nuclear fission when hit by protons with energies above 35 MeV; the foil was insensitive to electrons.

Below: An image of Saturn assembled from Voyager 2 pictures taken 13 million miles away. The Voyagers both conduct interplanetary studies, including celestial mechanics, occultation, infrared and ultraviolet spectroscopy, photo polarimetry, magnetometry, radio astronomy, radiometry, cosmic ray investigation and plasma analysis.

Cosmic Ray Energy Spectra Experiment
Pioneer 10/11 (1972/73)

The instrument consisted of three three-element solid-state telescopes. The high-energy telescope measured the flux of protons between 56 and 800 MeV. The medium-energy telescope measured protons with energies between 3 and 22 MeV and identified the ten elements from hydrogen to neon. The low-energy telescope measured the flux of electrons between 0.05 and 1 MeV and of protons between 0.05 and 20 MeV.

The cosmic ray telescope used for this experiment was designed to monitor solar and galactic cosmic ray particles and to track the high-energy particles from the Sun. The instrument could determine which nuclei of the ten lightest elements are the cosmic ray particles. Before saturation by radiation when near Jupiter and Saturn, the cosmic ray telescope measured high-energy particles in the radiation belts of these planets.

Cosmic-Ray Investigation
Voyager 1/2 (1977)

The cosmic-ray investigation had four principal scientific objectives:
- To measure the energy spectrum of electrons and cosmic-ray nuclei;
- To determine the elemental and isotopic composition of cosmic-ray nuclei;
- To make elemental and isotopic studies of Jupiter's radiation belts and to explore Saturn's environment, whose possible radiation belts have not yet been positively detected from Earth;
- To determine the intensity and directional characteristics of energetic particles as a function of radial distance from the Sun, and determine the location of the modulation boundary.

It used multiple-solid state detector telescopes to provide large solid-angle viewing. The Voyager low-energy telescope system covered the range from 0.5 to 9 million electron volts (MeV) per nucleon. The high-energy telescope system covered the range from 4 to 500 MeV. The Voyager electron telescope system covered the range from 7 MeV. The cosmic-ray instrument weighed 16.5 pounds and used 8.25 watts of power, including 2.8 watts for supplementary heaters.

Flux-Gate Magnetometer Experiment
Pioneer 11 (1973)

The instrument, mounted on the main body of the spacecraft, used two magnetic ring cores that were driven to saturation by associated oscillators at a frequency of 8 kHz. The presence of an external magnetic field created an imbalance in the sensors which was detected by four coil windings; the coil windings were oriented perpendicular to each other. This instrument was designed to measure the intense planetary fields of Jupiter and Saturn and to extend the measuring capability of the spacecraft beyond the range provided by the helium vector magnetometer. The scientific objectives were to study the intrinsic magnetic fields of Jupiter and Saturn by carrying out measurements during the closest approach phases of the Pioneer 11 mission. The knowledge acquired allowed a comprehensive study of the general problem of how planets, including Earth, generate their magnetic fields, and a determination of the detailed geometry of their inner magnetospheres.

Infrared Radiometer (see photo on page 59)
Pioneer 10/11 (1972/73)

The two-channel radiometer instrument not only determined the temperature across the disks of Jupiter and Saturn (and Saturn's ring system) but also provided important information to aid in determining the thermal structure and chemical composition of each planet's atmosphere.

Like the ultraviolet photometer, the infrared radiometer used a fixed telescope that scanned the surface of the planetary cloudtops as the spacecraft rotated. Because of the fixed viewing angle, the infrared instrument could view the planets for only limited times during approach.

Designed with a three-inch diameter Cassegrain (see Glossary) optical system, the instrument relied on 88-element, thin-film, bimetallic thermopiles to detect infrared radiation. Its field of view was about 450 by 1500 miles on Jupiter's cloud surface at about the time of closest approach. Its resolution at the distance of closest approach was about 1500 miles.

Infrared Spectroscopy and Radiometry Investigation
Voyager 1/2 (1977)

The IRIS instrument was designed to perform spectral and radiometric measurements of the Jovian and Saturnian planetary systems and targets of opportunity during the cruise phase of the mission.

Scientific objectives for IRIS are:
- Measurement of the energy balance of Jupiter and Saturn.
- Studies of the atmospheric compositions of Jupiter, Saturn, Titan and other satellites.
- Temperature structure and dynamics of the atmospheres.
- Measurements of composition and characteristics of clouds and aerosols.
- Studies of the composition and characteristics of ring particles (at Saturn) and the surfaces of those satellites the instrument will observe.

The instrument provided broad spectral coverage, high spectral resolution and low noise equivalence radiance through use of Michelson interferometers. These characteristics of the instrument, as well as the precision of the radiometer, allowed scientists to acquire information about a wide variety of scientific questions concerning the atmospheres of the planets and satellites, local and global energy balance and the nature of satellite surfaces and the rings of Saturn.

Two versions of the IRIS instrument were prepared for possible use on the spacecraft. The first, known simply as IRIS, was designed for use at the Jupiter and Saturn planetary systems. It was an improved version of the IRIS instrument which flew to Mars on Mariner 9 in 1971-72 (see pages 40–41). The second, known as the Modified IRIS, or MIRIS, was designed later to be able to perform farther out in the Solar System at Uranus. Either instrument could be flown on the spacecraft because the principal mechanical and electrical interfaces are identical. The MIRIS instruments were flown on both Voyager spacecrafts because they offered advantages at Jupiter and Saturn as well as at Uranus.

Interplanetary Solar Wind (Plasma) Experiment
Pioneer 10/11 (1972/73)

The Pioneer spacecraft each carried a plasma analyzer to evaluate the solar wind. It looked toward the Sun through a hole in each spacecraft's large dish-shaped antenna. The solar wind particles entered the plasma analyzer's apertures between two quadraspherical plates where the direction of arrival, the energy (speed), and the number of ions and electrons making up the solar wind were measured.

A voltage was applied across the quadraspherical plates in a maximum of 64 steps, at a rate of one step/revolution of the spacecraft, to count particles in discrete energy ranges. The direction of particle travel was determined from instrument orientation and by knowing which of the detector targets the particle struck. The instrument had a high-resolution analyzer and a medium-resolution analyzer to detect particles of different energy levels. The high-resolution analyzer had 26 continuous channel multipliers (CCM) to measure the number of ions per second with energies from 100 to 8000 electron volts (eV). The medium-resolution analyzer had 5 electrometers to count ions in the energy range from 100 to 18,000 3V and electrons from 1 to 500 eV.

The solar wind consists of streams of protons, electrons, and some helium nuclei emitted by the Sun in all directions. Particles in the solar wind affect electrical and communication systems on Earth and may give rise to long-term weather cycles. This wind was unknown until spacecraft began to explore space beyond Earth's magnetosphere in the late 1950s. Some of the charged particles of the solar wind become trapped in radiation belts by Earth's magnetic field. They also account for the aurora borealis, the aurora australis, and other phenomena that baffled scientists until the radiation belts were discovered by experiments carried out by Earth satellites.

Low-Energy Charged-Particle Investigation (see photo at right)
Voyager 1/2 (1977)

Scientific objectives of the Low-Energy Charged Particle Investigation included studies of the charged particle composition, energy-distribution and angular distribution with respect to:

♦ Saturn's magnetosphere (exploratory) and Jupiter's magnetosphere (detailed studies);

♦ Interactions of charged particles with the satellites of Jupiter and Saturn and possibly with the rings of Saturn;

♦ Measurements of quasi-steady interplanetary flux and high-energy components of the solar wind;

♦ Determination of the origin and interstellar propagation of galactic cosmic rays (those that come from outside the Solar System);

♦ Measurements of the propagation of solar particles in the outer Solar System.

The investigation used two solid state detector systems on a rotating platform mounted on the scan platform boom. One system was a low energy magnetospheric particle analyzer with large dynamic range to measure electrons with energy ranging from 15,000 electron volts (15 KeV) to greater than 1 MeV; and ions in the energy range from 15,000 KeV per nucleon to 160 MeV per nucleon.

The second detector system was low-energy particle telescope that covers the range from 0.15 MeV per nucleon to greater than about 10 MeV per nucleon.

The Low-Energy Charged-Particle Investigation weighed 16.5 pounds and drew 9.46 watts including 4.66 watts for supplementary heaters.

Magnetic Fields Experiment
Pioneer 10/11 (1972/73)

This experiment used a sensitive magnetometer mounted on the tip of a lightweight boom extending 21.5 feet from the center of the spacecraft to reduce the effects of even the minute amount of residual magnetic field of the spacecraft and to help balance the spin-stabilized Pioneer spacecraft. The helium vector magnetometer measured the fine structure of the interplanetary field, mapped the fields of Jupiter and Saturn, and provided field measurements to evaluate the interaction of the solar wind with the two planets. The magnetometer operated in any one of eight ranges. The ranges were selected by ground command or automatically by the instrument as it reached the limits of a given range. The sensor for the magnetometer consisted of a cell filled with helium that was excited by electrical discharge at radio frequencies and by infrared optical pumping. Changes in helium absorption caused by magnetic fields passing through the magnetometer were measured by an infrared optical detector.

Magnetic fields permeate the plasma of electrically charged particles in interplanetary space as they spread out from the Sun across the Solar System. Before the Pioneer missions to Jupiter and Saturn, these effects had been observed and measured only to the orbit of Mars. Beginning here, it is a *new* experiment!

Magnetic Fields Investigation

The magnetic field of a plane is an externally measurable manifestation of conditions deep in its interior.

The magnetic fields instruments on Voyager 1 and 2 determined the magnetic and magnetospheric structure at Jupiter and Saturn; they studied interaction of the magnetic field and the satellites that orbit the planets inside that field studied the interplanetary-interstellar magnetic field.

Four magnetometers are carried aboard Voyager. Two are low-field, three-axis instruments located on a boom to place them as far from the spacecraft's magnetic field from the external field that is to be measured. The other two magnemometers are high-field three-axis instruments mounted on the spacecraft body.

Total weight of the magnetic fields investigation was 12.3 lb. The instruments used 2.1 watts of power.

Dr Norman Ness of NASA's Goddard Space Flight Center was principal investigator.

Meteoroid Detector
Pioneer 10/11 (1972/73)

Associated with the Particles and Dust in Space Investigation, this experiment consisted of 13 panels, each containing 18 pressurized cells. The cells were filled with a mixture of argon and nitrogen. These panels had an area of 6.5 square feet and were mounted on the back of the dish antenna.

When a cell was punctured by a particle in interplanetary space, it lost gas at a rate proportional to the size of the hole made in the cell wall. The loss in pressure was detected when the pressure reached a

At top, above: This instrument is a Low Energy Charged Particle detector (LECP unit), and has seen use on both Voyager 1 and 2. Generally, it measures charged particle radiation around a planet, and thereby discerns that planet's magnetic fields, radiation belts and radiation sources (see text, this page). *Above:* Voyager scientists discuss the LECP unit. For a full discussion of the LECP unit, as well as other instruments essential to interplanetary scientific study missions, please see the text pages 49–62.

certain threshold value. Cells on Pioneer 10 recorded impacts with particles with masses as small as one billionth of a gram; on Pioneer 11 the cell walls were thicker so that only more massive particles would be detected.

Occultation Experiment
Pioneer 10/11 (1972/73)

The radio signals from the spacecraft were used in another experiment to probe the atmospheres of Jupiter and Saturn and the innermost large satellite of Jupiter, Io. Passage of each spacecraft's S-band radio signal through the atmospheres of the planets when the Pioneers swung behind them as viewed from Earth directly measured the vertical structure of their ionospheres and provided information on the density of the atmospheres to a pressure level of about one-tenth Earth's atmosphere.

As the spacecraft flew behind the planets (and Pioneer 10 behind a satellite of Jupiter), radio signals from the spacecraft had to pass through the planetary (and satellite) atmospheres on their way to Earth. As the spacecraft flew behind Io and Jupiter, its radio signals were modified by the ionosphere and then cut off by the surface of Io and by the dense atmosphere of Jupiter. Changes in the radio signals as they passed through the atmospheres of these bodies provided valuable information about atmospheric structures, temperatures, compositions, and charged particles.

Particles And Dust In Space Investigation
Pioneer 10/11 (1972/73)

This investigation consisted of two distinct experiments, using different experimental techniques. One technique detected light reflected from particles, the other detected particle impacts.

The instrument for the first experiment consisted of four nonimaging telescopes that detected sunlight reflected from meteoroids passing through their fields of view. Each telescope had an eight-inch diameter primary mirror, secondary optics, and a photomultiplier hue that converted light to electrical signals. When a particle passed through the telescope's eight-degree field of view, reflected light from it was detected by the photomultiplier tube. The fields of view for the four telescopes overlapped slightly. If a particle was 'seen' simultaneously by any three of the telescopes, the instrument recorded an event. From these data, the particle's distance, trajectory, velocity, and relative size were calculated.

These telescopes could detect objects ranging from distant asteroids (miles in diameter) to minute sunlit particles of dust several feet from the telescope.

Photopolarimetry Investigation
Voyager 1/2 (1977)

A great deal of information about the composition of an object can be learned from the way that object reflects light. The Voyager spacecraft's photopolarimeter observed how light reflected from Jupiter, Saturn and their satellites is polarized by the chemicals and aerosols in the atmospheres and on the surfaces.

The photopolarimeter measured methane, molecular hydrogen and ammonia above the cloud tops. It studied aerosol particles in the atmospheres of the planets and satellites; the textures and compositions of the surfaces of satellites; size, albedo, spatial distribution, shape and orientation of particles in Saturn's rings; measured optical and geometric thickness of the rings; and observed the sky background to search for interplanetary and interstellar particles.

The instrument is made up of a 60 inch Cassegrain telescope, aperture sector, polarization analyzer wheel, filter wheel and a photomultiplier tube detector. The filter wheel carries eight filters ranging from 2,350-Angstrom to 7,500-Angstrom wavelength; three linear polarizers (0 degrees, 60 degrees and 120 degrees) plus 'open' or blank. The instrument's field of view can be set at three and one-half degrees, one degree, one-fourth degree and one-sixteenth degree.

The photopolarimeter weighed 9.7 pounds and used 2.6 watts average power.

Planetary And Interplanetary Charged Particles Experiment
Pioneer 10/11 (1972/73)

This instrument measured the intensities, energy, spectra, and angular distribution of energetic electrons and protons in interplanetary space and near Jupiter and Saturn. On Pioneer 10, the instrument

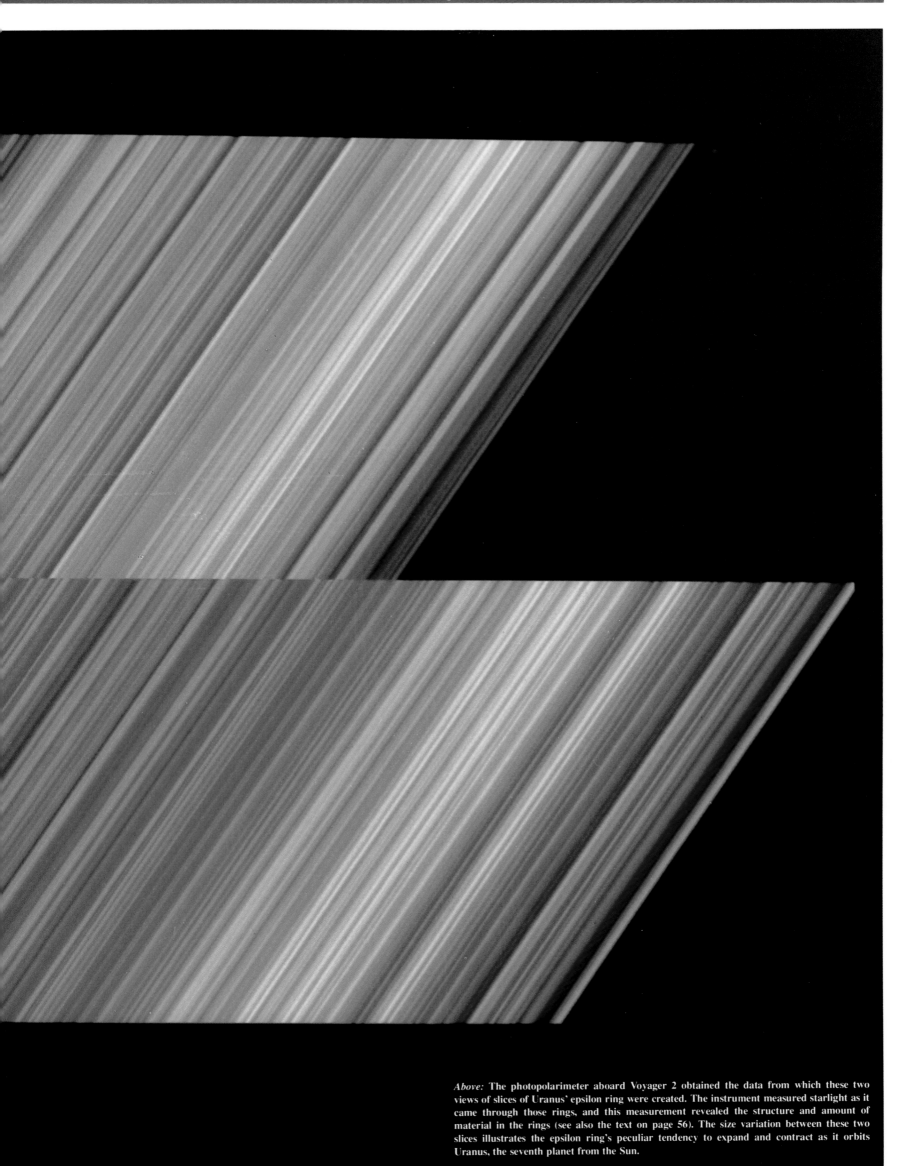

Above: The photopolarimeter aboard Voyager 2 obtained the data from which these two views of slices of Uranus' epsilon ring were created. The instrument measured starlight as it came through those rings, and this measurement revealed the structure and amount of material in the rings (see also the text on page 56). The size variation between these two slices illustrates the epsilon ring's peculiar tendency to expand and contract as it orbits Uranus, the seventh planet from the Sun.

used an array of seven miniature Geiger-Mueller tubes, collectively known as a Geiger tube telescope (GTT). Each tube was a small gas-filled cylinder. When a charged particle passed through the gas, an electrical pulse was generated by the applied voltage. Individual pulses from five of the tubes and coincident pulses from three combinations of seven tubes were transmitted. Protons of energy greater than 5 MeV and electrons with energies greater than 40 MeV were detected.

On Pioneer 11, one Geiger-Mueller tube was replaced by a thin silicon wafer to detect protons in the specific energy range 0.61 to 3.41 MeV. Other minor changes were made to improve the characteristics of the detector system.

The trains of pulses were passed through quasi-logarithmic data processors and then to the radio telemetry system of the spacecraft. Angular distributions were measured as the spacecraft rotated.

Planetary Radio Astronomy Investigation
Voyager 1/2 (1977)

The Planetary Radio Astronomy Investigation consisted of a stepped frequency radio receiver that covered the range from 20 kHz to 40.5 mHz and two monopole antennas 33 feet long to detect and study a variety of radio signals emitted by Jupiter and Saturn.

Scientific objectives of the investigation included detection and study of radio emissions from Jupiter and Saturn and their sources and relationship to the satellites, the planets' magnetic fields, atmospheric lightning and plasma resonances. The instrument also measured planetary and solar radio bursts from new directions in space and related them to measurements made from Earth.

Jupiter emits enormous bursts of radio energy that are not clearly understood. They appear to be related to the planet's magnetosphere, its rotation and even to passage of the satellite Io. The energy released in the strongest bursts is equivalent to that of multi-megaton hydrogen bombs.

The receiver was designed to provide coverage in two frequency bands—one covering the range from 20.4 kHz to 2345 kHz, the second from 1228.8 kHz to 40.5 mHz. The receiver bandwidth was 1 kHz in the low-frequency range and 200 kHz in the high-frequency band. There were three signal input attenuators to provide switchable total attenuation from 0 to 90 decibels.

The instrument weighed 17 pounds and drew 6.7 watts of power.

Planetary Trapped Radiation Experiment
Pioneer 10/11 (1972/73)

Telescopes different from those described in the Planetary Charged Particle Experiment were used in a trapped radiation detector covering a broader range of electron and proton energies. The greater range of this instrument was obtained through use of several different kinds of detectors. An unfocused Cerenkov counter, which measures the light produced by charged particles, detected the light emitted in a particular direction as particles passed through it. It recorded electrons with energies from 0.5 to 12 MeV. An electron scatter detector was activated by electrons with energies from 100 to 400 thousand electron volts (keV).

The instrument also included a minimum ionizing detector consisting of a solid-state diode that measured minimum ionizing particles (*ie*, less than 3 MeV) and protons in the range 50 to 350 MeV. Sensitive materials of different types in two scintillation detectors distinguished between electrons of less than 5 keV and protons of less than 50 keV. These five different 'eyes' of the instrument provided basic information about several of the fundamental features of the planetary radiation belts, including the types of particles within the belts, their distribution, energy, and intensity.

Plasma Investigation (*see photo at right*)
Voyager 1/2 (1977)

Plasma, clouds of ionized gases, moves through the interplanetary region and comes from the Sun and from the other stars. The plasma investigation used two Faraday-cup plasma detectors, one pointed along the Earth-spacecraft line, the other at right angles to that line.

Scientific objectives of the plasma investigation were:
♦ Determine properties of the solar wind, including changes in the properties with increasing distance from the Sun;
♦ Study of the magnetospheres intrinsic to the planets themselves and that corotate with the planets independent of solar wind activity;

Charged Particle Detector (Pioneer 10/11)

Infrared Radiometer (Pioneer 10/11)

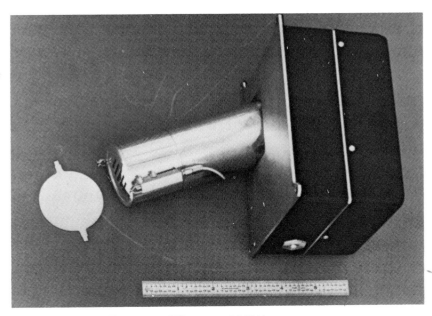

Ultraviolet Radiometer (Pioneer 10/11)

Plasma Investigation hardware (Voyager 1/2)

♦ Study of the satellites of Jupiter and Saturn and the plasma environment of Io;

♦ Detection and measurement of interstellar ions.

The Earth-pointing detector uses a novel geometrical arrangement that makes it equivalent to three Faraday cups and determines macroscopic properties of the plasma ions. With this detector, accurate values of the velocity, density and pressure can be determined for plasma from the Earth (1 AU) to beyond Saturn (10 AU). Two sequential energy scans were employed to allow the instrument to cover a broad range of energies—from 10 ev to 6 KeV). Significant measurements can be made between subsonic and supersonic speeds in cold solar wind or hot planetary magnetosheath.

The variable energy resolution allowed scientists to detect and sort out ions that flow with the solar wind at the same time they measured the solar wind's properties.

The instrument had a large (180 degree) field of view at planetary encounters and a 90 degree field of view in the solar wind. No electrical or mechanical scanning is necessary.

The other Faraday cup, a side-looking or lateral detector, measures electrons in the range of 10 eV to 6 KeV and should improve spatial coverage for any drifting or corotating positive ions during planetary encounters.

The instrument was designed primarily for exploring planets' magnetospheres. It was capable of detecting hot subsonic plasma such as has been observed in the Earth's magnetosphere and is expected from ions originating in the McDonough-Brice ring of Io. The instrument's large angular acceptance allowed detection of plasma flows well away from the direction of the Sun, such as plasma flows that corotate with the planet.

The plasma instrument weighed 21.8 pounds and drew 9.9 watts of power.

Plasma Wave Investigation
Voyager 1/2 (1977)

Scientific objectives of the plasma wave investigation were measurements of thermal plasma density profiles at Jupiter and Saturn, studies of wave-particle interactions and study of the interactions of the Jovian and Saturnian satellites with their planets' magnetospheres (*see Figures 22 and 23*).

The plasma wave instrument measured electric-field components of local plasma waves over the frequency range from 10 Hz to 56 kHz.

The instrument shared the two extendible 33 foot electric antennas provided by the planetary radio astronomy experiment team. The two groups use the antennas in different ways. The plasma wave investigation uses the antennas to form a V-type balanced electric dipole, while the radio astronomy investigation uses them as a pair of orthogonal monopoles.

In the normal format, the plasma wave signals were processed with a simple 16-channel spectrum analyzer. At planetary encounters, the system provided a spectral scan every four seconds.

The plasma wave system had a broadband amplifier that used the Voyager video telemetry link to give electric field waveforms, with a frequency range from 50 Hz to 10 kHz, at selected times during planet encounters.

The investigation was designed to provide key information on the wave-particle interaction phenomena that control important aspects of the dynamics of the magnetospheres of Jupiter and Saturn. Wave-particle interactions play extremely important roles at Earth and scientists understand that at least the inner magnetosphere of Jupiter is conceptually similar to that of Earth despite the vast difference in size and in energy of the trapped particles.

In addition, the satellites of Jupiter and saturn appear to provide important localized sources of plasma and field-aligned currents and they should significantly affect the trapped-particle populations.

The instrument weighed 3.1 pounds and drew 1.6 watts of power.

Radio Science Investigation
Voyager 1/2 (1977)

The spacecraft's communications system was used to conduct several investigations by observing how the radio signals are changed on their way to Earth.

By measuring the way signals died out and return when the

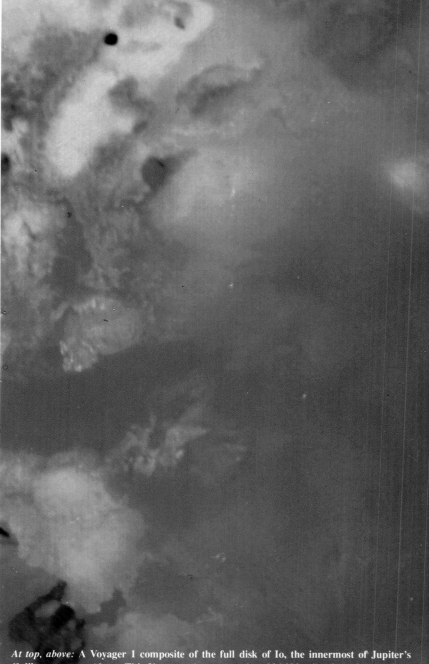

At top, above: A Voyager 1 composite of the full disk of Io, the innermost of Jupiter's Galilean moons. *Above:* This Voyager photo was taken 226,200 miles from Io's surface. This moderately-sized moon is the most volcanically active body in the Solar System, and spews sulfurous material at speeds of up to 3280 feet per second, and at altitudes of up to 130 miles! Io has no conventional atmosphere; it has a donut-shaped torus, or tube of electrically charged particles that traces Io's orbit around Jupiter (see the boxed illustrations on page 61). The torus consists of ionized sulfur and oxygen atoms, and it is theorized that it has its origins in the material spewed out during Io's intense eruptions.

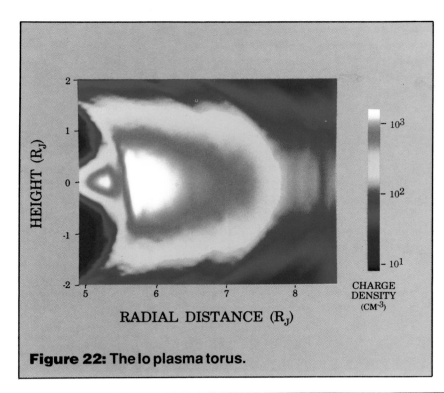

Figure 22: The Io plasma torus.

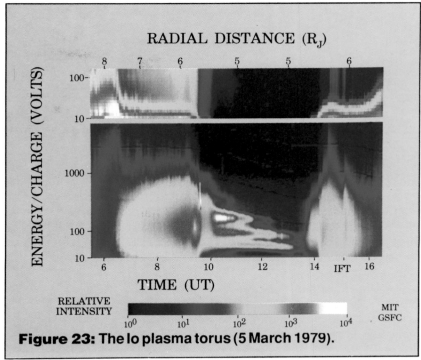

Figure 23: The Io plasma torus (5 March 1979).

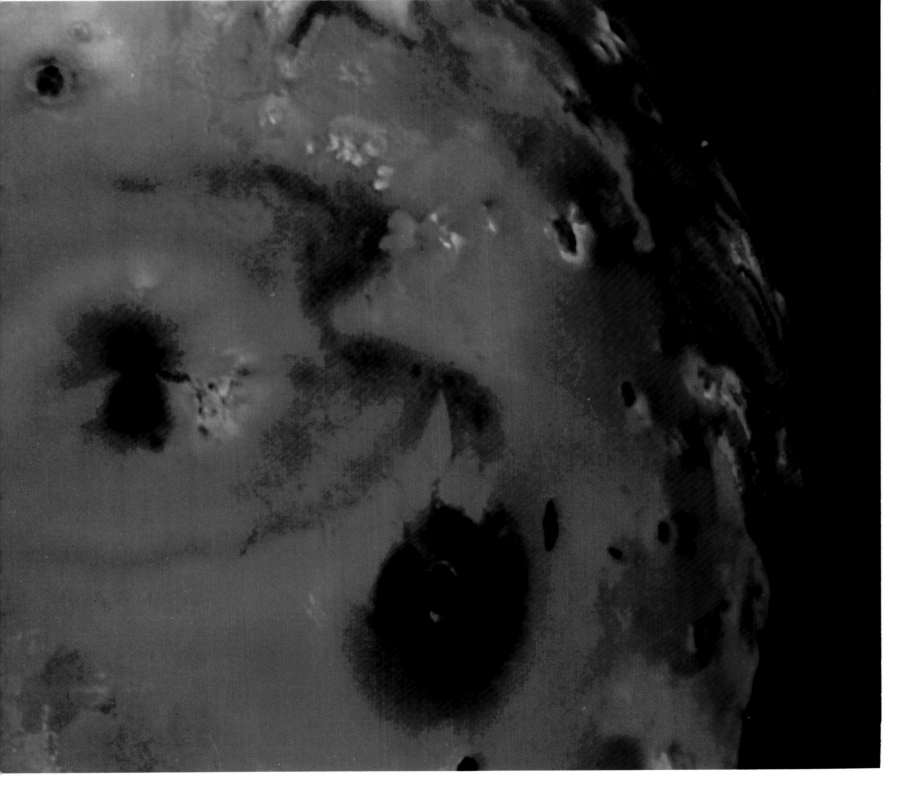

spacecraft disappeared behind a planet or satellite and then reappeared, the radio science team could determine the properties of planetary and satellite atmospheres and ionospheres.

The radio signals also allowed scientists to make precise measurements of the spacecraft's trajectory as it passed near a planet or satellite. Post-flight analyses allowed determination of the mass of a body and its density and shape.

The rings of Saturn were also explored by the radio science team by measuring the scattering of the radio signals as they traveled through the rings. This provided measurements of ring mass, particle size distribution and ring structure.

The investigation used the microwave receivers and transmitters on the spacecraft as well as special equipment at the Deep Space Network tracking stations. The spacecraft transmitters were capable of sending 9.4, 20 or 28.3 watts at S-band, and 12 or 21.3 watts at X-band. The spacecraft antenna is a 12 foot parabola and was aimed by special maneuvers performed during planet occultations.

Ultraviolet Photometer (see photo on page 59)
Pioneer 10/11 (1972/73)

The ultraviolet photometer carried onboard Pioneers 10 and 11 measured the scattering of solar ultraviolet light or emission of ultraviolet light from interplanetary hydrogen, helium, and dust; from the atmospheres of Jupiter and Saturn; and from some of their satellites (see Figure 24, below).

Radiotelescopes have shown that the Solar System is immersed in and traveling through an interstellar gas cloud of cold, neutral (uncharged) hydrogen. By measuring the scattering of the Sun's ultraviolet light in space, the ultraviolet photometer measured the amount of neutral hydrogen within the Solar System. The presence of neutral hydrogen (already measured near Earth) could be the result of the neutralization of fast solar wind hydrogen ions at the boundary of the heliosphere (the limit of the Sun's influence on the universe), their conversion into fast uncharged hydrogen atoms, and diffusion of the neutral atoms back into the heliosphere. Or the source of the neutral hydrogen might be in the galaxy itself. The hydrogen penetrates the Solar System as a result of the System's relative velocity to the interstellar gas of 45,000 mph.

The experiment was intended to gather data to resolve the origin of the neutral hydrogen and to establish the boundaries of the heliosphere. From measurements of the interplanetary helium, experimenters hoped to determine also the percentage of helium in the interstellar medium. This was expected to throw more light on the question of whether the universe originated in a 'big bang,' a single creative event, or if it is a continuous creation still going on.

The viewing angle of the ultraviolet photometer was fixed so that the spin of the spacecraft caused the photometer to scan the celestial sphere. When near Jupiter and Saturn, the photometer scanned the medium above the cloudtops. By measuring the changes in intensity of ultraviolet light reflected into two photocathodes (cathodes which emit electrons when exposed to radiant energy, especially light) of the instrument—one measuring radiation at 1216–Angstrom, the other at 584–Angstrom—the photometer detected light emitted by excited hydrogen and helium atoms, respectively (see Figure 25, below).

Within the systems of Jupiter and Saturn, the instrument measured the scattering of solar ultraviolet light by the atmospheres of the planets. This scattering provided information about the amount of atomic hydrogen in the upper atmospheres, the mixing rates within the atmosphere, the amount of helium in each, and therefore the helium/hydrogen ration within the atmospheres of these huge gas giants. Virtually all theories of the origin of these two planets and their subsequent development make assumptions about the amount of helium in the planetary atmospheres, but before the Pioneer missions, helium had not been identified in the atmosphere of either Jupiter or Saturn.

By measuring changes in the ultraviolet light glow, the instrument checked to see if Jupiter and Saturn had polar auroras at the times of flyby. Such auroras are bright, glowing regions in the upper atmospheres caused by precipitation of particles along magnetic field lines from space toward the poles of the planet.

Ultraviolet Spectroscopy Investigation
Voyager 1/2 (1977)

The ultraviolet spectrometer looked at the planets' atmospheres and at interplanetary space.

Scientific objectives of the investigation were:

♦ To determine distributions of the major constituents of the upper atmospheres of Jupiter, Saturn and Titan as a function of altitude;

♦ To measure absorption of the sun's untraviolet radiation by the upper atmospheres as the Sun is occulted by Jupiter, Saturn and Titan;

♦ To measure ultraviolet airglow emissions of the atmospheres from the bright discs of the three bodies, their bright limbs, terminators and dark sides;

♦ Determine distribution and ratio of hydrogen and helium in interplanetary and interstellar space.

The instrument measured ultraviolet radiation in 1200-Angstrom bandwidth in the range from 400 to 1800-Angstroms. It used a grating spectrometer with a microchannel plate electron multiplier and a 128-channel anode array. A fixed position mirror reflecting sunlight into the instrument during occulation. The instrument had a 0.86-degree by 0.6-degree field of view during occultation and a 0.86- by 2-degree field of view for airglow measurements.

The ultraviolet spectrometer weighed 9.9 pounds and used 2.5 watts.

At right: Pioneer 11 is shown here with a mockup of its launch capsule prior to its launch in 1973. On board was an ultraviolet photometer, which measured the scattering of solar ultraviolet light, or the emission of ultraviolet light from interplanetary hydrogen, helium and dust. Other ultraviolet studies conducted with the photometer have resulted in important discoveries—and important theories—about the atmospheres of Jupiter and Saturn.

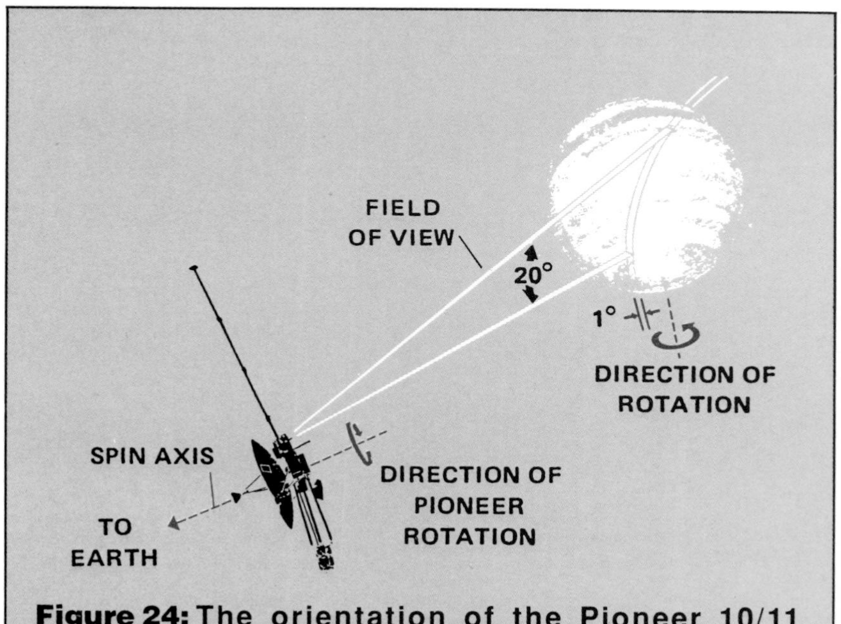

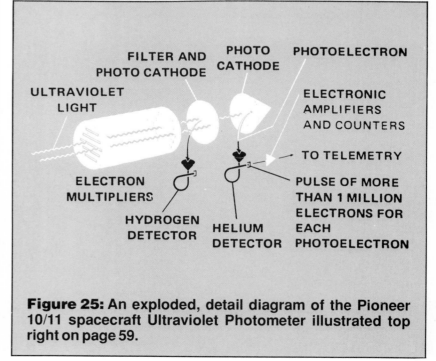

Figure 24: The orientation of the Pioneer 10/11 spacecraft in relation to Jupiter, with the Ultraviolet Photometer scanning the planet's cloud tops.

Figure 25: An exploded, detail diagram of the Pioneer 10/11 spacecraft Ultraviolet Photometer illustrated top right on page 59.

Above: This oblique view of Mars was taken by the Viking 1 Orbiter. Shown here is the smooth plain which is known as Argyre Planitia. From the foreground to the horizon here is a distance of approximately 12,000 miles. *Below:* This Viking 2 Orbiter photo was taken just as the line of dawn was racing across the face of Mars. The photo has been computer enhanced to bring out contrast and detail, such as the dormant volcano at upper left and the water ice plumes at right. *Above right:* The huge summit craters of Mars' gigantic, 16-mile high Olympus Mons seem to rise up toward the Viking cameras in this true-color photo. *Below right:* The Viking 10 and 11 spacecraft were identical lander/orbiter combinations. Here, the encapsulated lander rides on top, and the orbiter (note its solar panels) is on bottom. See also the photos and illustrations on pages 11, 66–67 and 71.

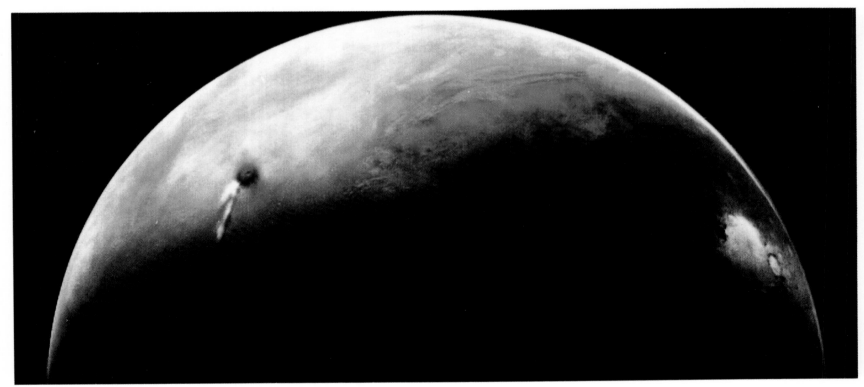

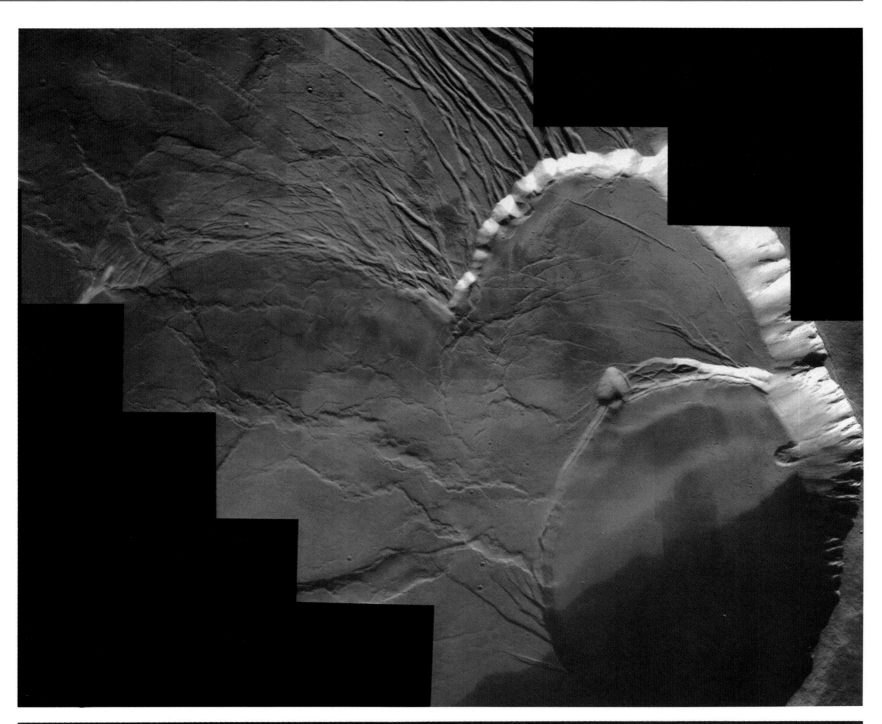

The Viking Orbiters

Each Viking spacecraft was launched by a Titan/Centaur—a Centaur upper stage combined with the Titan 3 booster. Centaur was the first United States high-energy liquid hydrogen/liquid oxygen rocket. It developed 30,000 pounds of thrust at liftoff. This was the first successful operational flight of the Titan launch vehicle with a Centaur upper stage. Each Viking was divided into an orbiter portion and a lander.

The 5125-pound orbiter vaguely resembled a scaled-up Mariner spacecraft, since the arrangement of components was generally similar and Mariner design philosophy was employed throughout. The orbiter main structure was a flat, octagonal prism with unequal sides 85 by 99.2 inches along diagonals. Louvers around the periphery of the octagon opened and closed automatically to provide individual thermal control to 16 equipment bays. Four solar panels were hinged at their bases to outrigger structures and hinged again halfway out. Together the panels provided 23,250 square inches of solar cells. At Mars' distance they generated 620 watts of power. Supplementary power for peak loading and for dark times was provided by two 30-ampere-hour nickel-cadmium batteries.

The orbiter's communication system was used as a relay between the lander on the Martian surface and the Earth. A parabolic, high-gain antenna, 57.9 inches in diameter, was motor-

(1) Orbiter Assembly
(2) Spacecraft Adapter Installation
(3) Lander Capsule Adapter Installation
(4) Pyrotechnic Installation
(5) Antenna Installation
(6) High Gain Antenna
(7) Solar Panel Installation
(8) Science Installation

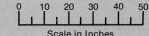

Scale in Inches

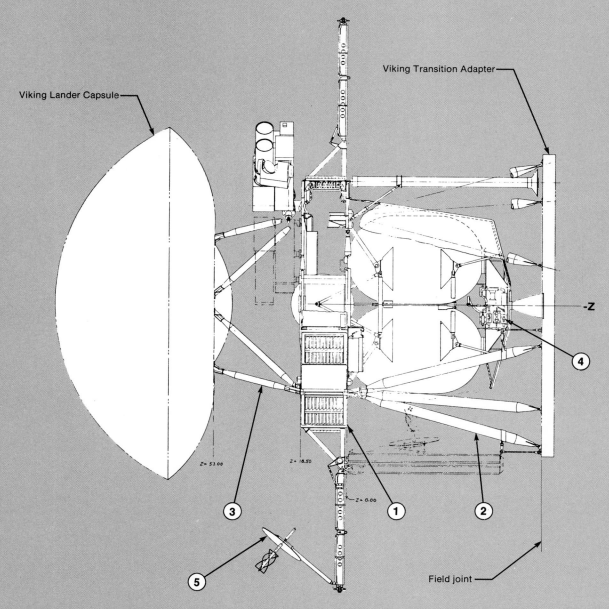

Figure 26: A schematic side view of the Viking Orbiter Spacecraft with solar panels and science installation (camera platform) deployed for the mission.

driven about two axes. A rod-like low-gain antenna on the sunlit side of the spacecraft allowed limited two-way communications with Earth over greater than hemisphere coverage. A third antenna, mounted on the end of one solar panel, was for communication between orbiter and lander. The orbiter's transmitter power was about 20 watts, allowing transmission of 4000 bits per second to a 210-foot-diameter DSN station.

The orbiter carried three instruments, and performed four experiments. Two narrow-angle television cameras provided high-resolution imaging and was first used for landing-site verification. An atmospheric water detector mapped the super-dry atmosphere of Mars for what water vapor may be there. (Mariner 9 showed signs of water vapor escaping the atmosphere.) An infrared thermal mapper also covered the planet's surface for signs of warmth. And the spacecraft radio provided data for an occulation experiment to provide data on the planet's size, gravity, mass, density and other physical characteristics.

The accompanying 2353-pound lander became the first US spacecraft to land on another planet. (US and Soviet spacecraft had landed on the Moon, a satellite of Earth. Soviet spacecraft have landed on Mars and Venus.)

Viking 1 was launched on 20 August 1975 from Kennedy Space Center at Cape Canaveral, Florida and inserted into Mars orbit on 19 June 1976. The Viking 1 lander was detached from the orbiter and successfully landed on the Martian surface on 20 July 1976 from where it continued to transmit data and photographs until November 1982. The Viking 1 orbiter continued to transmit data until 7 August 1980. (*see pages 64–65*)

Viking 2 was launched from Kennedy Space Center on 9 September 1975 and inserted into Mars orbit on 7 August 1976. The Viking 2 lander was detached and successfully landed on Mars on 3 September 1976 from where it continued to transmit data and photographs until 12 April 1980. The Viking 2 orbiter continued to transmit data until 25 July 1978. (*see pages 64–65*)

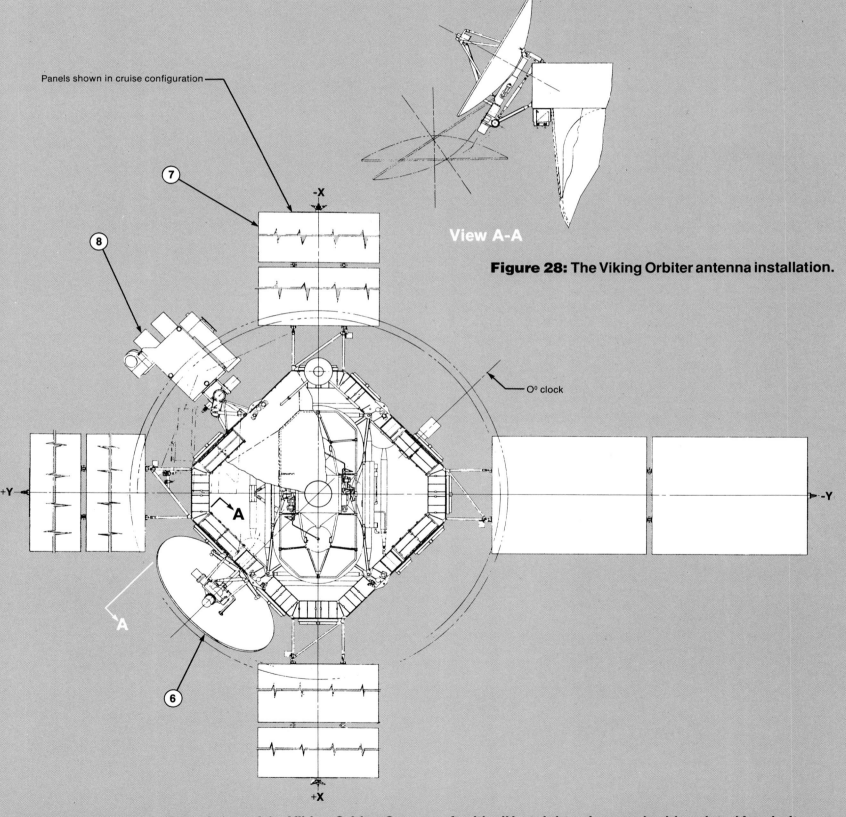

Panels shown in cruise configuration

View A-A

Figure 28: The Viking Orbiter antenna installation.

0° clock

Figure 27: A schematic end view of the Viking Orbiter Spacecraft with all but right solar panels abbreviated for clarity.

Above: False-color photography does much to bring out planetary features which otherwise might remain hidden to Earth-based receptors of information which is transmitted from an interplanetary spacecraft. In addition, such variant techniques as ultraviolet spectrometry reveal the presence, each by its 'signature' color, of the constituent elements of a planet's atmosphere. This particular image of Saturn shows, among other things, large bright spots in the planet's North Temperate Belt, which may well be large convective storms in an already turbulent atmosphere. Saturn's banded atmosphere and spectacular rings are only part of its fascinating and complex system, which includes 20 moons as well! The 'kinks,' or vertical lines, in this photograph reveal where separate images were joined to create one composite. The dark, transverse markings on the rings evidence the mysterious 'spoke' features.

F. ELECTRICAL SYSTEM

Power Budget

After having determined the components that will be included in the spacecraft, it is necessary to develop a power budget—a tally of the electrical power that will be required to operate these components and subsystems. This tally should first include a list of all the subsystems (*see Part One-E4*) that will be used throughout the eight to ten years of the mission—the computers, cameras, heaters, antenna, etc—and the wattage they will need for the routine part of the mission. Next, the tally should include the peak power requirements of the planetary encounter. At this time all the subsystems noted above will be working much harder than at any other time and their power requirements will be much higher. The antenna/transmitter subsystem, for example, will be transmitting a tremendous quantity of data, including all the digitized photographs taken by the camera platform.

It may be that only two watts of output would be required for routine housekeeping transmissions for most of the flight because these transmissions might contain no more than 1000 bits of information. At planetary encounter, however, both bit rate and output requirement could increase 10-fold. Scientific components—dormant for much of the mission—will be 'awakened' during the encounter and they will add their needs to the total requirement.

Power Source

The selection of a power source would have to be predicated on two important factors beyond the simple output requirements. One of these is the duration of the mission and the other is the distance from the Sun. Because of the latter, solar energy—a major power source in many Earth-orbit satellites—would have to be ruled out. Solar voltaic cells (*see pages 72–73*) are simply not effective beyond the orbit of Jupiter. A system which used solar cells for the early part of the mission and switched to another source later on might be worth considering. However, the effective range of solar power is very limited compared to the distance that must be covered, and the added complexity simply might not be worth it.

Other potential power sources would include nuclear (*see page 74*) and chemical (*see page 76*) batteries.

continued on page 74

Solar power was fine for the lunar orbiter spacecraft in 1966–67 *(below)*, but while the Viking Mars Orbiter carried solar panels, the Viking Mars Lander had a nuclear power generator. The Viking Orbiter/Lander combination *(at right,* and see also Figure 26 on page 66) had respectable service lives for their respective modules. The Viking 1 Lander was the last of the Viking 1 and 2 units to be shut down by mission control, after more than six years in operation. See also the photos on pages 11 and 69, and the illustrations on pages 66–67.

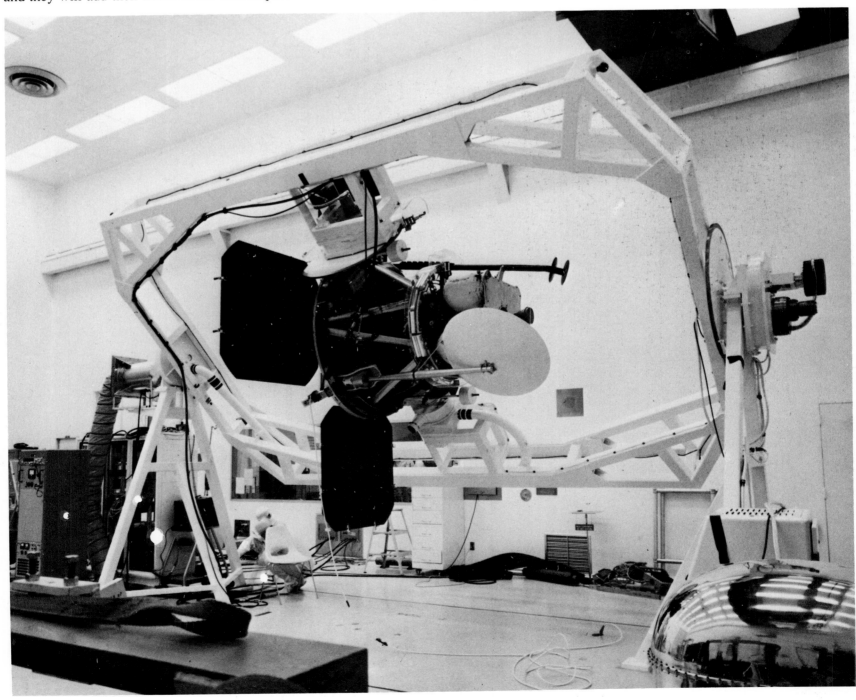

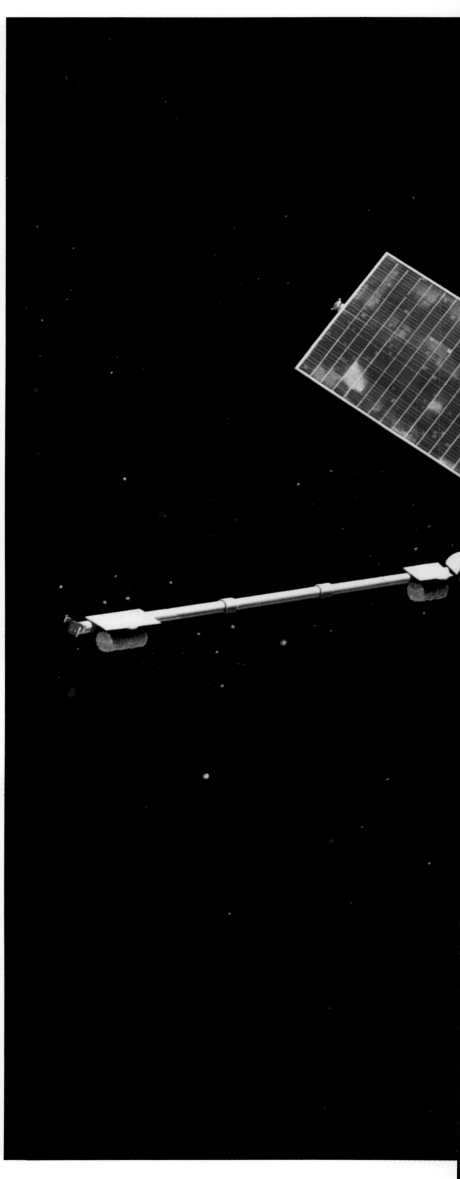

Solar power in service. *Above*, the Hughes Intelsat 6 spacecraft body's exterior is covered with the solar panels that power its various systems. *Below:* The much-anticipated Hubble Space Telescope is shown in this conception with its edge mounted panels. *At right:* The Boeing Mariner 10 spacecraft with its end-mounted 106-inch paddle panels; acquisition sun sensors mounted at their tips helped to keep them properly oriented. Five of the craft's 10 electronics compartments were louvered and insulated against inner Solar System heat. Solar power was ideal for Mariner 10's investigations of Mercury.

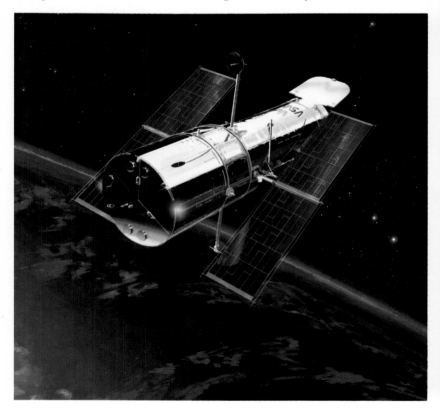

Nuclear Power and Voyager's Requirements

The use of nuclear power was common in many spacecraft that were produced in the 1960s and 1970s and that required a reliable long-term power source. Voyager, for example, was built with an array of three radioisotope thermoelectric generators (RTGs) which are detailed in Figures 30 and 31 *at right*, and which were developed by the US Energy Research and Development Administration (ERDA). (A propulsion module, active only during the brief injection phase of the mission, used a separate battery source.)

The RTG units, mounted in tandem on a deployable boom (*see Figure 29, below*) and connected in parallel, convert to electricity the heat released by the isotopic decay of plutonium-238. Each of those isotope heat sources had a capacity of 2400 thermal watts with a resultant maximum electrical power output of 160 watts at the beginning of the mission. There is a gradual decrease in power output. The minimum total power available from the three RTGs ranged from about 423 watts within a few hours after launch to 384 watts now that the spacecraft have both passed Saturn.

The spacecraft power requirements from launch to post-Saturn operations were characterized by this general power timeline: launch and post-launch, 235 to 265 watts; interplanetary cruise, 320 to 365 watts; Jupiter encounter, 384 to 401 watts; Saturn encounter, 377 to 382 watts; and post-Saturn, less than 365 watts. Telemetry measurements have been selected to provide the necessary information for power management by ground command, if needed.

The RTGs reached full power about seven hours after launch. During prelaunch operations and until about one minute after liftoff, the generator interiors were kept filled with an inert gas to prevent oxidation of hot components. Venting the generators to space vacuum is achieved with a pressure relief device actuated when the outside ambient pressure drops below 10 psi.

Power from the RTGs is held at a constant 30 volts DC by a shunt regulator. The 30 volts is supplied directly to some spacecraft user and is switched to others in the power distribution subassembly. The main power inverter also is supplied the 30 volts DC for conversion to *2.4* kilohertz (kHz) square wave power used by most spacecraft subsystems. Again, the AC power may be supplied directly to users or can be switched on or off by power relays.

Command actuated relays control the distribution of power in the spacecraft. Some relays function as simple on-off switches and others transfer power from one module to another within a subsystem.

Among the users of DC power, in addition to the inverter, are the radio subsystem, gyros, propulsion isolation valves, some science instruments, most temperature control heaters and the motors which deploy the planetary radio astronomy antennas. Other elements of the spacecraft use the 2.4 kHz power.

There are two identical 2.4 kHz power inverters—main and standby. The main inverter is on from launch and remains on throughout the mission. In case of a malfunction or failure in the main inverter, the power chain, after a 1.5-second delay, is switched automatically to the standby inverter. Once the switchover is made, it is irreversible.

A 4.8 kHz synchronization and timing signal from the flight data subsystem is used as a frequency reference in the inverter. The frequency is divided by two and the output is 2.4 kHz plus- or-minus 0.002 percent. This timing signal is sent, in turn, to the computer command subsystem which contains the spacecraft's master clock.

Because of the long mission lifetime, charged capacitor energy storage banks are used instead of batteries to supply the short-term extra power demanded by instantaneous overloads that would cause the main DC power voltage to dip below acceptable limits. A typical heavy transient overload occurs at turn on of a radio power amplifier.

Full output of the RTGs, a constant power source, must be used or dissipated in some way to prevent overheating of the generator units or DC voltage rising above allowed maximum. This is controlled by a shunt regulator which dumps excess RTG output power above that required to operate the spacecraft. The excess power is dissipated in resistors in a shunt radiator mounted outside the spacecraft and radiated into space as heat.

A major problem with RTGs—and indeed, any nuclear power source—are government regulations. Even though they pose virtually no hazard whatsoever, it would almost certainly be impossible to get a permit to launch an RTG-equipped spacecraft from the United States, and indeed from most countries. Even NASA has—since the Voyager days—become less inclined to use nuclear power sources. Nuclear batteries, because they have few common uses, would also be extremely expensive.

Voyager also used chemical batteries for powering the valves on the thrust vector control engines, and chemical batteries are discussed in the following section.

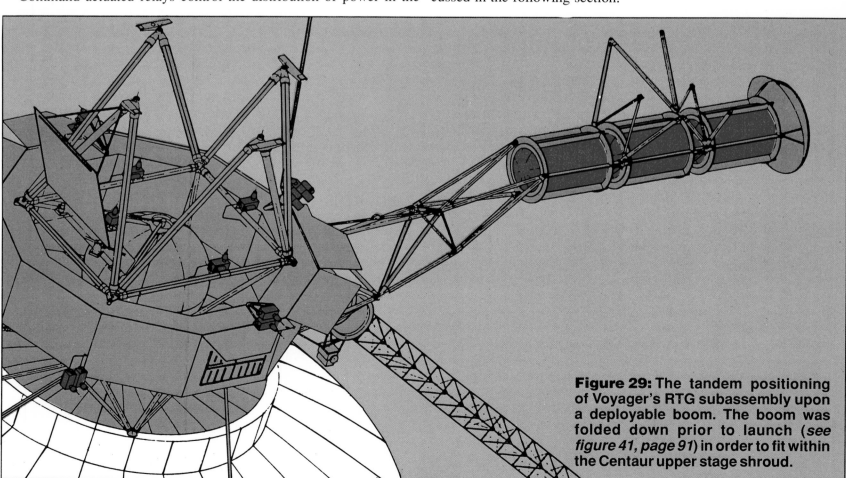

Figure 29: The tandem positioning of Voyager's RTG subassembly upon a deployable boom. The boom was folded down prior to launch (*see figure 41, page 91*) in order to fit within the Centaur upper stage shroud.

Figure 30: The Voyager Radioisotope Thermoelectric Generator (RTG).

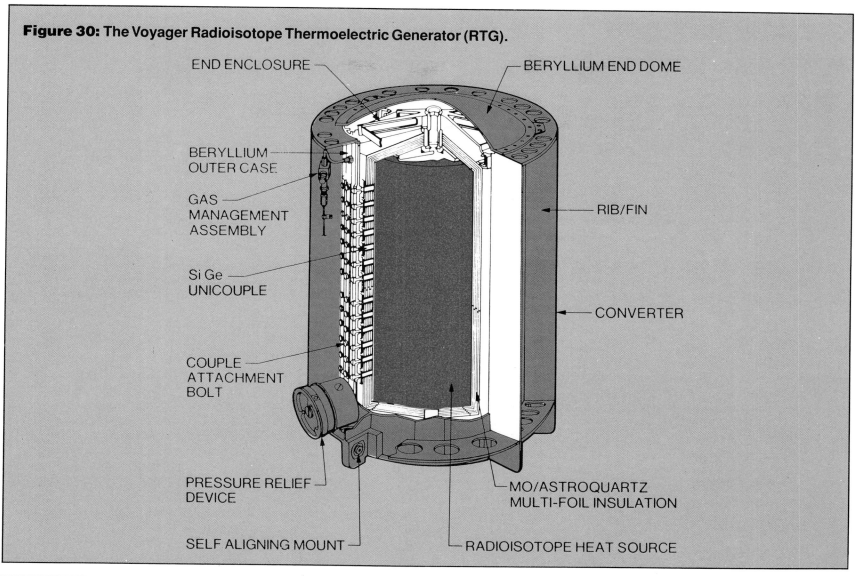

END ENCLOSURE

BERYLLIUM END DOME

BERYLLIUM OUTER CASE

GAS MANAGEMENT ASSEMBLY

Si Ge UNICOUPLE

COUPLE ATTACHMENT BOLT

RIB/FIN

CONVERTER

PRESSURE RELIEF DEVICE

SELF ALIGNING MOUNT

MO/ASTROQUARTZ MULTI-FOIL INSULATION

RADIOISOTOPE HEAT SOURCE

Figure 31: The heat source for the Voyager Radioisotope Thermoelectric Generator (RTG).

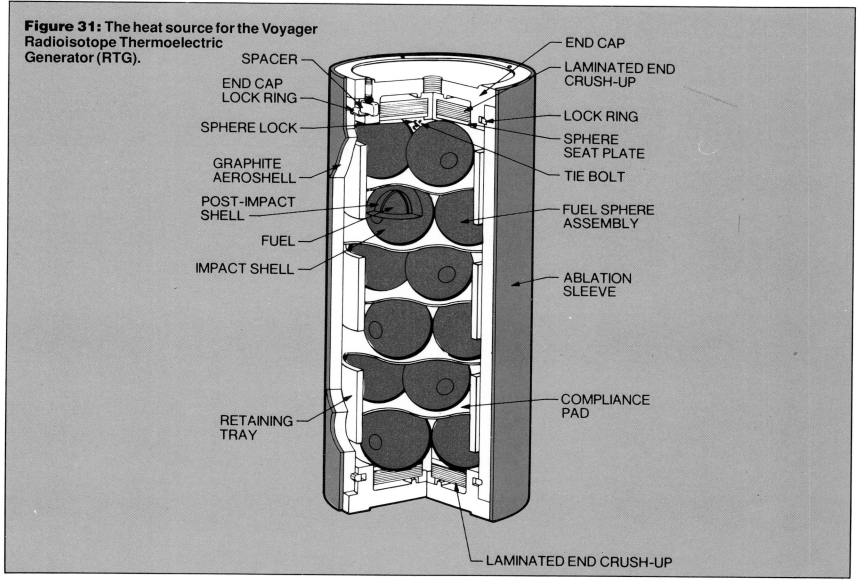

SPACER

END CAP LOCK RING

SPHERE LOCK

GRAPHITE AEROSHELL

POST-IMPACT SHELL

FUEL

IMPACT SHELL

RETAINING TRAY

END CAP

LAMINATED END CRUSH-UP

LOCK RING

SPHERE SEAT PLATE

TIE BOLT

FUEL SPHERE ASSEMBLY

ABLATION SLEEVE

COMPLIANCE PAD

LAMINATED END CRUSH-UP

Chemical Batteries

The optimum long-term power source—given the problems with solar and nuclear—would be chemical batteries. They can operate anywhere, without regard to the Sun, but they have the problem of duration. Solar and nuclear sources can potentially last forever, but—as anyone who has picked up a dim flashlight knows—chemical batteries wear out.

Batteries with shelf lives exceeding those zinc oxide flashlight batteries do exist, and choosing an appropriate one is a matter of selection: the watch-words are long life and higher storage capacity.

One probably doesn't want nickel cadmium (nicad) standard rechargeable batteries. (The standard zinc oxide flashlight batteries are not rechargeable.) Being rechargeable, nicads are also very low density and very low-powered. They don't store as many watts per pound as throw-away batteries, so they are definitely out because one would want the densest power possible. If one were to use a scheme of disposable, but not recharging, batteries, then solar panels *could* be used, provided that the spacecraft switched over to them *before* reaching Saturn's orbit. Another possibility would be to use solar panels in diminishing mode and drain the nickel hydrad cells more slowly. Solar panels could be mounted directly on the antenna structure.

As we noted earlier, NASA used chemical batteries as a supplementary power source in Voyager. Two batteries were included, which independently supplied unregulated DC power to a remote driver module (RDM) for powering valve drivers to the thrust vector control engines on the propulsion module during the injection phase of the mission. The batteries and the RDM are located in the propulsion module which is jettisoned a few minutes after the mission module is injected onto a Jupiter transfer trajectory. Each battery is composed of 22 silver oxide-zinc cells with a capacity of 1200 ampere seconds at 28 to 40 volts, depending upon the load.

The basic requirement for the batteries is a high power for a short period—12 minutes. With a lifetime of only 66 minutes, Voyager's batteries were kept inert until just four seconds before separation from the shroud containing it atop the launch vehicle and 20 seconds before solid rocket ignition. After activation, in which an electrolyte is injected into the cells, the batteries were at full voltage in one-half second and ready for use in two seconds.

Another source of batteries for an interplanetary spacecraft that is both promising and innovative would come from the heart pacemaker industry. By definition, pacemaker batteries *must* provide continuous, reliable electrical power for periods up to 10 years. This is exactly what is needed for an interplanetary spacecraft. The Promeon Division of Medtronic, Incorporated is a world leader in the development and production of high reliability pacemaker batteries. During the development of this book, Promeon was contacted about the use of their batteries for this type of application and they responded with a great deal of interest.

The Promeon product line includes three types of lithium-thionyl 1 chloride (Li-SOCl$_2$) and seven types of lithium iodide (Li-I$_2$) batteries. The lithium-thionyl chloride batteries range in weight from 10 to 18 grams and each deliver 3.6 volts. The lithium iodide batteries, in turn, range in weight from two to 27 grams and each deliver 2.9 volts.

The Mirel T (*Figure 32, below*), Alpha 36T (*Figure 33, below*) and Zeta 26T lithium-thionyl chloride batteries are premium primary cells in nonconventional shapes. Designed to provide a highly reliable source of power, these batteries feature exceptional energy density, highly reproducible discharge performance, and long shelf life. Completely welded construction and use of a high reliability glass-to-metal feedthrough developed and manufactured by EnerTec ensure hermeticity. Lithium-thionyl chloride chemistry gives them exceptionally stable load voltage throughout discharge, and the design features an outstandingly low self-discharge rate. It has accepted short circuit, over-charge, and over-discharge conditions without rupturing. Proprietary design features reduce the voltage delay phenomenon in these cells. The thin, flat configuration makes these batteries ideal for many unique applications.

Members of the Alpha and Zeta families of Lithium/iodine batteries are premium primary cells in nonconventional shapes. Designed to be a highly stable, long-lived source of low power for medical devices, this product line has a proven reliability record. Exceptional energy density, highly reproducible discharge performance, and long shelf life are all features of both families. A completely welded construction and use of an EnerTec feedthrough ensure that they are hermetically sealed. These products are currently licensed for medical applications only.

Each Telstar 3 spacecraft *(at right)* was built with communications systems capable of handling 21,600 simultaneous telephone calls as well as numerous voice, video and digitized data transmissions. These systems were solar powered when the craft was out of the Earth's shadow, and battery operated when the craft was in the Earth's shadow. The nickel-cadmium batteries were recharged via the craft's solar cells. Each Telstar 3 spacecraft—three in all—has performed well within its mission life designation of 10 years.

Promeon Enertec Power Sources				
Battery Name	Chemistry	OCV (Volts)	Capacity (Amp-hrs)	Application Current (mA)
Mirel T	Li-SOCl$_2$	3.6	2.9	.10-50
Alpha 36T	Li-SOCl$_2$	3.6	2.5	.10-50
Zeta 26T	Li-SOCl$_2$	3.6	1.3	.10-100
Alpha 333*	Li-I$_2$	2.8	2.7	.001-.050
Beta 263*	Li-I$_2$	2.8	2.6	.001-.050
Alpha 335*	Li-I$_2$	2.8	2.2	.001-.050
Alpha 283*	Li-I$_2$	2.8	2.2	.001-.050
Alpha 28*	Li-I$_2$	2.8	1.7	.001-.050
Zeta 265*	Li-I$_2$	2.8	1.3	.001-.050
Zeta 205*	Li-I$_2$	2.8	0.9	.001-.032

Battery Name	Cell Dimensions (mm) Thickness	Height	Width	Weight (Grams)
Mirel T	9.2	24.0	48.0	18
Alpha 36T	7.9	36.0	27.4	16
Zeta 26T	5.2	26.0	36.6	10
Alpha 333	7.9	33.4	27.4	27
Beta 263	8.3	26.2	36.6	23
Alpha 335	7.9	33.4	27.4	27
Alpha 283	7.9	28.4	27.4	19
Alpha 28	7.9	28.4	27.4	17
Zeta 265	5.2	26.0	36.6	14
Zeta 205	5.2	20.0	36.6	10

*Licensed for Medical Device Applications Only

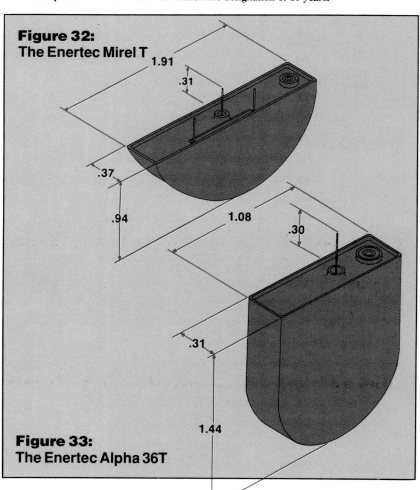

Figure 32:
The Enertec Mirel T
1.91 .31 .37 .94 1.08 .30 .31 1.44

Figure 33:
The Enertec Alpha 36T

Peak Power Auxiliaries

For the peak power requirements of the planetary flyby, one might consider the type of thermal batteries that are used in weapons like artillery shells and air-to-air missiles to power the motors and steer the fins, and to handle the arming, warhead triggering and radar. They are fired pyrotechnically like an explosive bolt. While many such batteries last for only two seconds, some last for up to 40 minutes or more. They put out a fair amount of heat, and they also put out a lot of power. In one case a 10-pound battery put out 5 Kw across a very wide range, from 150 volts down to 6 volts.

They are routinely available and not classified. Pacific American uses them in the Liberty launch vehicles for primary electrical power. Because the booster's lifetime is so short—90 seconds to two minutes—they provide whatever battery power is needed.

The camera would require a fraction of a watt, but the transmitter would need 20 to 50 watts of pulse power to transmit digitally-encoded video over the course of two hours, and to *repeat* it several times to make sure the ground station gets it. For this application, a thermal battery like this might be ideal. Two hours of imagery could be stored, and then transmitted several times in a few minutes. These batteries are very lightweight for their power and there could be several of them.

In a flyby, the period of peak power is a few hours, or at most a couple of days. The real peaks of power, especially transmission, can easily be provided by thermal batteries. They deliver a lot of power for a short period of time, but if the requirement lasted up to a couple of days, eight or twelve thermal batteries could be installed to help warm things up, then discharged one at a time from a mounted ring outside of the spacecraft. These twelve thermal batteries would provide eight hours of continuous power for transmission *and* for recharging storage batteries.

If one were able to conduct a Pluto flyby using thermal batteries for peak power, it may also be possible to use them in an orbital mission. However, they can't be used very long. One might use them to charge conventional batteries for a longer mission, but not for more than one or two weeks because of the power required to put the spacecraft *into* orbit. A second array of thermal batteries might be installed and fired after orbital insertion, and thus several days after the first array.

The thermal battery was developed in 1946 by Catalyst Research Corporation (a division of Mine Safety Appliances Company) in cooperation with the US Bureau of Standard's Ordnance Development Division (now Harry Diamond Laboratories).

The thermal battery is a pyrotechnically initiated battery. At ordinary temperatures, the cell electrolyte is an inert solid which provides no electrical power. When power is required, heat source is ignited by either an electric match or a mechanically actuated percussion primer. The heat source melts the electrolyte and electrical power is generated for periods of a few seconds to minutes. Because of these qualities thermal batteries have many of the storage properties of munitions rounds, including shelf life.

Thermal batteries are widely used by the military as 'one-shot' electrical power sources for target acquisition, guidance and control applications in missile systems. They are also extensively employed as fusing and activation devices in artillery shells, bombs, torpedoes and mines. Other applications have included airborne expendable jamming devices, aircraft escape seats, parachute release devices, and as power supplies on lunar modules and the space shuttle. Thermal batteries have been used in almost all engineered environments where batteries are required to be highly reliable, maintenance free, instantly activated, and have a long storage capability. In terms of longevity, Frederick Tepper and David Yalom wrote in the *Handbook of Batteries and Fuel Cells* (McGraw Hill, 1984) that the 'shelf life of thermal batteries is greater than ten years, and batteries of more recent manufacture are expected to last at least twenty years.' This characteristic easily answers the time requirements of a mission to the outer Solar System.

Catalyst Research has produced over 5 million batteries, all designed to meet the varied needs of specific programs and environments. Their various operational requirements specify that the batteries be capable of:

- Operation over temperature ranges from -80 F to 180 F
- Sizes ranging from a .38 caliber shell to 18 inches in diameter
- Electrical characteristics ranging from 1000 volts for 60 seconds to 200 volts for 200 seconds to 30 volts for 40 minutes
- Withstanding shock 100,000 x normal gravity
- Operation at altitudes of 240,000 miles (lunar orbit)
- Operation at depths of 2000 ft.

The electrochemical system of a thermal battery consists of an active metal anode, a fused salt electrolyte and an oxidizing agent in conjunction with a relatively inert metal as a cathode. Thermal batteries manufactured by Catalyst Research use two different types of active anodes with calcium anode thermal batteries providing a moderate current drain for periods ranging from milliseconds to a few minutes.

With its molten lithium active anode permitting higher current drains and longer discharge durations, the lithium-iron disulfide thermal battery (LAN) (*Figure 35, below*) is replacing the calcium and calcium chromate chemistry (*Figure 34, below*) as the industry workhorse. Typically, power and energy densities of 3 to 7 times that of $Ca/CaCrO_4$ are possible with Li/FeS_2 over a wider range of temperatures and environments than is possible with the earlier technology. The most widely used Li/FeS_2 batteries are those designed and manufactured by Catalyst Research using several of its patented lithium anode designs, and these have been in use for over ten years.

The LAN cell design consists of an anode assembly, a two layer electrolyte-catholyte pellet and a pelletized wafer or pill of iron-based pyrotechnic.

The electrolyte-catholyte cathode pellet is pelletized powder made by the compaction of two distinct powers in separate layers. The electrolyte layer is required to electrically isolate the anode from the iron pyrite cathode layer which is electrically conductive. The electrolyte is a mixture of lithium-potassium chloride eutectic electrolyte and ceramic binder. The cathode is a mixture of iron pyrite and electrolyte. The iron-based pyrotechnic is a pelletized wafer or pill of iron powder and potassium perchlorate.

The anode assembly, as designed by Catalyst Research, consists of an iron cup which is crimped around an elemental lithium carrier matrix. This assembly is called the LAN anode. Here, a binding agent is used which binds the lithium by surface tension in a manner similar to the 'gelling' of electrolyte by ceramic binders.

Figure 34: A cross section of a Catalyst Research calcium-potassium dichromate thermal cell.

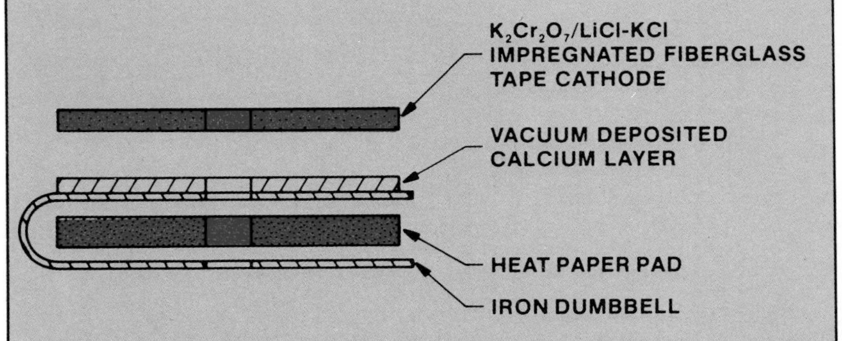

$K_2Cr_2O_7$/LiCl-KCl IMPREGNATED FIBERGLASS TAPE CATHODE

VACUUM DEPOSITED CALCIUM LAYER

HEAT PAPER PAD

IRON DUMBBELL

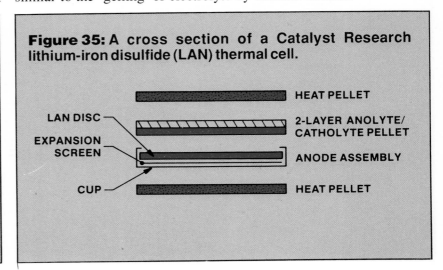

Figure 35: A cross section of a Catalyst Research lithium-iron disulfide (LAN) thermal cell.

HEAT PELLET

LAN DISC

2-LAYER ANOLYTE/ CATHOLYTE PELLET

EXPANSION SCREEN

ANODE ASSEMBLY

CUP

HEAT PELLET

Above: Thermal batteries are at home in this environment, both steering the fins of this AIM-7 Sparrow air-intercept missile, and standing ready in the ejection seat over long periods in constantly-changing temperatures for the possibility that the pilot may one day suddenly need to 'punch out' of his supersonic McDonnell Douglas F-15 Eagle fighter.

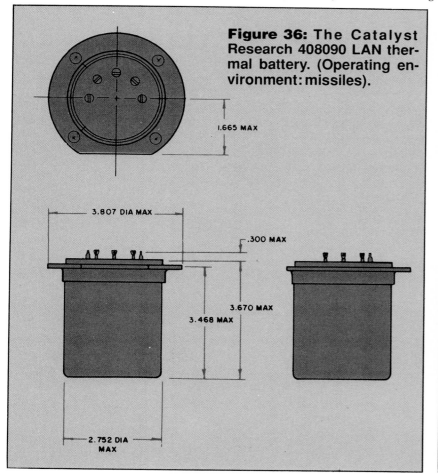

Figure 36: The Catalyst Research 408090 LAN thermal battery. (Operating environment: missiles).

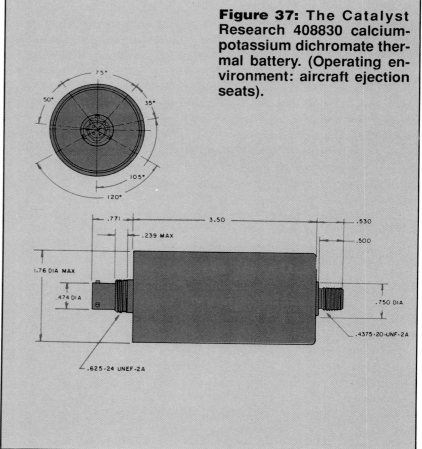

Figure 37: The Catalyst Research 408830 calcium-potassium dichromate thermal battery. (Operating environment: aircraft ejection seats).

Heating

Heating is a simple, albeit vital part of planning for any spacecraft project. A Kapton blanket (*see Glossary*) with copper on it could be laid out with a pattern of heating elements (photo-etched just like a printed circuit board). This amounts to a thin flexible sheet, out of which come computer leads. It is glued down where needed and leads are put down to power the power source. That's all there is to it. It would go on propellant lines and on the bottoms of the propellant tanks (*see page 26*). It is very versatile.

If it were not for the camera and science experiments, one probably would not need to heat the electronics because they would be functioning continuously and as such would generate their own heat adequate to the task. It wouldn't matter if things like the the motors cooled when they weren't doing anything, as long as they had sufficient warm-up time. One would have to arrange to heat them before use. On the other hand, one of the thermal batteries could be dedicated to this function. An hour before encounter a prewired thermal battery could automatically supply power to warm everything. (As a matter of course, a second thermal battery could be used as a redundant feature.)

Earth-orbit spacecraft typically operate at between 40 and 80 degrees. Once in Earth's orbit they encounter normal solar incidence. In the case of our hypothetical interplanetary mission temperatures between 40 and 50 degrees F would be adequate. The CCD camera, for instance, can function at 23 degrees F. It is purely a function of the spacecraft; its size, its color (burnished metal or not) and whether or not it is in sunlight.

In deep space, of course, sunlight would not be an issue. Pluto is forty times farther from the Sun than is the Earth, so it is going to be very cold. For instance, Pluto's surface temperature is estimated at -350 degrees F and the Sun would appear scarcely brighter than a very bright star (*see pages 20–21*).

The two Voyager spacecraft were designed to remain operable farther from Earth than any previous manmade object, and the less sophisticated Pioneer craft are still functioning well beyond Pluto's orbit. For these spacecraft, survival depends greatly upon keeping temperatures within operating limits while they traverse an environmental range of one solar constant (the Sun's heat at the Earth distance) to only four percent of that intensity at Jupiter and less than one percent at Saturn.

Unprotected surfaces at the Saturn range, nearly one billion miles from the Sun, can reach -321 degrees F—the temperature of liquid nitrogen.

Both the top and bottom of Voyager's 10-sided structure are enclosed with multilayer thermal blankets to prevent the rapid loss of heat to the cold of space. The blankets are sandwiches of aluminized Mylar, sheets of Tedlar for micrometeroid protection, and outer black Kapton covers, which are electrically conductive to prevent the accumulation of electrostatic charges (*see pages 86–91*).

Also extensively blanketed are the instruments on the scan platform. Smaller blankets and thermal wrap cover eight electronics bays, boom and body-mounted instruments, cabling, propellant lines and structural struts. Only a few exterior elements of the spacecraft are not clad in the black film: the high gain antenna reflector, plasma sensors, sun sensors and antenna feed cones.

Temperature control of four of the ten electronics compartments is provided by thermostatically-controlled louver assemblies, which provide an internal operating range near room temperature. The louvers are rotated open by bimetallic springs when large amounts of heat are dissipated. These bays contain the power conditioning equipment, the radio power amplifiers and the tape recorder. Mini-louvers are located on the scan platform, cosmic ray instrument and the sun sensors.

Radioisotope heating units (RHU), small nonpower-using heater elements which generate one watt of thermal energy, are located on the magnetometer sensors and the sun sensors. Of course, no RHUs are used near instruments that detect charged particles.

Electric heaters are located throughout the spacecraft to provide additional heat during certain portions of the mission. Many of these heaters are turned off when their respective valves, instruments or subassemblies are on and dissipating power.

Below: This artist's conception shows Pioneer 10 as it passed out of the known Solar System on 13 June 1983. The Sun, nearly three billion miles distant, would be a mere bright speck of light, and temperatures would be in the -350 degrees range! Therefore, insulation and heat control are crucial to the ongoing success of any outer Solar System mission. The artist's concept *at right* shows a Voyager craft witnessing a Jovian eclipse of the Sun! Heating was well provided for in the Voyager missions. Please see the text, this page.

Weight Budget (*Continued from page 46*)		**920.0 lb**
Propellant		720.0 lb
Propellant stage hardware		
Rocket motor	15.0 lb	
Fuel tank	6.6 lb	
Oxydizer tank	6.6 lb	
Fixtures and fittings	2.8 lb	
Residuals (unburned propellant)	7.2 lb	
Bracketry	12.0 lb	
Subtotal:		50.2 lb
Attitude control subsystem		
Cold gas system	5.0 lb	
Fixtures, fittings and bracketry	15.0 lb	
Subtotal:		20.0 lb
Propellant stage, optional enhancements		9.8 lb
Computer, casing and wiring		40.0 lb
Antenna		
TA 550 scaled twice up (less stand)		45.0 lb
Camera system		
Two Sony DXC-102s		3.5 lb
Platform		5.0 lb
Additional Subsystems (estimated)		15.0 lb
Batteries		
20 Enertec Alpha 36Ts		0.7 lb
12 Thermal batteries (array 1)		35.0 lb
12 Thermal batteries (array 2)		35.0 lb
Total (*See discussion, below*)		**959.2 lb**

G. Summary and Weight Factor

Having completed an inventory of spacecraft components (shown in Figure 38 at right), it can now be noted in the table above, that we are 39.2 pounds (or 4.3 percent) in excess of the original weight budget of 920 pounds. This problem can be addressed in a number of ways. A 4.3 percent weight reduction might be considered for all components across the board, but in some cases this might not be practical. (The Enertec batteries have a fixed weight, and cannot be scaled down, and furthermore, 689 pounds of propellant would simply be inadequate.)

Alternatively, certain subsystems could be reduced substantially. The use of wood or plastic in such things as bracketry and computer casing might save as much as ten pounds overall. Furthermore, the use of two Apple MacIntosh computers or two IBM PS-2s, instead of a pair of IBM XT- or AT-based computers, could save up to 20 pounds. The scientific subsystems could be scaled down or miniaturized, although their total elimination would run counter to the whole purpose of the spacecraft.

The elimination of one thermal battery array could in itself, however, make up for the majority of the excess weight. This would then, of course, have to be considered in light of the impact on the mission of losing an extra eight hours of high voltage transmission power.

As this exercise demonstrates, the factor of weight is a consideration that looms over the shoulder of the spacecraft designer at every turn in the road. A mission cannot fly if the spacecraft is overweight, but on the other hand, the mission is not *worth* flying if it can't carry the components necessary for that mission. It is a situation of constant tradeoffs, where a few ounces can be critical. In the 1960s and 1970s, this led to the miniaturization of many spacecraft components, and the spin-offs in commercial technology gave us the likes of such things as home computers and hand-held calculators, technology which has come full circle, making consideration of a 120-pound interplanetary spacecraft produced with off-the-shelf components not such a far-fetched idea.

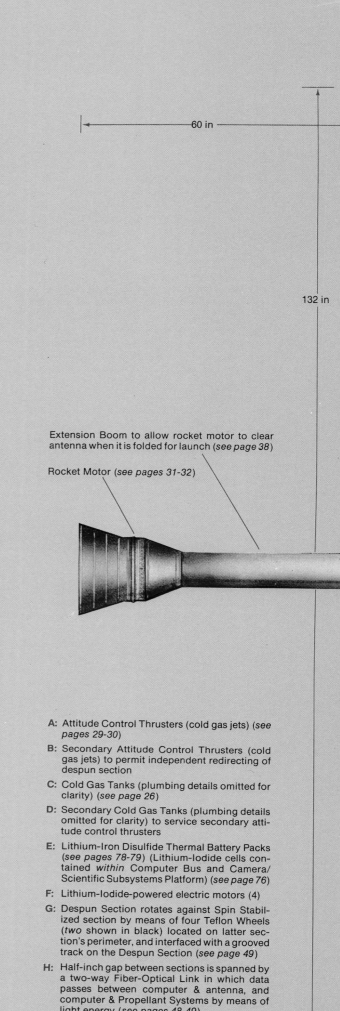

Extension Boom to allow rocket motor to clear antenna when it is folded for launch (*see page 38*)

Rocket Motor (*see pages 31-32*)

A: Attitude Control Thrusters (cold gas jets) (*see pages 29-30*)

B: Secondary Attitude Control Thrusters (cold gas jets) to permit independent redirecting of despun section

C: Cold Gas Tanks (plumbing details omitted for clarity) (*see page 26*)

D: Secondary Cold Gas Tanks (plumbing details omitted for clarity) to service secondary attitude control thrusters

E: Lithium-Iron Disulfide Thermal Battery Packs (*see pages 78-79*) (Lithium-Iodide cells contained *within* Computer Bus and Camera/Scientific Subsystems Platform) (*see page 76*)

F: Lithium-Iodide-powered electric motors (4)

G: Despun Section rotates against Spin Stabilized section by means of four Teflon Wheels (*two* shown in black) located on latter section's perimeter, and interfaced with a grooved track on the Despun Section (*see page 49*)

H: Half-inch gap between sections is spanned by a two-way Fiber-Optical Link in which data passes between computer & antenna, and computer & Propellant Systems by means of light energy (*see pages 48-49*)

Figure 38: The hypothetical spacecraft developed in this section in generalized final form. (*See also Figures 7, 12, 14, 19 and 20*).

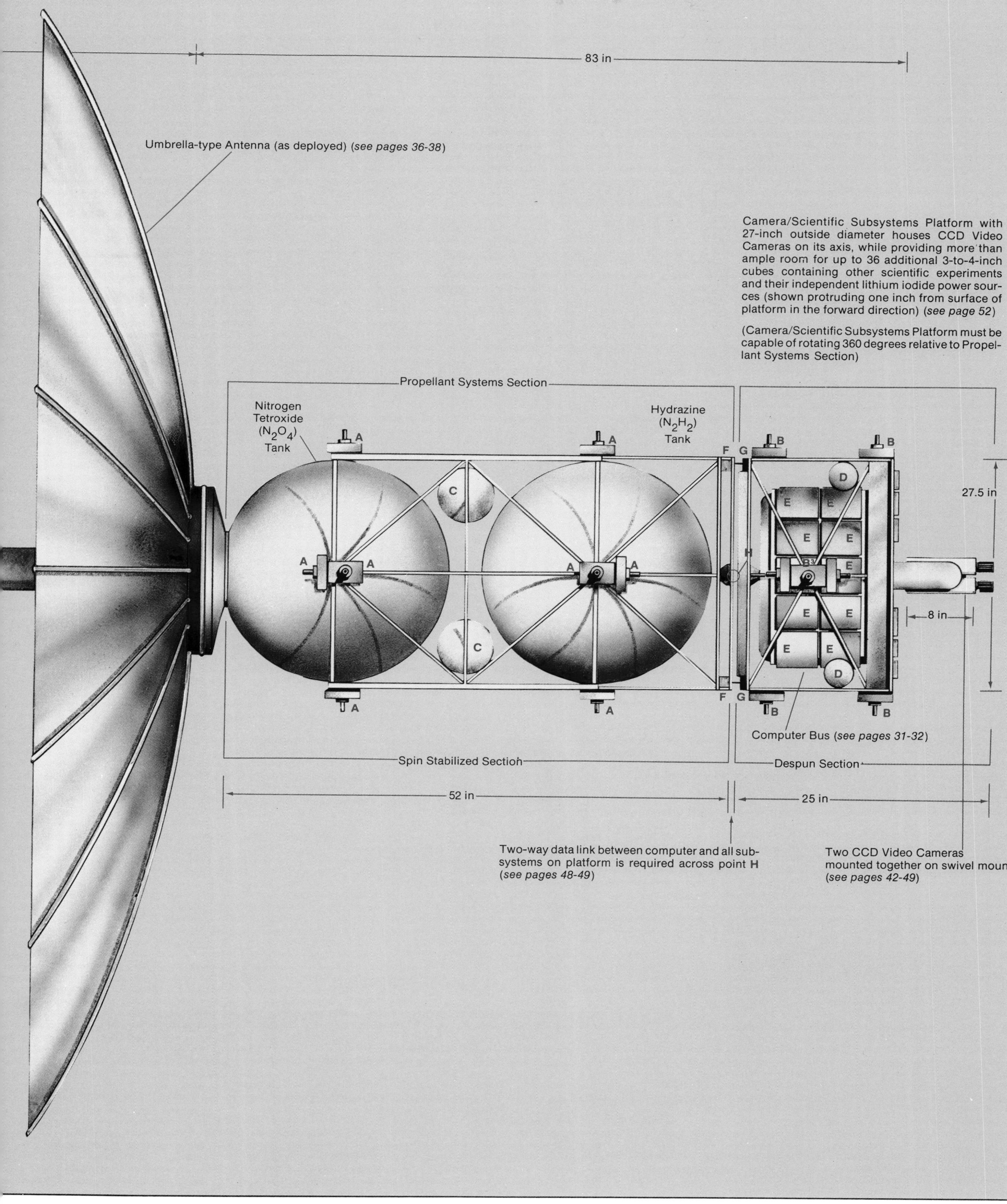

Umbrella-type Antenna (as deployed) (*see pages 36-38*)

Camera/Scientific Subsystems Platform with 27-inch outside diameter houses CCD Video Cameras on its axis, while providing more than ample room for up to 36 additional 3-to-4-inch cubes containing other scientific experiments and their independent lithium iodide power sources (shown protruding one inch from surface of platform in the forward direction) (*see page 52*)

(Camera/Scientific Subsystems Platform must be capable of rotating 360 degrees relative to Propellant Systems Section)

Propellant Systems Section

Nitrogen Tetroxide (N_2O_4) Tank

Hydrazine (N_2H_2) Tank

83 in

27.5 in

8 in

Computer Bus (*see pages 31-32*)

Spin Stabilized Section

Despun Section

52 in

25 in

Two-way data link between computer and all subsystems on platform is required across point **H** (*see pages 48-49*)

Two CCD Video Cameras mounted together on swivel mount (*see pages 42-49*)

83

Technical Profiles of Great Interplanetary Spacecraft
Voyager 1 and Voyager 2

Still functional more than a decade after they were launched, the two identical Voyager spacecraft are designed to operate at greater distances from Earth and the Sun than required by any previous space mission. Communications capability, hardware reliability, navigation, and temperature control are among the major challenges that had to be met to operate over the lifetime of the mission, due to the distances between Earth and the spacecraft and the wide range of environmental conditions the Voyagers encounter.

The spacecraft themselves weigh 1819 pounds including a 258 pound instrument payload. Like the Mariner spacecraft and Viking Mars Orbiters, the Voyagers are stabilized on three axes using the Sun and a star as celestial references.

Hydrazine gas jets provide thrust for stabilization and trajectory-correction maneuvers. A nuclear power source—three radioisotope thermoelectric generators—provides electrical power for the spacecraft.

The pointable science instruments are mounted on a two-axis scan platform at the end of the science boom. Other instruments fixed to the body of the spacecraft and attached to booms are aligned to provide for proper interpretation of their measurements.

Data storage capacity on the spacecraft's tape recorders is about 536 million bits—approximately the equivalent of 100 full-resolution photos. Dual-frequency communications links—S-band and X-band—provide accurate navigation data and large amounts of science information during planetary encounter periods (up to 115,200 bits per second at Jupiter, 44,800 bps at Saturn, and 21,600 bits at Uranus).

The basic spacecraft structure is a 54 pound 10-sided aluminum framework with 10 packaging compartments. The structure is 18.5 inches high and 70 inches from longeron to opposite longeron. The electronics assemblies are structural elements of the 10-sided box.

A spherical propellant tank contains fuel for hydrazine thrusters used for attitude-control and trajectory-correction maneuvers. It occupies the center cavity of the decagon. Propellant lines carry hydrazine to 12 small attitude-control and four trajectory-correction maneuver thrusters.

The dominant feature of the spacecraft is the 12 foot diameter high-gain antenna which is pointed almost continuously at Earth. While the antenna dish is white, most visible parts of the spacecraft are black—blanketed or wrapped for thermal control and micrometeoroid protection. A few small areas are finished in gold foil or have polished aluminum surfaces to reflect heat.

Sun sensors protrude through a cutout in the antenna dish. An X-band feed horn is at the center of the reflector. Two S-band feed horns are mounted back-to-back with the X-band subreflector on a three-legged truss above the dish. Louver assemblies provide temperature control for the electronics compartments. The top and bottom of the 10-sided structure are enclosed with multi-layer thermal blankets. Two Canopus Star Trackers are mounted side-by-side and parallel atop the upper ring of the decagon.

Three radioisotope thermoelectric generators are assembled on a boom hinged on outrigger struts attached to the basic structure. The RTG boom is constructed of steel and titanium. Each RTG unit, contained in a beryllium outer case, is 16 inches in diameter, 20 inches long and weighs 86 pounds.

The science boom, supporting the instruments most sensitive to radiation, is located 180 degrees from the RTG boom. The boom, 7.5 feet long, is a bridgework of graphite-epoxy tubing. Attached at its midpoint are the cosmic-ray and low-energy charged-particle instruments. Farther out on the boom is the plasma-science instrument.

The two-axis scan platform is mounted at the end of the boom and points four remote-sensing instruments—the ultraviolet spectrometer, infrared interferometer/spectrometer and radiometer, photopolarimeter, and a two-camera imaging-science subsystem. The total gimballed weight of the platform is 220 pounds.

Two 33 foot whip antennas are part of the planetary radio astronomy (PRA) instrument package and are shared with the plasma-wave instrument (PWS). The PRA and PWS assemblies are body-mounted one atop the other. The magnetic-fields experiment consists of four magnetometers—two high-field sensors affixed to the spacecraft and two low-field sensors mounted on a 43 foot boom. The boom is made of epoxy glass and forms a rigid triangular mast with one magnetometer attached to its end plate and another 20 feet closer to the spacecraft. A four-square-foot shunt radiator/science-calibration target faces outward from the propulsion module truss adapter toward the scan platform. The structure radiates into space, any excess heat from the electrical system. The outer surface also serves as a photometric calibration target for the instruments on the scan platform.

Communications with the Voyagers are conducted through a radio link between Earth tracking stations and the dual-frequency radio aboard the spacecraft (*see pages 116–120*).

The uplink operates at S-band only, carrying commands and ranging (for distance measurements) signals from ground stations to one of a pair of redundant receivers. The downlink is transmitted from the spacecraft at both X-band and S-band frequencies.

Only one receiver is powered at any one time, with the redundant receiver at standby. The receiver operates continuously during the mission at about 2113 megahertz. The receiver can be used with either the high-gain or low-gain antenna. Voyager 2's primary receiver failed on 5 April 1978, and the spacecraft is operating on its backup receiver, which itself suffered a partial failure of the portion of the receiver that acquires and tracks the frequency of the signal transmitted from Earth. Despite this, mission results have been spectacular.

The Voyager power subsystem generates, converts, conditions, and switches power on the spacecraft. The power source is an array of three radioisotope thermoelectric generators (RTGs). The RTG units, mounted in tandem on a boom and connected in parallel, convert to electricity the heat released by the isotopic decay of plutonium-238. Each isotope heat source has a maximum power output of 160 watts at the beginning of the mission. There is a gradual decrease in power throughout the mission. Power from the RTGs is held at a constant 30 volts DC by the shunt regulator. The 30 volts are supplied directly to some spacecraft users and are switched to others in the power-distribution subassembly. Because of the long mission lifetime, charged capacitor energy-storage banks are used instead of batteries to supply the short-term extra power demanded by instantaneous overloads that would cause the main DC power voltage to dip below acceptable levels (*see pages 74–75*).

The heart of the on-board control system is the computer-command subsystem (CCS), which provides a semi-automatic capability to the spacecraft. The CCS includes two independent memories, each with a capacity of 4096 data words. Half of each memory stores reusable fixed routines that do not change during the mission. The second half is programmable by updates from the ground. Most commands to other spacecraft subsystems are issued from the CCS memory, which, at any given time, is loaded with the sequence appropriate to the mission phase. The CCS also can decode commands from the ground and pass them on to other spacecraft subsystems. Under control of an accurate on-board clock, the CCS counts hours, minutes or seconds until a preprogrammed interval has elapsed, then branches into subroutines stored in the memory that result in commands to other subsystems (*see pages 31–32*).

Thrusters used for trajectory-correction maneuvers are started with a tandem command from both CCS processors and stopped with a parallel command. (*continued on page 90*)

Figure 39: A three-quarter view of the overall Voyager spacecraft configuration highlighting important details discussed in the text on pages 86–91. (*See also the photograph on pages 88–89*).

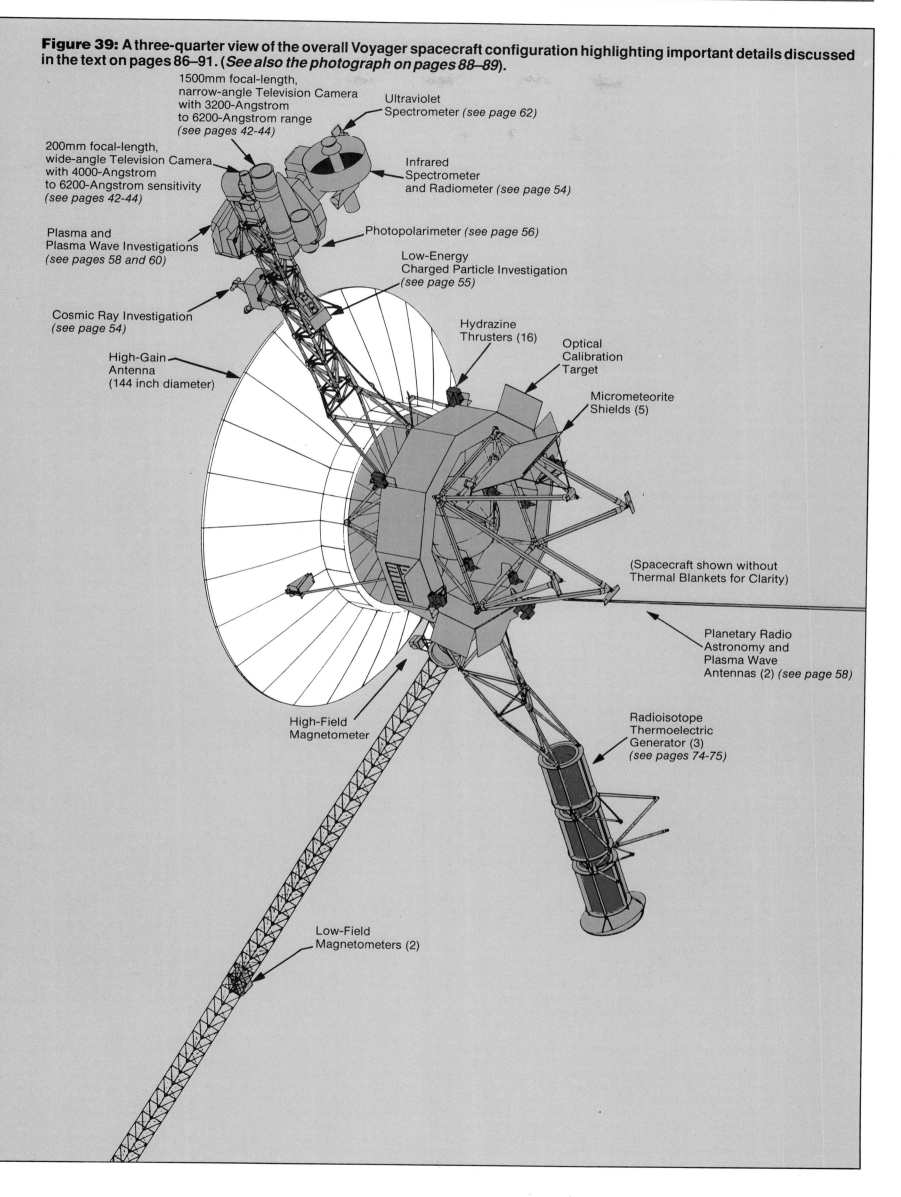

1500mm focal-length, narrow-angle Television Camera with 3200-Angstrom to 6200-Angstrom range (*see pages 42-44*)

Ultraviolet Spectrometer (*see page 62*)

200mm focal-length, wide-angle Television Camera with 4000-Angstrom to 6200-Angstrom sensitivity (*see pages 42-44*)

Infrared Spectrometer and Radiometer (*see page 54*)

Plasma and Plasma Wave Investigations (*see pages 58 and 60*)

Photopolarimeter (*see page 56*)

Low-Energy Charged Particle Investigation (*see page 55*)

Cosmic Ray Investigation (*see page 54*)

Hydrazine Thrusters (16)

Optical Calibration Target

High-Gain Antenna (144 inch diameter)

Micrometeorite Shields (5)

(Spacecraft shown without Thermal Blankets for Clarity)

Planetary Radio Astronomy and Plasma Wave Antennas (2) (*see page 58*)

High-Field Magnetometer

Radioisotope Thermoelectric Generator (3) (*see pages 74-75*)

Low-Field Magnetometers (2)

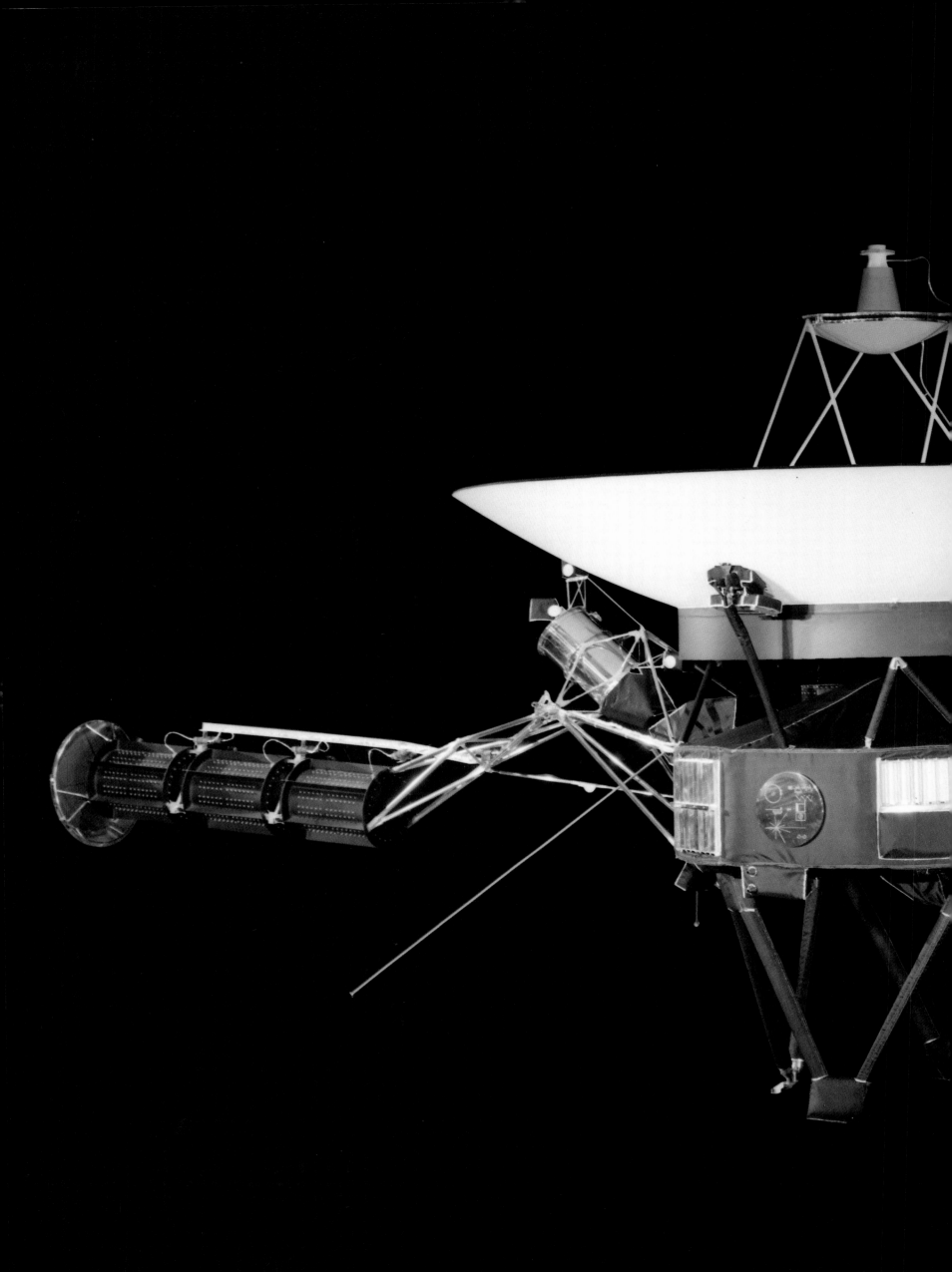

Above: The Voyager spacecraft were designed to operate farther from Earth than any previous man-made object. With Voyager 1 having been purposely slung out of the ecliptic plane after its flyby of Saturn and the giant moon Titan, Voyager 2 was slung around Uranus and is due to encounter Neptune in August of 1989—after which it, too, will pass out of the Solar System. In addition to their scientific payloads, both craft bear a golden plaque, plainly seen here, which was designed to enable any (hopefully) friendly galactic neighbors to locate the origin of the spacecraft. In addition, to get them into the swing of things, mission specialists included a 'Sounds of Earth' recording, which comprised both natural and man-made sounds, including music.

All 24 hydrazine thrusters use a catalyst that spontaneously initiates and sustains rapid decomposition of the hydrazine.

The spacecraft hydrazine supply is contained within a 28 inch diameter spherical titanium tank, separated from the helium pressurization gas by a Teflon-filled rubber bladder. The tank, located in the central cavity of the spacecraft bus, contained 230 pounds of hydrazine at launch and was pressurized at 420 psi. As the propellant is consumed, the helium pressure will decrease to a minimum of about 130 psi.

The 16 thrusters on the spacecraft itself each deliver 0.2 pounds of thrust. Four are used to execute trajectory-correction maneuvers; the others, in two redundant six thruster branches, stabilize the spacecraft on its three axes. Only one branch of attitude-control thrusters is needed at any time.

The AACS includes an onboard computer system called HYPACE (Hybrid Programmable Attitude Control Electronics), redundant sun sensors, redundant Canopus Star Trackers, three two-axis gyros, and scan actuators to position the science platform. The HYPACE contains two redundant 4096-word plated-wire memories—part of which is fixed and part programmable—redundant processors and input/output driver circuits.

The sun sensors look through a slot in the high-gain antenna dish. They are electro-optical devices that send attitude position error signals to HYPACE, which in turn signals the appropriate attitude-control thrusters to fire and turn the spacecraft in the proper direction. Sun-lock stabilizes the spacecraft on two axes (pitch and yaw).

The star Canopus, one of the brightest in the galaxy, is usually the second celestial reference for three-axis stabilization. Two star trackers are mounted so that their lines-of-sight are parallel. Only one is used at a time. The star tracker, through HYPACE logic, signals the thrusters to roll the spacecraft about the already-fixed Earth or Sun-pointed roll axis until the tracker is locked on Canopus. Three-axis stabilization with celestial reference is the normal attitude-control mode for cruise phases between planets.

The spacecraft can be stabilized on one axis (roll) or all three axes with the AACS' inertial reference unit consisting of three gyros. Inertial reference is used whenever the spacecraft is not on Sun/star celestial lock (*see page 112*).

Voyager's two television cameras, ultraviolet spectrometer, photopolarimeter and infrared spectrometer/radiometer are mounted on the scan platform, which can be rotated about two axes for precise pointing. Controlled by the attitude and articulation control subsystem (AACS), the platform allows multiple pointing directions of the instruments. The platform's two axes of rotation are described as the azimuth angle motion about an axis displaced seven degrees from the spacecraft roll axis (perpendicular to the boom centerline) and elevation angle motion about an axis perpendicular to the azimuth axis and rotating with the azimuth axis. Angular range is 360 degrees in azimuth and 210 degrees in elevation (*see pages 42–44*).

The platform is slewed one axis at a time with selectable slew rates in response to computer command subsystem commands to the AACS.

After Voyager 2's Saturn encounter, a problem was experienced with the scan platform's motion in azimuth. Long and detailed diagnosis and prognostic work led the Mission Planning Office to put constraints on the use of the scan platform's slewing mechanism, so that no high-speed slews were made during the Uranus encounter.

Both the top and bottom of the spacecraft's basic decagon structure are enclosed with multilayer thermal blankets to control loss of heat to space. The blankets are sandwiches of aluminized mylar, sheets of Tedlar for micrometeoroid protection, and outer black Kapton covers. Also extensively blanketed are the instruments on the scan platform. Smaller blankets and thermal wraps cover eight electronics bays, boom and body-mounted instruments, cabling, propellant lines and structural struts. Only a few exterior elements of the spacecraft are not clad in the black film—the high-gain antenna reflector, plasma sensors, sun sensors and antenna feed-cones.

Radioisotope Heating Units (RHU), small non-power-using heat elements that generate one watt of thermal energy, are located on the magnetometer sensors and the sun sensors. No RHUs are used near instruments that detect charged particles. Electric heaters are located throughout the spacecraft to provide additional heat. Many heaters are turned off when their respective valves, instruments or subassemblies are on and dissipating power.

Voyager 1 was launched from Cape Canaveral on 5 September 1977 and targeted toward Jupiter, which it encountered at a dis-

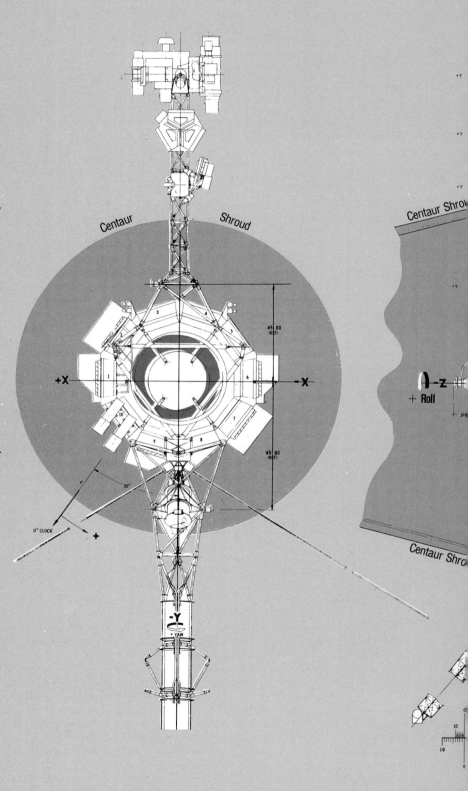

Figure 40: A sectional end view (section A-A of Figure 41) of the Voyager spacecraft configuration with deployable booms in the deployed postion.

tance of 177,720 miles, on 5 March 1979. A gravity-assist from Jupiter slung the spacecraft on to its next destination, Saturn, which it observed from as close as 77,000 miles on 12 November 1980. Mission objectives at Saturn, including a very close flyby of the giant moon Titan, precluded Voyager 1 from continuing on to any other planets. The spacecraft was boosted up and out of the ecliptic plane of the solar system by Saturn's gravity-assist.

Voyager 2 was launched 20 August 1977, about two weeks before the launch of Voyager 1. Flying a longer trajectory, it reached Jupiter coming as close as 399,560 miles on 9 July 1979, four months after Voyager 1's flyby. Like its twin spacecraft, Voyager 2 was slung on to Saturn, which it encountered at a distance of 63,000 miles on 25 August 1981. At that time, Voyager 1 had been directed North, past Saturn's moon Titan, while the decision was made to send Voyager 2 to an aimpoint at Saturn which would permit it to follow a course toward Uranus that allowed it to pass within a half million miles of that planet on 24 January 1986 and continue outward in the Solar System toward an encounter with Neptune in August 1989 (*see page 107*).

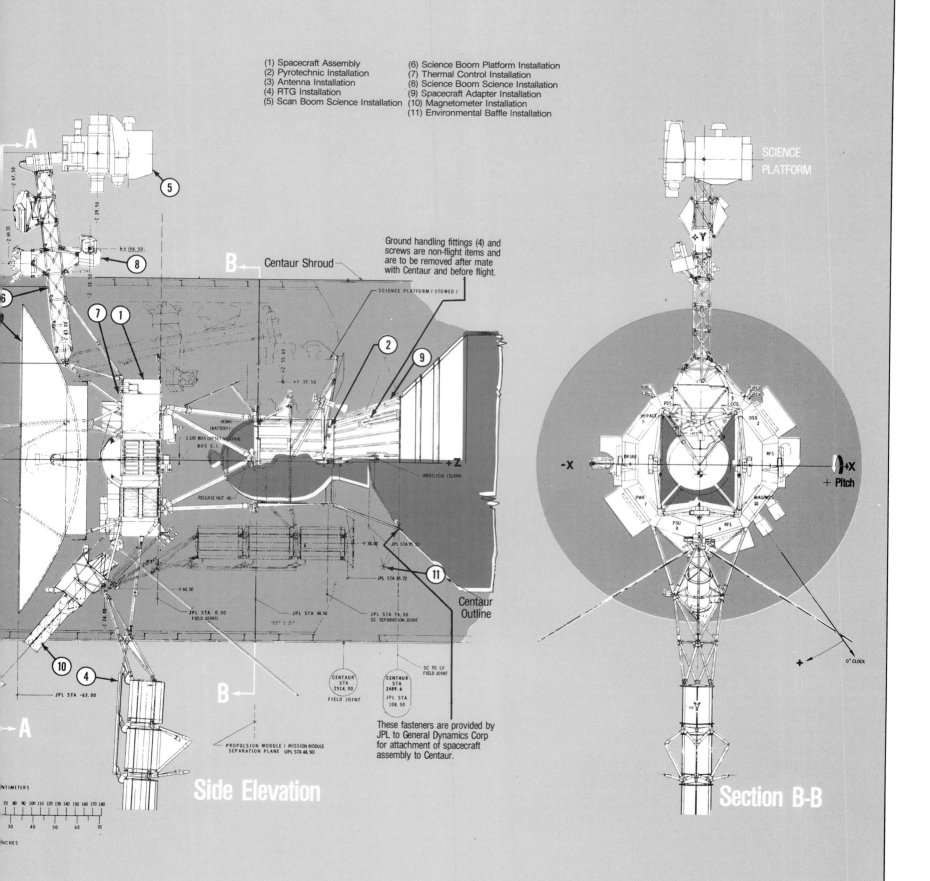

(1) Spacecraft Assembly
(2) Pyrotechnic Installation
(3) Antenna Installation
(4) RTG Installation
(5) Scan Boom Science Installation
(6) Science Boom Platform Installation
(7) Thermal Control Installation
(8) Science Boom Science Installation
(9) Spacecraft Adapter Installation
(10) Magnetometer Installation
(11) Environmental Baffle Installation

Side Elevation

Section B-B

Figure 41: A schematic side view of the Voyager spacecraft configuration, showing the stowed and deployed position of the deployable booms.

Figure 42: A sectional end view (section B-B of figure 41) of the Voyager Spacecraft configuration with deployable booms in the deployed position.

At left: The awesome vastness of Saturn is apparent in this 3 November 1980 Voyager 1 photo, taken from eight million miles out. Also visible here are two of the giant planet's many moons, Tethys (above) and Dione. The shadows of Saturn's rings and Tethys are cast onto the planet's cloud tops. *Above:* This computer-generated photo of the Encke Division in Saturn's outer 'A' ring was created from Voyager 2 photo polarimeter data (see text, page 56). The computer generation technique creates stunning visual images. *Below left* is a Voyager image of the Saturn moon Enceladus. Enceladus is 242.3 miles in diameter, and evidences surface faulting with its very visible 'grooves.' *Below right* is a Voyager color mosaic of the Saturn moon Dione. A variety of information gathering systems—cameras, sensors and computers—combined to ensure the Voyager successes.

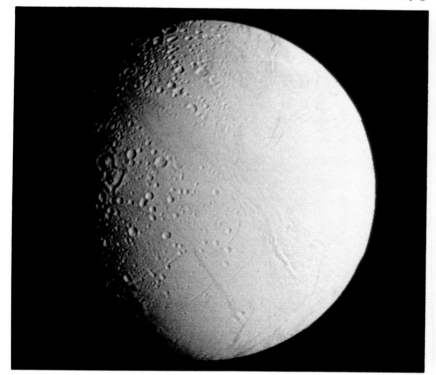

PART TWO

THE LAUNCH

A. Overview

The Liberty 1C (*see Figures 43–45, below and right*) with an upper stage would be adequate to launch a 110 pound spacecraft, and its 800 pound propellant stage (*see pages 22–29*), into a Pluto flyby trajectory (*see pages 6–9 and 98–100*).

The launch location depends on what is available at any given time. A launch can be set up in a few weeks time at most—probably a few days time to launch from any site in the world. This cannot be done from just any patch of desert, however, because of Department of Transportation licensing regulations involving launch sites. Typically, one cannot get a license to do an inland launch because in case of an aborted flight the first and second stages would fall in areas where you might not want them to go. Possible launch sites include Johnston Island, other Pacific islands or Hawaii.

It may be possible to launch from the US Navy site at Barking Sands on Kauai, but it might be too small. There are a number of suitable islands off the California coast like St Nicholas, which is also a Navy base. Of course NASA's Wallops Island, Virginia launch facility might be a good possibility. There are various international sites which might be optimum for this. The Japanese have some sites and the Chinese have three. One can always find a site. All that would be required is an *over-water trajectory*, although one would need to worry about one's position, in respect to the equator, which is why the Pacific Island sites are good.

The Liberty 1C launch vehicle package *includes* a mission operation center module that could be used to control the entire launch sequence (*see Figure 46, right*). A number of companies have built similar things in the past. DSI, which built the small satellite launch for the shuttle, has a work station based on an IBM personal computer, which is less elaborate, and probably less expensive than Liberty's. One could use one of these for the entire launch sequence and also for the insertion into the planetary trajectory. After that, one could keep the console to use as 'mission control,' and to collect and enter data from remote sites, since there wouldn't be a direct communications link. The data could be displayed and processed on the original launch control facilities.

As Pacific American's part of the mission, they would conduct the entire launch, with the standard off-the-shelf launch van and console (*see Figure 46*), and then turn it over to the user.

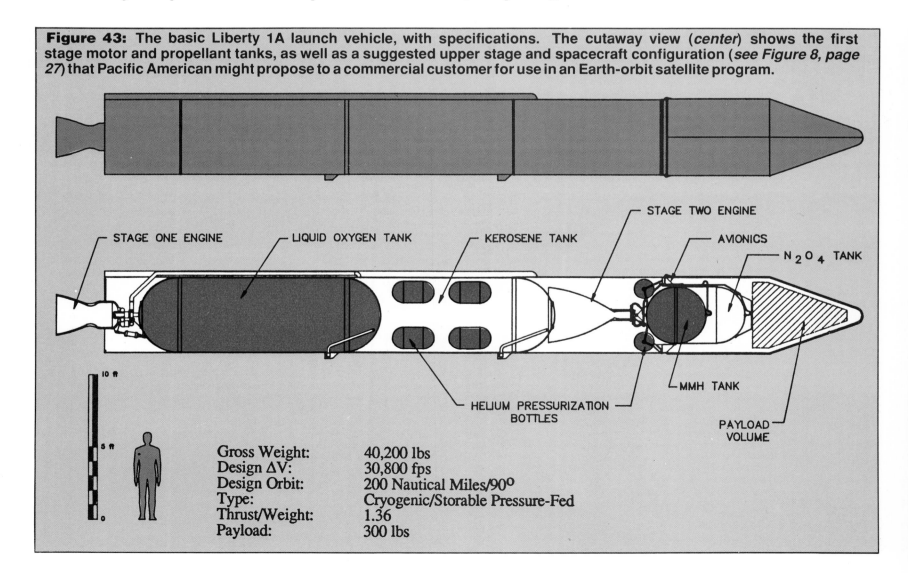

Figure 43: The basic Liberty 1A launch vehicle, with specifications. The cutaway view (*center*) shows the first stage motor and propellant tanks, as well as a suggested upper stage and spacecraft configuration (*see Figure 8, page 27*) that Pacific American might propose to a commercial customer for use in an Earth-orbit satellite program.

STAGE ONE ENGINE — LIQUID OXYGEN TANK — KEROSENE TANK — STAGE TWO ENGINE — AVIONICS — N₂O₄ TANK — MMH TANK — PAYLOAD VOLUME — HELIUM PRESSURIZATION BOTTLES

Gross Weight:	40,200 lbs
Design ΔV:	30,800 fps
Design Orbit:	200 Nautical Miles/90°
Type:	Cryogenic/Storable Pressure-Fed
Thrust/Weight:	1.36
Payload:	300 lbs

Figure 44: The Pacific American Liberty launch vehicle family.

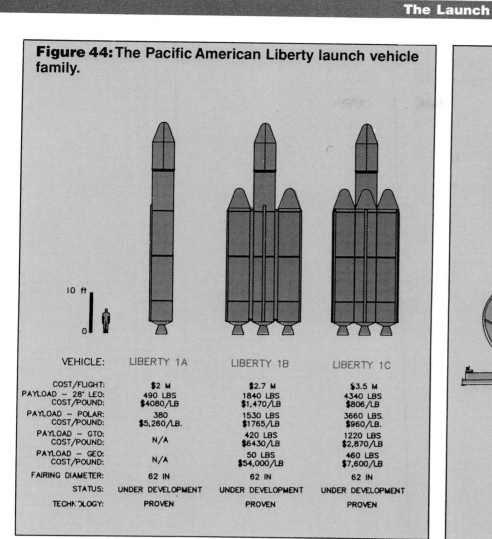

VEHICLE:	LIBERTY 1A	LIBERTY 1B	LIBERTY 1C
COST/FLIGHT:	$2 M	$2.7 M	$3.5 M
PAYLOAD – 28° LEO:	490 LBS	1840 LBS	4340 LBS
COST/POUND:	$4080/LB	$1,470/LB	$806/LB
PAYLOAD – POLAR:	380	1530 LBS	3660 LBS
COST/POUND:	$5,260/LB.	$1765/LB	$960/LB.
PAYLOAD – GTO:	N/A	420 LBS	1220 LBS
COST/POUND:		$6430/LB	$2,870/LB
PAYLOAD – GEO:	N/A	50 LBS	460 LBS
COST/POUND:		$54,000/LB	$7,600/LB
FAIRING DIAMETER:	62 IN	62 IN	62 IN
STATUS:	UNDER DEVELOPMENT	UNDER DEVELOPMENT	UNDER DEVELOPMENT
TECHNOLOGY:	PROVEN	PROVEN	PROVEN

10 ft

0

Figure 46: Pacific American launch control hardware.

Gee, you can launch one of these with a PC and a truck! *At right:* The Mission Operations and Control Center for the Libert 1C, and *above right,* the system's Mobile Launch Control Center. This system sets up in less than one day, and is a completely integrated ground station—with full S-Band Telemetry, Command and Control; Simulation; Data Acquisition; Data Archiving; Data Reduction; Data Presentation; and, if necessary, Command Destruction. Launch systems in the 1950s–early 1960s used computers as big as a basketball court; these days, a suitcase-size home computer might do the same job even better!

Figure 45: A detailed cutaway view of the basic Liberty 1A launch vehicle first stage.

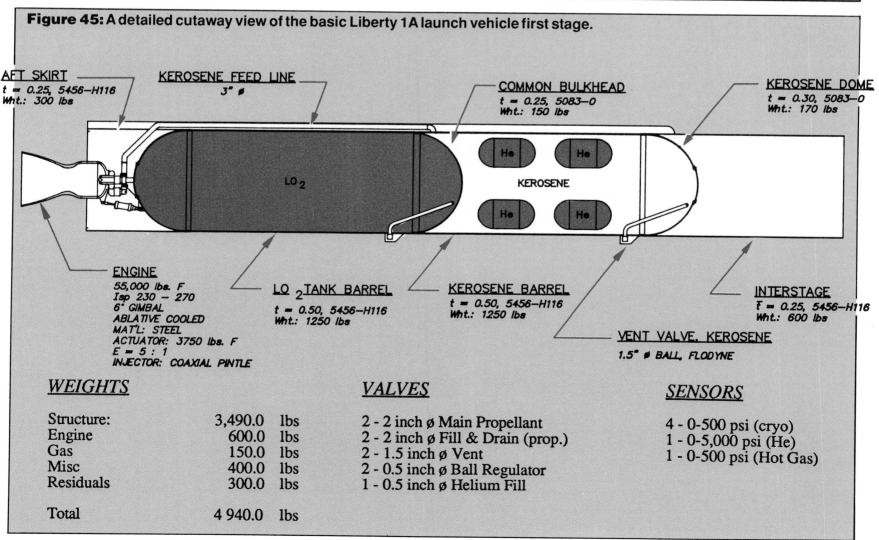

AFT SKIRT
t = 0.25, 5456–H116
Wht.: 300 lbs

KEROSENE FEED LINE
3" ø

COMMON BULKHEAD
t = 0.25, 5083–0
Wht.: 150 lbs

KEROSENE DOME
t = 0.30, 5083–0
Wht.: 170 lbs

LO₂

He   He

KEROSENE

He   He

ENGINE
55,000 lbs. F
Isp 230 – 270
6° GIMBAL
ABLATIVE COOLED
MAT'L: STEEL
ACTUATOR: 3750 lbs. F
E = 5 : 1
INJECTOR: COAXIAL PINTLE

LO₂ TANK BARREL
t = 0.50, 5456–H116
Wht.: 1250 lbs

KEROSENE BARREL
t = 0.50, 5456–H116
Wht.: 1250 lbs

VENT VALVE, KEROSENE
1.5" ø BALL, FLODYNE

INTERSTAGE
t = 0.25, 5456–H116
Wht.: 600 lbs

WEIGHTS

Structure:	3,490.0	lbs
Engine	600.0	lbs
Gas	150.0	lbs
Misc	400.0	lbs
Residuals	300.0	lbs
Total	4 940.0	lbs

VALVES

2 - 2 inch ø Main Propellant
2 - 2 inch ø Fill & Drain (prop.)
2 - 1.5 inch ø Vent
2 - 0.5 inch ø Ball Regulator
1 - 0.5 inch ø Helium Fill

SENSORS

4 - 0-500 psi (cryo)
1 - 0-5,000 psi (He)
1 - 0-500 psi (Hot Gas)

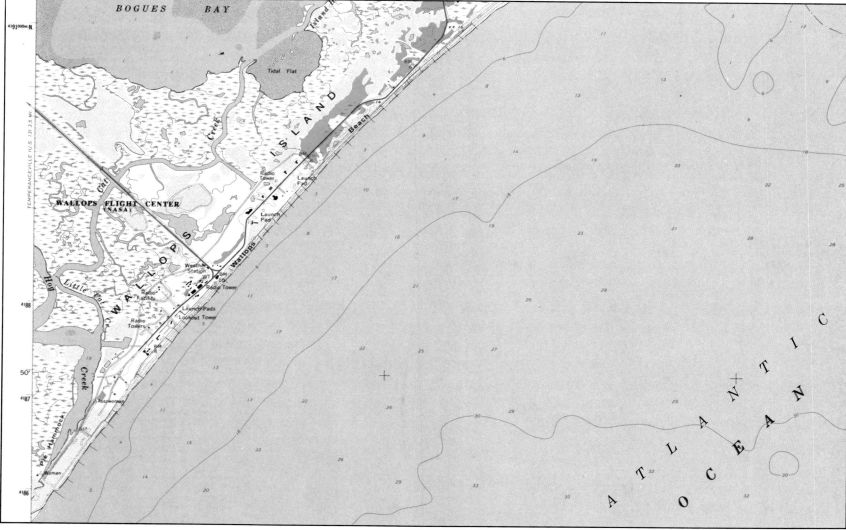

At left and at top, above: This is what launch sites look like. The site at left—Pad 39 at the Kennedy Space Center in Florida—is probably the most complicated launch site in the Western World, where many of NASA's cost-intensive projects have been launched over the years, including the Space Shuttle. The launch site detailed *at top and above* — located at Wallops Island off the coast of Virginia—is where NASA launches its low-budget projects. Both sites offer over-water trajectories in the Atlantic Ocean. Equipment transportation to either site would be no problem, but Kennedy is definitely the high-rent neighborhood for budget-conscious space explorers.

PART THREE

TRAJECTORY

A. Planning

The path that a spacecraft takes is called its 'trajectory' and it is determined by when and with what force the rocket motors fire (*see pages 22–29*). The principles of space flight are complicated but most of the equations required can be understood by using high school algebra and calculus, while all the mathematics can be readily found in available text books. To send a spacecraft from Earth to Pluto, the rocket motors must accomplish three distinct tasks:

1) Push the spacecraft from the Earth's surface up into a stable Earth orbit.
2) Push the spacecraft beyond the Earth's gravity, into an orbit around the Sun.
3) Push and guide the spacecraft so that at a precise moment in time, it crosses Pluto's orbit when the planet is in position for the rendezvous.

For a launch into Earth orbit, the three decisions to be made are what direction to launch, where the launch will occur, and how high the orbit will be.

Before these decisions are made concerning the planning of an interplanetary mission, one must consider several facts about Earth-or-biting satellites. The most important is that for all of them, the altitude of the orbit is related to how often they pass closest to the Sun and not their speed relative to the surface of the rotating Earth. It doesn't matter if they orbit west-to-east or east-to-west, or over the poles. It also doesn't matter how massive they are.

Because the Moon is 240,000 miles from Earth, it must pass closest to the Sun once every *28 days*. Any manmade satellite at 240,000 miles must also orbit the Earth once every 28 days. An altitude of 22,000 miles requires a *24 hour* rotation rate. Since the Earth revolves on its axis once every 24 hours, a satellite orbiting at this altitude over the equator would always be over the same point on the equator. This is a geosynchronous orbit (*see Glossary*) since it is synchronized to the Earth's rotation. That is precisely where the weather and communications satellites are 'parked'—so they can always view a particular part of the Earth. This applies if they orbit from west-to-east. With both the north-south (polar) orbit and the east-to-west orbit, they would pass over the same point every 12 hours—once in the daytime and again in the night.

Although this all may seem trivial, it is a fact from which we can benefit. If a launch is made from a point on or near the equator, the

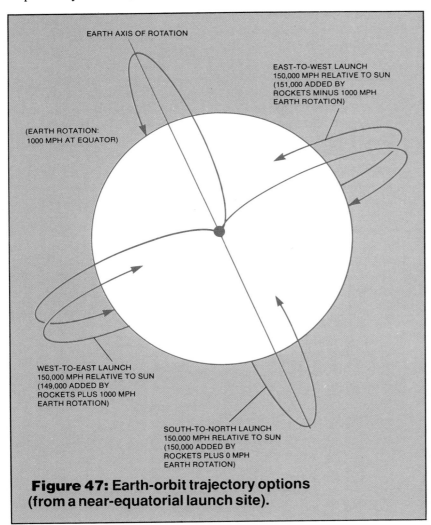

Figure 47: Earth-orbit trajectory options (from a near-equatorial launch site).

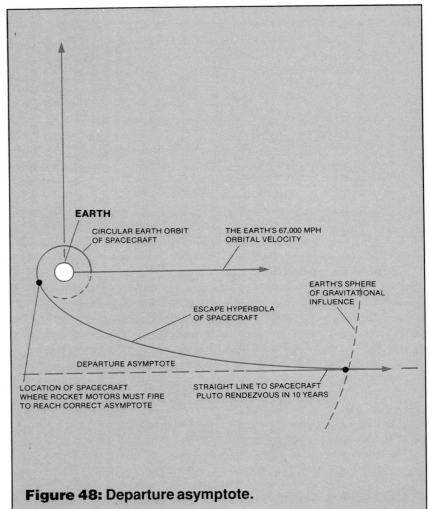

Figure 48: Departure asymptote.

spacecraft is traveling west-to-east at a speed over 1000 miles per hour (25,000 miles Earth circumference/24 hours). From as far north as Florida that speed is still over 900 miles per hour. Even in Anchorage, Alaska it is 500 miles per hour.

However, this holds true only if one launches west-to-east. If one were to launch to the north, one can use none of this momentum— 1000 mph has gone to waste. For an east-to-west launch, this rotational momentum has to be overcome and there is a 1000 mph deficit (see Figure 47).

Two decisions are easy—one should launch to the east and as close to the equator as is practical. The last decision concerning altitude is important only in that a launch must get above the atmosphere.

No matter how many thousands of miles above the Earth's surface the orbit is established, an interplanetary spacecraft must still be pushed billions of miles 'higher', or farther out toward Pluto. If it is placed in too low an orbit, however, the spacecraft will reenter the atmosphere and burn up. Only a trace of atmosphere exists above 120 miles but there is enough at this altitude for frictional drag to decay the orbit, slowing it down until the spacecraft falls back to Earth.

Timing the launch into Earth orbit is important, however. Once a stable Earth orbit is established, the spacecraft must wait for its 'launch window,' which involves critically precise timing. Since the Earth is a satellite of the Sun, it revolves around the Sun with a natural momentum which the spacecraft can again utilize. Instead of 1000 mph, this bonus is 67,000 mph. Unlike the case of an Earth orbit launch, however, an interplanetary spacecraft will be 'shot out' in a straight line, so the Earth must be traveling directly *toward* Pluto when this next leg of the journey begins.

To know when this will occur we must know the current location of Pluto. This information can be obtained from astronomical charts. For example, these charts will show that Pluto was in conjunction with the Sun on 29 April 1987, meaning that at midnight on that date, Pluto was directly overhead. Nevertheless, on that date the Earth's momentum in its orbit was not directed *toward* Pluto. That point would occur nine months later, early in February 1988.

At that time, the spacecraft must be sent on its way to Pluto along a curved line, called its departure *asymptote*. The journey up from the circular Earth orbit to the *asymptote* is the escape hyperbola and

must be extremely precise. Any error in this portion of the launch will require a great deal of fuel to correct because of the tremendous speed of the spacecraft at this point (see Figure 48).

Even at this incredible speed, which will decrease along the journey, the trip is four billion miles long and will require 10 years. In those 10 years, Pluto will have continued to move on in its orbit around the Sun. Remembering that the departure asymptote is set to reach Pluto in 10 years, the reignition of the rocket motors to leave Earth orbit must occur one quarter revolution (three months) before the point where Pluto will be over the Earth in 1997, such as on 29 February 1988, or one year and three days later on 3 March 1989 (see Figure 49). Here it should be pointed out that this isn't the *only* trajectory possible to reach Pluto. Weighing the advantages and disadvantages of each, the flyby choice has the most to offer (see table below).

As we discussed on page 31, and continue to discuss in Part Four, the craft will be in occasional contact with Earth for 10 years after the launch to allow monitoring of its condition and its location. Midcourse maneuvers (see page 110) will be required to adjust the trajectory. A change in direction as minute as the width of a hair held at arm's length might result in a million mile course change by the time the spacecraft reaches Pluto.

Even if the trajectory were computed and executed exactly, one might still need to correct for a quirk in Pluto's orbit. Most of the planets orbit the Sun within 3.39 degrees of the same ecliptic plane. That is, if we went beyond Pluto and looked back we could draw a line along which most of them would be located at all times in their orbits. Nevertheless, two planets' orbits are tilted more accurately— Mercury at seven degrees and Pluto at 17 degrees (see Figure 59).

If the spacecraft were launched perfectly and no midcourse maneuver were possible, Pluto would still pass one billion miles under the spacecraft as it crossed the orbit of the planet. In making the midcourse correction, a rule of thumb is, 'the sooner the better' in terms of using up fuel. Redirecting the spacecraft 17 degrees as it travels 1000 mph is much easier, if it can be completed early enough, than waiting until the correction must be 30 degrees at 10,000 mph.

In describing the factors involved in determining the trajectory of such a journey the reader may wonder why few numbers were involved. Exactly when and for how long do these critical rocket firings occur? The reason that they weren't given is that they depend

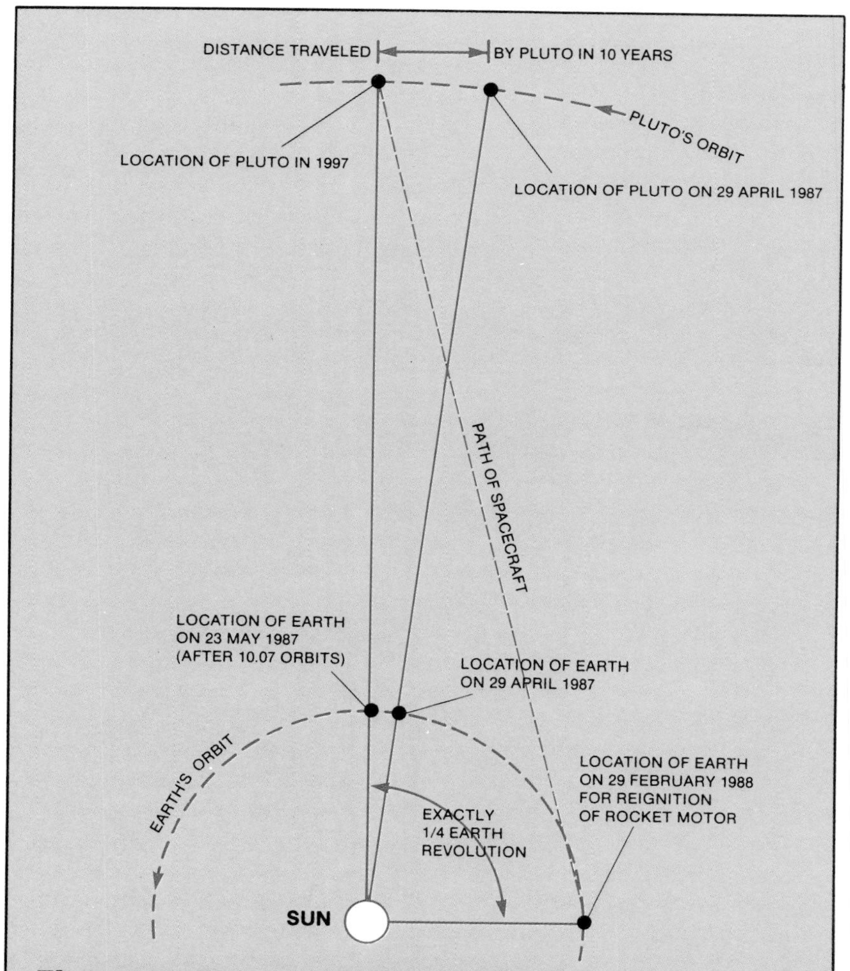

Figure 49: Pluto mission trajectory options.

Possible Journeys to Pluto

Option	Advantages	Disadvantages
Flyby (our choice)	Requires less precision and fuel. Spacecraft will become 3rd to pass out of Solar System. Less time required to get pictures—10 years. Can store data in computer to relay back after passing Pluto	Less time to take pictures because spacecraft is moving so fast
Collision with Pluto	Requires less fuel. Spacecraft will become 1st to reach surface of any of 5 outer planets. Less time to get pictures—10 years. Closest pictures possible just before collision	Less time to take pictures because spacecraft is moving so fast
Establish permanent Pluto orbit	Can orbit for years and photograph entire planet	Requires 46 years to reach Pluto. Requires much more fuel.
Pass around Pluto and return to Earth	Retrieval of maximum artifacts for museum	Requires almost 100 years to reach Pluto and return to Earth. Requires the most fuel. Must be brought through Earth atmosphere after reestablishing Earth orbit

on factors that won't be known until before the firings occur. The most critical factor in these firings is the mass of the spacecraft, (including the remaining fuel). The term mass is used because while the spacecraft has weight on the launch pad, it has none in space. With forces acting counter to the gravity of the Earth and the Sun, the spacecraft is weightless in outer space.

The key to computing these firings is a simple equation: impulse = momentum; (ft = MV). This means that the force that the rocket exerts on the spacecraft multiplied by the time it is applied equals the mass of the spacecraft multiplied by the increase in its velocity (speed).

Because the mass of the spacecraft will depend on what is launched and will even change as the fuel is used, the industry rates its hardware in terms of available impulse. In addition, we can compute the initial velocity that a spacecraft will require to reach its destination. If a catapult could throw a spacecraft off its launch pad at 35,000 feet per second, it would establish an Earth orbit. If in orbit, another catapult could toss it again at 7000 fps, it would escape Earth orbit and orbit the Sun alone.

With another catapult adding another 10,000 fps we could journey to Pluto at a speed of over 25,000 mph. The change in velocity will be 52,000 feet per second—that must be supplied by the rocket motor. If one doubles the mass of the craft one can either *double the force required* or *double the time that the force is exerted* to obtain the same trajectory (*see Figure 50, below*).

There are really two different scenarios to get to Pluto. If one were to do a flyby of Pluto—strictly a flyby—then one could use Jupiter's gravitational field as a slingshot because that would be worth the savings in time and it would also probably provide a little better Pluto flyby velocity. It would also save three to four years. Without a Jupiter flyby the time to Pluto could be 11 years.

However, as we discussed at some length on page 16 and page 32, a Jupiter flyby would subject the spacecraft to serious radiation danger. As noted on page 99, the problem has to do with *when* the spacecraft is launched. Because Pluto's orbit is so inclined and eccentric, one really can't calculate any meaningful numbers until one specifies the launch date. At one launch date a 120 pound spacecraft could be launched, but at another date, one might only be able to launch 60 pounds.

The difference in spacecraft weight between a Pluto flyby—or any outer planet flyby—and a mission within the asteroid belt (such as Mars or Venus) is minimal. A Jupiter orbit that would allow us to

look at that planet's intriguing Galilean moons, would be the same for all practical purposes of Delta V requirements. The Liberty 1C can put just over 100 pounds into any of those trajectories (*see Figure 50, below*).

The Delta V is the change in velocity necessary to attain an orbit-trajectory. (Delta is the Greek letter for 'change.') These are measured in thousands of feet per second. There are two terms we need to know. One is *Ideal Delta V* and the other is *Characteristic Delta V*. Characteristic Delta V is the lower of the two and it is the actual energy or velocity necessary to do the mission. Ideal Delta V includes all the losses that occur—such as that of climbing up out of the gravitational pull of Earth, the drag losses that are experienced, the atmosphere passage, thrust-vector losses (*see Figure 50, below*).

Typically, everything that slows the spacecraft down until it gets into outer space will add another 4000-5000 feet per second to these numbers, so when one designs the stage, or the vehicle, one must take 50,000 feet per second as the target velocity and add about 5000 feet per second to it for each of these factors. Then one may start computing the performance of the upper stage, or the specific impulse needed in the engine, and how much of a payload is being carried.

Because Pluto is closer until the end of the 20th century than it will be for 200 years, it is advisable to get something off the ground before 1999. Although it is closer in 1995, the flyby velocity must be higher. If one were to intersect Pluto farther out, however, the flyby velocity would be a lot lower. But it would take one about a year longer to get there. One must make tradeoffs. If one were to launch in 1992, the trip would take roughly nine years, versus 10 years if launched in 1999.

The *ideal* transfer could take 19 years to get to Pluto, but nobody is going to want to take *that much time*. This is where Jupiter comes in. A Jupiter flyby reduces the time required for the mission by at least three or four years. Using Jupiter's gravitational force would mean a travel time to Pluto of *as little as five or six years* in a 1992 launch, and then seven or eight years after that. One must still play a delicate matching game because if one were to launch for the earliest arrival time, one also has the highest relative Delta V, which means there will have to be a much bigger rocket motor to slow down. If one waits another turn, the next smaller rocket could be used.

A discussion of the use of Jupiter, in connection with the *Gravity Assist Principle* during the Voyager program, begins on page 102.

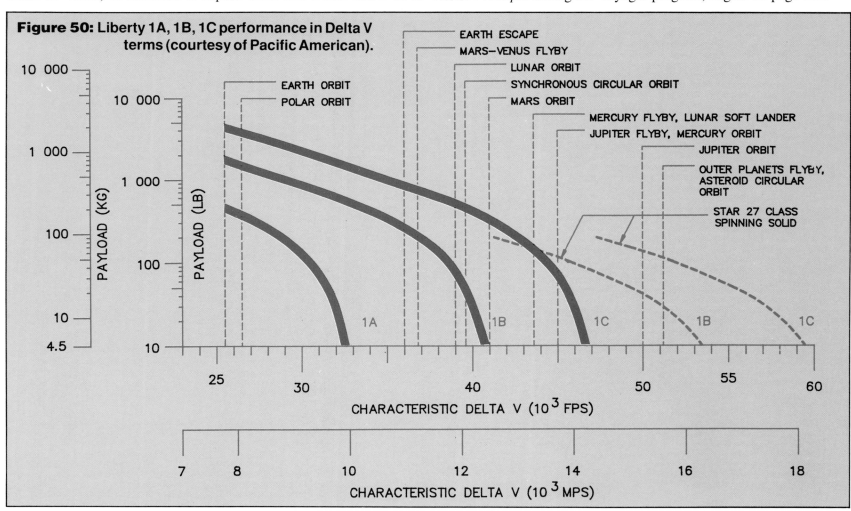

Figure 50: Liberty 1A, 1B, 1C performance in Delta V terms (courtesy of Pacific American).

Above: A composite of Jupiter and its four innermost satellites. A spacecraft to Pluto could use Jupiter's intense gravitational field as a slingshot to save time and to gain extra velocity. The problem, as has been discussed, is Jupiter's destructive radioactivity. Given the right launch date on Earth, the problem could be avoided—see the text, page 100.

B. The Gravity Assist Principle in Interplanetary Missions

Adapted from a report prepared in 1981 at the Jet Propulsion Laboratory, California Institute of Technology, under contract NAS-100 sponsored by the National Aeronautics & Space Administration.

By Andrey B Sergeyevsky

Member, Technical Staff, Voyager Trajectory Analysis Task Leader, Jet Propulsion Laboratory (NASA)

Multiple planet flybys, utilizing the gravity assist (G/A) principle have over the last two decades been growing in stature from the early first circumlunar 'free return' concept (1957), used on the Apollo Mission translunar leg (1968-1972), through the Mariner 10 of 1973 and the Pioneer 11 Jupiter/Saturn tour (1973-1979), through the Voyager 2 Mission destined to encounter Neptune in 1989.

All of these sophisticated missions owe their very existence to efforts of a long line of theoreticians throughout the last two centuries. The nature of the grouping of cometary orbits with respect to the major planets brought 19th century classical celestial mechanicians to recognize the concept of the natural gravitational perturbation maneuver, which could transform a very long period incoming comet into a much less eccentric, short period object, by way of a close encounter with a major planet (F Tisserand, A Poincare). With the advent of the 20th century and the dawn of flight came new visionaries contemplating manmade objects in orbits similar to those of classical celestial mechanics. Thus was born a new discipline of engineering, which eventually came to be known as Astrodynamics. It brought forth a new wave of investigators with a very pragmatic outlook on the future.

Among these were some who quickly recognized the enormous potential of the gravitational swingby maneuver, which could not only change direction of flight, but could also gain or shed spacecraft velocity by means of a pre-planned momentum interchange with the planet or moon to be encountered. Suffice it to mention the names of YV Kondratyuk (1919), FA Tsander (1925), VA Firshoff (1954), DF Lawden (1954), MA Minovitch (1963), GA Flandro (1965), JC Niehoff (1966), JM Deerwester (1966), and BW Silver (1967), to encompass the grand effort of those pioneers on whose shoulders present mission designer's accomplishments rest.

The gravity assist method, as applied to Outer Planet missions, was found to be so attractive because it allowed the use of low launch energies, barely sufficient to reach the first encounter planet, Jupiter in our case, on an elliptical trajectory. Beyond that point the orbit would become hyperbolic, flight times to subsequent easily targetable planets would be substantially shorter than they would have been on a direct mission. Such a direct mission would have to use a much higher nominal launch energy, just to reach these bodies, if it were not for the gravity assist phenomenon.

On multiple planet gravity assist flyby missions, only two independent variables are available to the mission designer to shape the trajectory. Usually these are launch and first encounter dates, but other combinations could be useful and acceptable, such as launch energy and, say, second encounter flyby distance, to avoid ring material.

On the Voyager 2 mission, the ballistic arrival times at Saturn, Uranus and Neptune are, in principle, totally determined by the dates on which Earth launch and Jupiter encounter had occurred. The downstream arrival dates can, however, be changed within modest limits by minor 'deterministic' propulsive trajectory correction maneuvers (TCMs) following each encounter. These velocity changes are performed to speed up or slow down the spacecraft, thus changing the time required to reach the next planet, in order to synchronize the arrival with an optimal satellite configuration at that next encounter, resulting in an enhanced science return. Naturally, the modified arrival time maps back onto the target plane* at the preceding body, ie the effect of such burns affects the computation of aim-

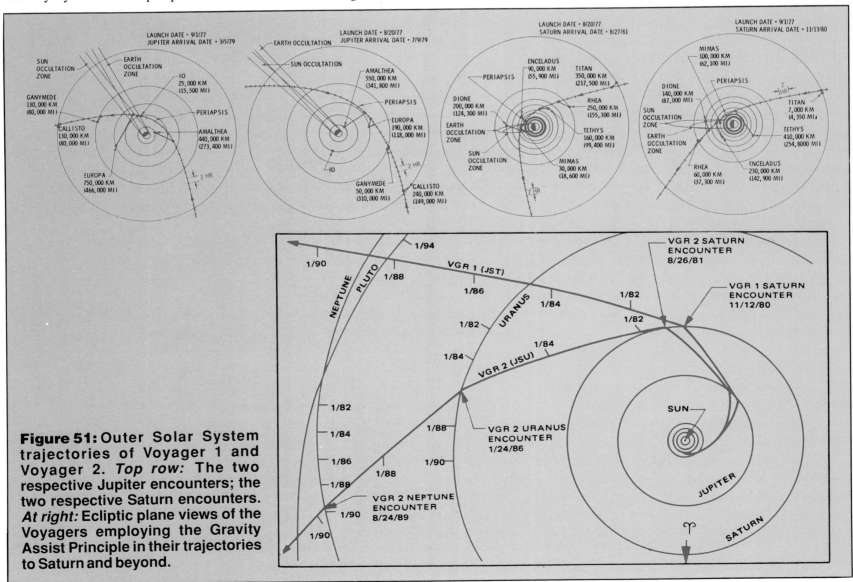

Figure 51: Outer Solar System trajectories of Voyager 1 and Voyager 2. *Top row:* The two respective Jupiter encounters; the two respective Saturn encounters. *At right:* Ecliptic plane views of the Voyagers employing the Gravity Assist Principle in their trajectories to Saturn and beyond.

points at Saturn and Uranus, such that the amount and direction of turn would come out just right for the envisioned continuation of the mission to Uranus and Neptune, respectively. In this sense, it may be said that these aimpoints are entirely defined, and thus fixed, by the need to continue the mission to the two specified target bodies.

A number of objectives and constraints significantly curtail the mission designers' freedom in choosing aimpoint and/or arrival time at any of the planets on a given tour:

(1) The orientation of at least one of the Deep Space Network (DSN) stations on the rotating Earth must be such, that the spacecraft may be tracked at sufficiently high antenna elevation angles to support high transmission bit rates at all significant encounter events, especially, however, during geocentric (radio) occulations of a planet or its satellites, as these events cannot be tape-recorded on the spacecraft, due to their very nature. Whenever a spacecraft is located at high (north or south) geocentric declination, station coverage becomes highly uneven among the three DSN station complexes, causing periods of poor or no coverage at all, during significant portions of each day.

As both Uranus and Neptune are now and throughout the rest of this century, at their most negative declinations because of their celestial position near the negative ecliptic Y-axis, this situation favors southern hemisphere stations, making DSN Station 43 tracking from Canberra, Australia an asset, DSN Station 14 at Goldstone, California a supportive station, because of partial overlap with DSN Station 14, and DSN Station 63 at Madrid, Spain practically ineffective. Stations 43 and 14 thus form a desirable observing time block, a 'DSN window.' Station 63 tracking periods and adjacent low elevation coverage intervals represent 'undesirable' Earth-receive event times. For typical examples compare Figures 56 and 57.

---

* Target plane, or B-plane, is a highly useful aimpoint design tool. It is an imaginary plane passed through the center of a celestial body.

(2) The encounter time must be synchronized with the position of the satellites to be closely approached, as previously discussed. On the target plane, each satellite can be represented by a locus of aimpoints that would cause impact, or passage at a specified occulation distance, for every specific planet closest approach time. Two families of oval or hat-shaped loci usually exist, one for close, high-turn-angle flybys and another for distant, low-bend-angle encounters. Suitable arrival times may be chosen from these or equivalent representations.

If the aimpoint is fixed, as it is at Saturn and Uranus, the problem is simplified and a plot of planet closest approach epoch versus satellite closest approach distances is sufficient to choose an optimal arrival time.

(3) The aimpoint must lie in a region of the B-plane where geocentric and heliocentric planetary occulation is realizable. These regions can be mapped into the target plane, usually assuming the shape of a planet-sized strip in one half-plane, with a bulbous region about the planet itself. Diametric planet occulation occurs along the center line of each such zone (see Figures 53 and 54). Geocentric diametric occulation is preferred by radio science experimenters, as it facilitates limb-tracking of the refracted Earth-point through the entire occulation event.

If rings about a planet are suspected, equatorial entry (or exit) becomes an asset, as it is desirable to separate atmospheric and ring occulation measurements, avoiding mutual data overlap.

(4) For reasons of spacecraft safety, regions containing ring, ringlet or rock material in orbit about the planet must be avoided by the spacecraft at all costs. This type of assorted debris seems to occur in orbit near the equatorial planes of most giant planets. At Uranus, stellar occulations (appulses) have indicated that ring

continued on page 106

The Grand Tour Concept

By 1970, serious interest in a Grand Tour mission was aroused within the aerospace community. Led by enthusiasts at the Jet Propulsion Laboratory—JE Long, RD Bourke, GA Flandro, MA Minovitch, PA Penzo, RA Wallace, and A Avizienes—work started on planning the 1977 JSP (Jupiter-Saturn-Pluto) and 1979 JUN (Jupiter-Uranus-Neptune) missions. At one time these were to be launched on a Saturn-S and utilize a new Thermoelectric Outer Planets Spacecraft (TOPS), equipped with a Self-Test-and-Repair (STAR) computer. Industrial giants—Rockwell, Boeing, Martin and TRW—invested significant company funds on large in-house study teams to prepare themselves for the Grand Tour project bidding. The 17th Annual Meeting of the American Astronautical Society in June 1971, at Seattle, was entirely devoted to the Grand Tour and Outer Solar System Missions. The projected cost of the TOPS JSP/JUN mission soared to about one billion dollars. In the meanwhile the success of the Apollo Lunar Missions caused a flare-up of US public ecstasy, to be followed by the hangover of an expensive victory in the unopposed Moon race. The legislative and public apathy that resulted caused a funding demise, the effects of which are felt to this day. As a consequence, the Grand Tour was not included in the 1972 budget, the effort was officially canceled and the industrial teams were disbanded or laid-off.

Good, promising ideas do not die easily, however. The 179-year reoccurrence cycle of JSUN Grand Tour opportunities made the 1977 launch too precious an asset to bypass. The rarity of these opportunities for missions of this type also proved to be a very timely reminder for those who could not patiently sit by and see the 76-year Halley Comet opportunity in 1985-86 wither away unused, exchanged for more utilitarian and near-sighted goals.

A Mariner-type, low cost in-house JPL Mission to Jupiter and Saturn was approved by mid-1972 through the efforts of unbend-

ing space-science advocates in Congress, NASA and JPL. The twin spacecraft were tentatively called Mariner 11 and 12, both to be launched in August-September 1977 on Titan 3-D launch vehicles. The cost of the new Mariner-Jupiter-Saturn project (MJS77) was not to exceed 360 million dollars.

The two spacecraft missions were soon to be labeled JSI and JSG, indicating that their reconnaissance effort at Jupiter was to emphasize Io and Ganymede, respectively. At Saturn, intensive Titan and Ring investigations by both spacecraft were also contemplated.

By 1975, the astounding radiation belt intensities at Jupiter were sampled by the Pioneers 10 and 11, while another planned Mariner-Jupiter-Uranus Mission in 1979 (MJU79) was experiencing funding difficulties. The MJS project was redirected to become the current Voyager Missions: one to Io and Titan at Jupiter and Saturn, respectively, the other, to flyby Jupiter at no less than 8.5 Jupiter radii (JR) while retaining at Saturn the 'hip-pocket' option of going to Uranus. To mission designers this decision, of course, meant a green light to Neptune—the Grand Tour still had a chance to be accomplished, with all its promise of discovery in a single shot and only 12 years of flight.

In March 1977, the project and the spacecraft were renamed to Voyager 1 and 2 (see pages 86–91). This name was originally applied to a grand version of what later became a less expensive Viking Landing Mission to Mars (see pages 64–67). With the August and September 1977 launches, the two Voyagers joined the NASA fleet of trail-blazing spacecraft, laying the groundwork for the 21st century's great voyages (see pages 86–93).

—*Andrey B Sergeyevsky*

Voyager 2 used the Jupiter 'gravity whip' to assist its travels. *At right:* The rings and cloud bands of Uranus have both been highly emphasized in this painting. In real life, the rings are so dark that they are practically invisible, except from point-blank range. *Above:* An artist's concept of Voyager 2 passing beyond Neptune and its moon Triton, in September of 1989.

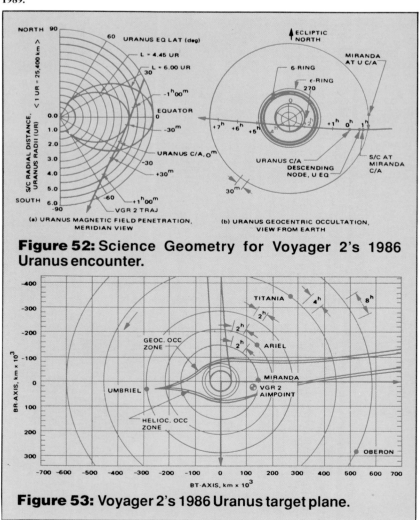

(a) URANUS MAGNETIC FIELD PENETRATION, MERIDIAN VIEW

(b) URANUS GEOCENTRIC OCCULTATION, VIEW FROM EARTH

Figure 52: Science Geometry for Voyager 2's 1986 Uranus encounter.

Figure 53: Voyager 2's 1986 Uranus target plane.

material definitely exists in the region from 1.6 to 2.0 planet radii. At Saturn, the visible rings end at about 2.4 radii, the so-called Roche limit. In the absence of any information on Neptune's ring structure, the same ring dimensions were assumed for the Neptunian system. Contours of limiting ring-plane crossing loci can be shown in the target plane by curves akin to satellite orbit impact mapping.

(5) Magnetic field penetration is desired to the deepest possible L-shell, a curved surface, somewhat like an onion shell, formed by a single magnetic field line, rotated about the dipole axis. The L measure is expressed in planet radii at the field line magnetic equator crossing point.

   The best way to illustrate spacecraft field penetration is a radius versus magnetic latitude plot, where the entire flyby is mapped into a single common meridian (*see Figures 52 and 55*). Charged particle radiation belts, if any, can also be shown on this type of plot.

(6) The twin Voyager spacecraft will eventually escape the Solar System some time following their terminal planetary encounter. The direction of such an escape is significant in terms of the achievable measurements of the solar and interstellar medium fields and particle characteristics. The orientation into the interstellar wind may be of great interest (*see Figure 58*).

(7) Lastly, the timing of significant events must avoid two interference events:
   a) Solar conjunction periods, when the Sun is positioned within five degrees of the Earth to spacecraft communication ray, and
   b) Lunar occultations, when the Moon blocks the line-of-sight between a tracking station and the spacecraft for short periods.

The totality of these considerations form the bulk of the criteria by which Tour trajectories were compared and selected.

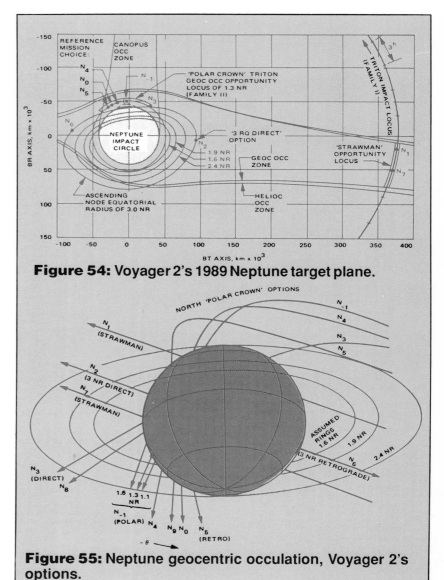

Figure 54: Voyager 2's 1989 Neptune target plane.

Figure 55: Neptune geocentric occulation, Voyager 2's options.

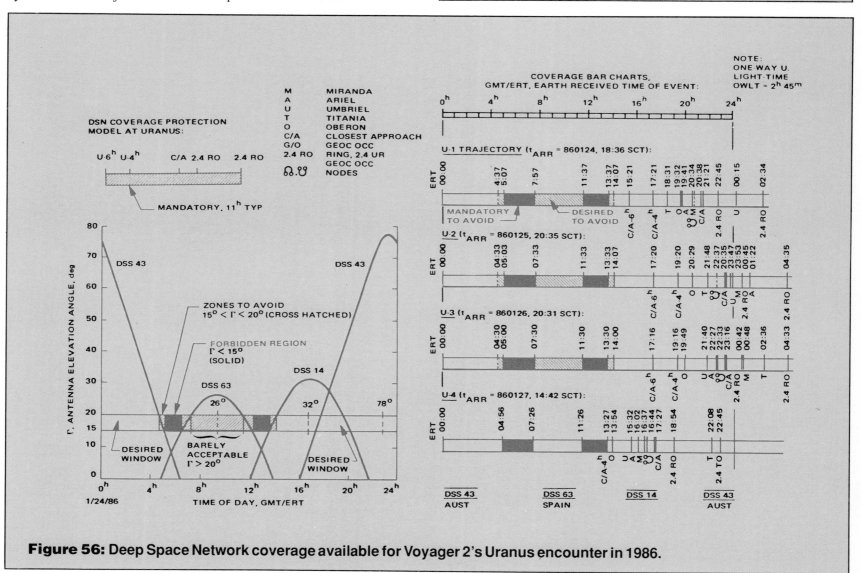

Figure 56: Deep Space Network coverage available for Voyager 2's Uranus encounter in 1986.

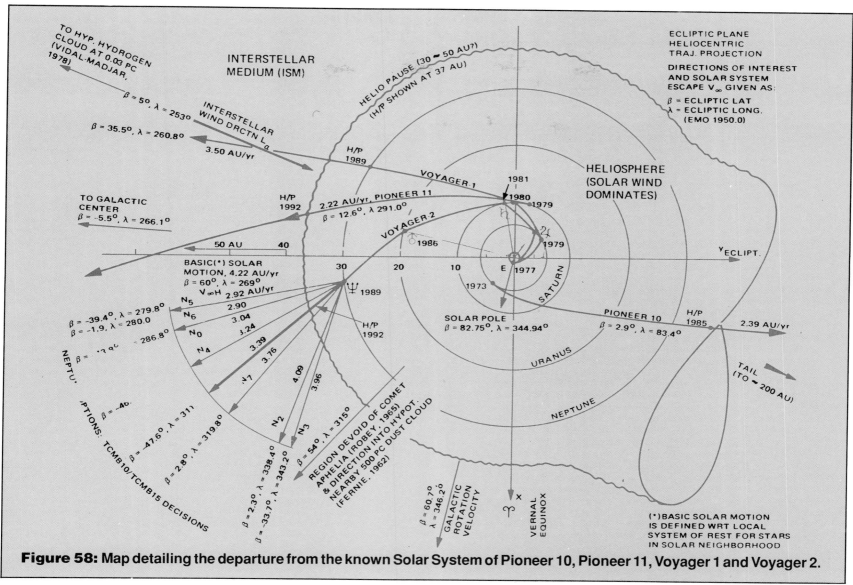

Figure 58: Map detailing the departure from the known Solar System of Pioneer 10, Pioneer 11, Voyager 1 and Voyager 2.

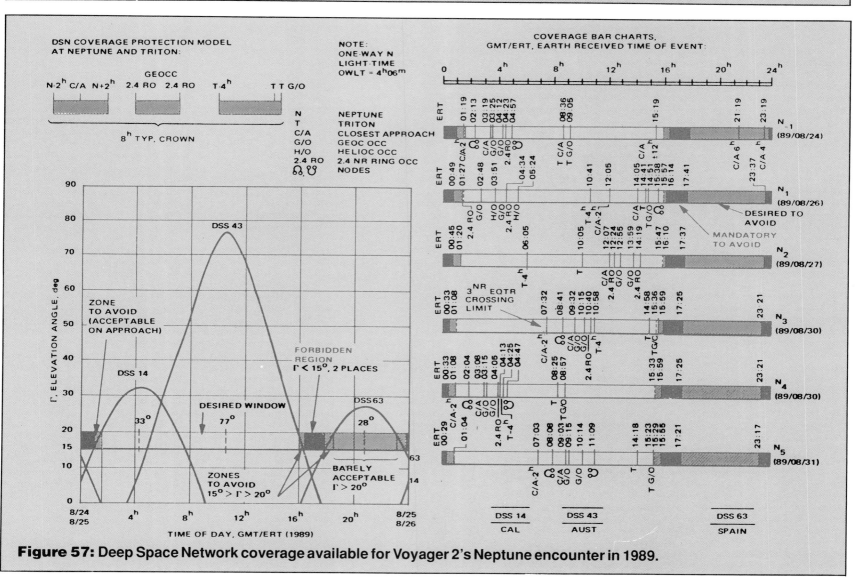

Figure 57: Deep Space Network coverage available for Voyager 2's Neptune encounter in 1989.

107

Above: Neptune, the next to last planet in the Solar System, and Triton, the larger of its two currently known moons appear in a conceptual portrait. Beyond these mysterious bodies lies the even more mysterious last planet, Pluto—our mission objective—and its mysterious moon, Charon.

Neptune is thought to be nearly the twin of Uranus, except that it, like Jupiter, actually generates more energy than it receives, and lies 950.5 million *more* miles from the Sun than does Uranus! Uranus itself is an average of 1.9 *billion* miles from the Sun.

By comparison, the extremely eccentric orbit of Pluto takes it as far out as 4.6 billion miles, and closes in, every 248 years, to an orbital radius which is actually 69.4 million miles less than Neptune's 2.8 billion mile orbital radius.

Pluto is now within that radius, and will be until the end of this century. Please see the text on page 100.

C. Midcourse Corrections

Throughout the several years of flight time, the onboard computer will be performing a systems and navigation check every 24 hours and these little bits of communications data from the spacecraft will build up into a database. When the spacecraft is a few months out, ground control will know where the spacecraft is in relation to the rest of the universe. By using Doppler shifting (*see Glossary*) and programs that have already been written by NASA's Jet Propulsion Laboratory for Pioneer and Voyager, one might say, 'Well, here we are four feet per second off trajectory.' Over the years, this drift will take the craft farther and farther from where it has to be, so if it is four feet per second off a few months into the mission it may mean that it is going to miss the target by 10 million miles.

There is an optimal point to make a midcourse correction, and if one can compute this ahead of time, one simply calls up the big radio astronomy receiver at Aracebo in Puerto Rico, for example, gives them the coordinates and the data that we want them to send—a couple of hundred words—and they could 'pulse it out' with all the power they've got. This tells the spacecraft that 30 days from now it will do such and such. That gives us 30 days for the spacecraft to come back and say, 'I received that message' (*see page 114*).

Provided nothing has gone wrong, at the end of 30 days the spacecraft executes the burn and it makes up the four feet per second correction and puts itself back on trajectory. It might be a tiny bit off, and maybe a year later it will need to be checked again. Given the data one might have to do a midcourse correction only two or three times over the course of an eight year voyage. The final correction may come roughly six months before the final planetary encounter.

The Voyager trajectories (*see pages 102–107*) were planned around eight trajectory correction maneuvers (TCM) with each spacecraft between launch and Saturn encounter. Mission requirements called for extremely accurate maneuvers to reach the desired zones at Jupiter, Saturn and the target satellites. Total velocity increment capability for each spacecraft is about 450 mph.

The first maneuver was planned for the period from launch-plus-five-days to launch-plus-15-days. The TCM was scheduled to take several hours, depending upon launch vehicle and injection phase trajectory errors and could be done in several parts if required by thermal constraints at this Sun-spacecraft distance. Three more maneuvers were executed prior to closest approach to Jupiter and four more between Jupiter and Saturn.

TCM sequencing is under control of the computer command subsystem (CCS) which sends the required turn angles to the AACS for positioning the spacecraft at the correct orientation in space and, at the proper time, sends commands to the AACS to start and stop the TCM burn. Attitude control is maintained by pulse-off sequencing of the TCM engines and pulse-on sequencing of two attitude control roll thrusters. Position and rate signals are obtained from the gyros. Following the burn, reacquisition of the cruise celestial references is accomplished by unwinding the commanded turns—repeating the turn sequence in reverse order. All Voyager TCMs have been enabled by ground command.

Above: **The Voyager trajectory from Earth via the largest planet, Jupiter, to Saturn flyby.**

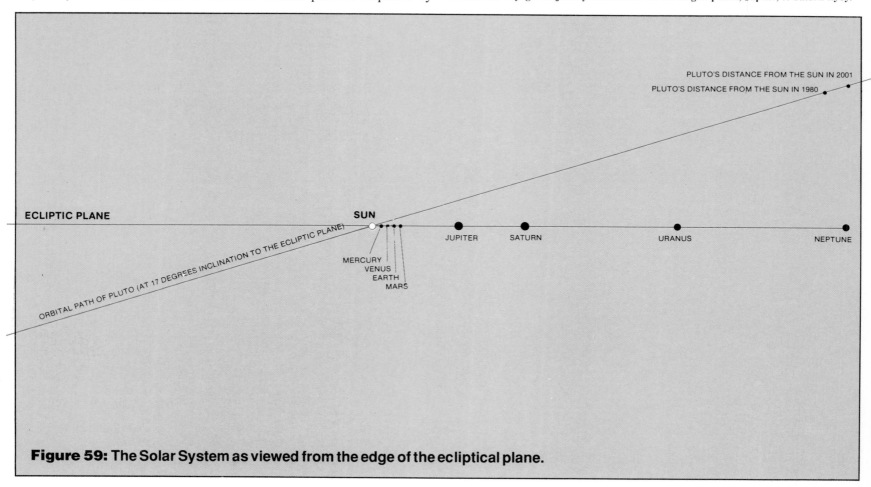

Figure 59: The Solar System as viewed from the edge of the ecliptical plane.

D. Orbital Insertion

An orbital mission is a different story because one needs the arrival Delta V (*see Figure 50, page 100*) to be as low as possible. The speed between the spacecraft and Pluto must be minimized. One *may* substitute a Saturn flyby for the Jupiter flyby. It would take a couple of years longer than a Jupiter flyby and there would not be as much extra boost, but you wouldn't have the radiation problem discussed on pages 16, 32 and 100.

It has been theorized that an orbital insertion pattern might be used in a flyby of Pluto at an altitude that would use the planet's gravitational pull to help slow the spacecraft and adjust the trajectory for a flyby of Charon. Using the gas thrusters, the spacecraft would then be trimmed for a half loop around Charon that would set it on a return trajectory to Pluto. By the time the spacecraft returned to Pluto, its velocity would be much slower than it had been for the flyby because of the combined slowing effect of the gravity of both planet and moon. The Pluto orbital insertion would then require less energy. This maneuver would also provide a good opportunity to obtain close-up photos of Charon (*see Figure 60, below*).

Whether or not the theoretical maneuver in the preceding paragraph was possible, after the spacecraft was settled into orbit around Pluto, the thermal batteries (*see page 78*) could be fired and the energy used for transmission of photos of (1) the initial Pluto flyby; (2) the approach to, and half loop around, Charon; and (3) the initial orbits around Pluto. Most of Pluto's surface could probably be photographed within 18-24 hours, so a second transmission could be scheduled for that time. In order to get progressively closer photos, one could then allow the orbit to decay steeply over the next 24 hours, ending with a final transmission just before the spacecraft impacted on Pluto's surface.

The problem with entering Pluto's atmosphere is that no one knows anything about it! We aren't sure of its composition, its density or whether Pluto even *has* an atmosphere. Methane has been detected, which probably exists in the form of ice and snow. Because of Pluto's small mass, its atmosphere is probably minimal if it exists at all, although it has been speculated that traces of gaseous methane do exist.

Much of the information about Pluto used in planning a planetary encounter would have to be gathered by the spacecraft itself because it will be traveling closer to Pluto than any manmade object in his-

tory. The cameras and spectrometer would be put into service three weeks prior to the initial flyby. Even the data received in the first 'on approach' transmission would increase the world's knowledge of this mysterious planet by a factor of at least 10. One would also have a much better idea of the atmospheric composition from the work of the spectrometer (*see pages 46–47*), while the cameras would reveal weather patterns that might exist if Pluto has any sort of cloud cover within its atmosphere.

For an orbiter that is going to allow itself to decay into an atmosphere, a spacecraft would probably need a deboost rocket, or retrorocket. Some believe, however, that any spacecraft going to go into this type of orbit around a planet with an atmosphere ought to be using an aero shell and not a rocket. An aero shell is simply a heat shield that encapsulates the spacecraft. For this kind of low velocity, one could probably use wood—polished, sealed oak. Aluminum with a ceramic exterior has also been used. Pluto's atmosphere density can only be guessed at. In any case, it would not be too thick but it doesn't take much atmosphere to kill speed. Large, fast-moving objects may hit the Earth's atmosphere and be burned up by friction within 50 miles. Planetary atmospheres are usually thicker than 50 miles. If one detects *any* atmosphere around Pluto from here—and we *think* we can—then it is certainly thicker than the uppermost 50 mile layer of the Earth's ionosphere, which will burn up 10 ton boulders in a few seconds, yet constitutes only 11 percent of the Earth's total atmosphere.

Wood is a cost-effective alternative to ceramic for the aero shell. The Soviet Union uses ironwood on many of their reentry vehicles, and so have the French and the Chinese. Every trace of moisture must be baked out of the wood to prevent damage during the long term exposure to temperatures close to absolute zero.

It's exciting to think about being able to use wood for this kind of high tech application. A more down-to-earth example is the very large wind tunnel at NASA's Ames laboratory where the new propellers are made of wood. The lab went back to using wood because steel was too heavy and the aluminum would have been too expensive to make a forging. The wood turned out to be just as strong and effective, as well as much easier and quicker to use. It was a case where aluminum and steel were clearly not advantageous in a modern application.

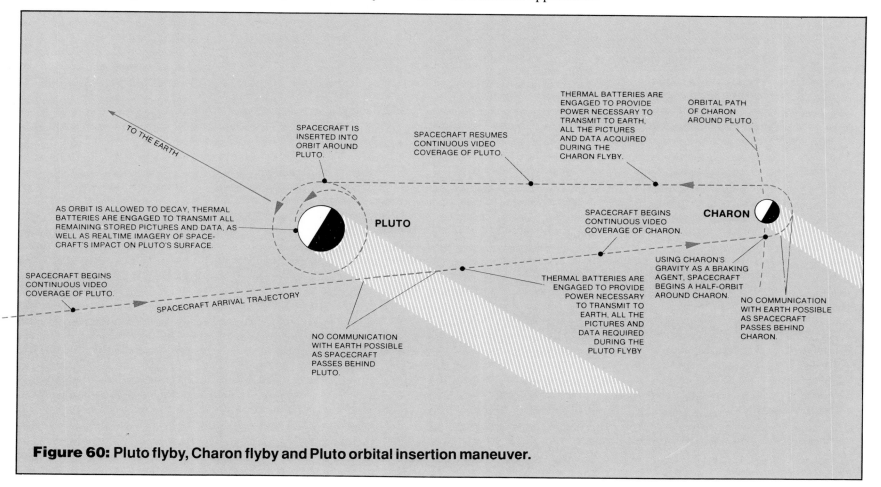

Figure 60: Pluto flyby, Charon flyby and Pluto orbital insertion maneuver.

E. Navigation/Star Tracker

If the spacecraft is spin-stabilized, it is suggested that one wouldn't need star trackers to know the precise position. One would be able to operate independently. The CCD camera, however, *is* an optical system and could be used as a star tracker with limited utility, which might be the thing to consider (*see pages 42–46*).

Most of the navigation would be done down on the ground with ground computer programs, where one would make measurements each day or each week, or as often as necessary to build up the plot. From this one would know whether the spacecraft was deviating from the planned trajectory or not (*see page 114*).

Knowing both the original velocity when the spacecraft was released from the booster and the direction in which it was pointed is essential to navigation computation. With that information one can know within a certain degree of error (which grows with the years) where the spacecraft is likely to be found. Then, with a Doppler (*see Glossary*) arrangement technique, one can tell how far away the spacecraft is from Earth at any given time because of the strength of the signal. As it moves away it changes in velocity and actually slows down as it is climbing out of the Sun's gravitational field. We can use that, knowing precisely at which original frequency the receiver-transmitter combination was set. We can tune in on the ground and determine that it has moved over two cycles, for example. If we know how long it has been flying we can compute very precisely where it is. NASA's Jet Propulsion Laboratory can do that within a few tens of miles of distance.

The Voyager spacecraft have sun sensors, which look through a slot in the high-gain antenna dish. These are electro-optical devices that send attitude position error signals to HYPACE (Hybrid Programmable Attitude Control Electronics, the computer language used) which, in turn, signals the appropriate attitude control thruster to fire and turn the spacecraft in the proper direction. Sun lock stabilizes the spacecraft on two axes (pitch and yaw).

The star Canopus, one of the brightest in the galaxy, is the second celestial reference for three-axis stabilization. Two Canopus Star Trackers (*as seen below*) are mounted so that their lines of sight are parallel, and only one is in use at any one time. The star tracker, through HYPACE logic, causes the thrusters to roll the spacecraft about the already fixed Earth or Sun pointed roll axis until the tracker is locked on Canopus. Brightness of the tracker's target star is telemetered to the ground to verify the correct star has been acquired (*see pages 86–91*).

To enhance downlink communications capability, the Sun sensor is electrically biased (offset) by commands from the computer command subsystem to point the roll axis at or as near the Earth as possible. The Sun sensor can be biased plus and minus 20 degrees in both pitch and yaw axes.

Three axis stabilization with celestial reference is the normal attitude control mode for cruise phases between planets.

Honeywell, Inc supplied the Canopus Star Trackers for the Voyagers. Each Voyager had two, mounted side-by-side as redundant systems in the upper part of the Voyager main bodies. The Canopus Star Tracker (*below*) is one of two conventional means of attitude control for interplanetary flights. By fixing on the bright star Canopus, the tracker monitors deviations from this reference point, and serves to correct such via commands to the spacecraft's attitude thrusters. It does this through use of Hybrid Programmable Attitude Control Electronics, or HYPACE, a computer logic by which the attitude thrusters are linked to the star tracker and to the spacecraft's sun sensors (the other means of attitude control). *At right:* An artist's conception of Voyager, with the antenna dish turned out, showing the sun sensor port at right of its central boom.

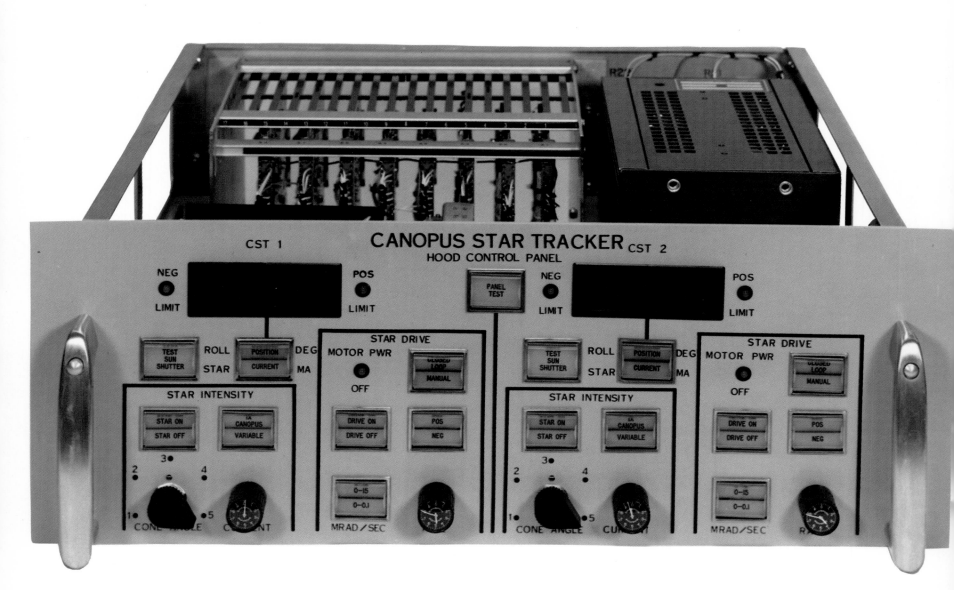

PART FOUR
Communications

A. Overview

Uplink transmission signals to the spacecraft would be limited by the aperture size of its antenna and by its power by distance. Thus, if one puts 100 Kw into a relatively small aperture one could transmit much farther. When receiving the signal, the aperture of this antenna is as important as the sensitivity of the receiver.

The 'uplink' operates at S-band, carrying commands and ranging signals from ground stations to one of a pair of redundant receivers. The 'downlink' is transmitted from the spacecraft at S-band and X-band frequencies. The power requirements for receiving *downlink* transmissions from a two watt transmitter—or even a 20 watt amplified transmitter—out as far as Pluto would make it exceedingly difficult and expensive to build a receiving station. This would not, however, be an insurmountable problem, because anyone who had gone to the work of launching a private enterprise interplanetary spacecraft would have no trouble convincing NASA to listen for that spacecraft with their Deep Space Network (DSN) (*see pages 121–124*).

Specifics depend on how much data this spacecraft would be sending back. For example, because of the five hour telemetry time, during a flyby there is no way to get real time data. One would have to set up a plan ahead of time. After the photos were taken, the computer's onboard memory would have captured as many frames as possible as the spacecraft flew by, and then it would spend whatever time necessary to transmit back to Earth all the video images that were taken.

One could use something significantly smaller than the DSN to send signals *to* the spacecraft because there are very few times when one would want to talk to the spacecraft. It will accelerate to its full velocity within the first 7000 miles and the antennas used to support the launch would certainly be powerful enough to communicate with the spacecraft for the first 20,000 miles. At that stage it's on its way, and the primary computer takes over (*see page 31*). Every 24 hours through the year this computer turns itself on, runs through a check-out routine, collects all the data that's been stored, and pulses all this data down to Earth over a minute's time at precisely midnight (for example) every day. It doesn't necessarily even have to be monitored every day (*see page 112*). One would put out a worldwide call giving the spacecraft's right ascension and declination at any given day of the year, and ask that any antenna free at midnight on any particular day, *and* that happens to have the spacecraft in its sky, to tune in. This is easy to do. It's sort of like getting amateur radio operators to be local listeners. These people would, in turn, take the data and send it back on a postcard.

It's like getting postcards from your spacecraft!

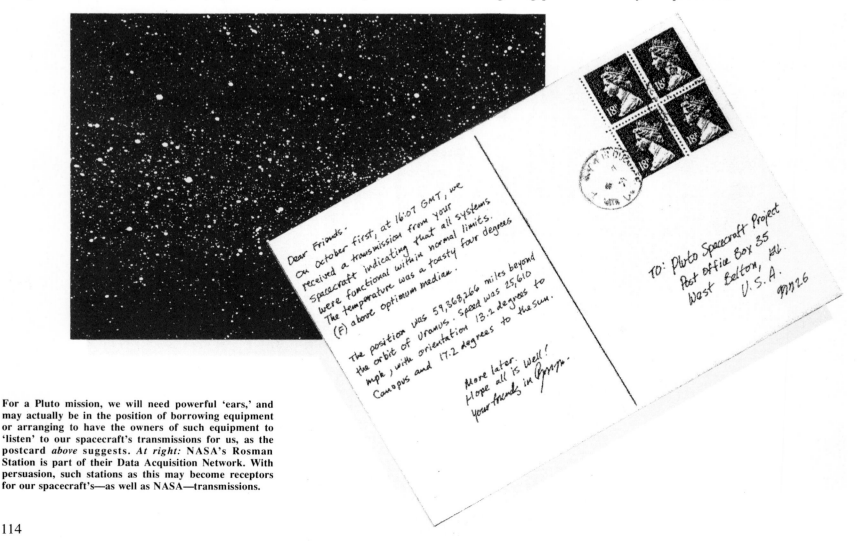

For a Pluto mission, we will need powerful 'ears,' and may actually be in the position of borrowing equipment or arranging to have the owners of such equipment to 'listen' to our spacecraft's transmissions for us, as the postcard *above* suggests. *At right:* NASA's Rosman Station is part of their Data Acquisition Network. With persuasion, such stations as this may become receptors for our spacecraft's—as well as NASA—transmissions.

B. Communicating With Voyager

Prepared by the NASA Jet Propulsion Laboratory

Communications between NASA and its Voyager spacecraft are by radio link between Earth tracking stations and a dual frequency radio system aboard the spacecraft.

The onboard communications system also includes a programmable flight data subsystem (FDS), modulation demodulation subsystem (MDS), data storage subsystem (DSS) and high-gain and low-gain antennas.

The FDS, one of the three onboard computers, controls the science instruments and formats all science and engineering data for telemetering to Earth. The telemetry modulation unit (TMU) of the MDS feeds data to the downlink. The flight command unit of the MDS routes ground commands received by the spacecraft.

Only one receiver is powered at any one time with the redundant receiver at standby. The receiver will operate continuously during the mission at about 2113 MHz. Different frequency ranges have been assigned to the radio frequency subsystems of each spacecraft. The receiver can be used with either the high-gain or low-gain antenna.

The S-band transmitter consists of two redundant exciters and two redundant power amplifiers of which any combination is possible. Only one exciter-amplifier combination operates at any one time.

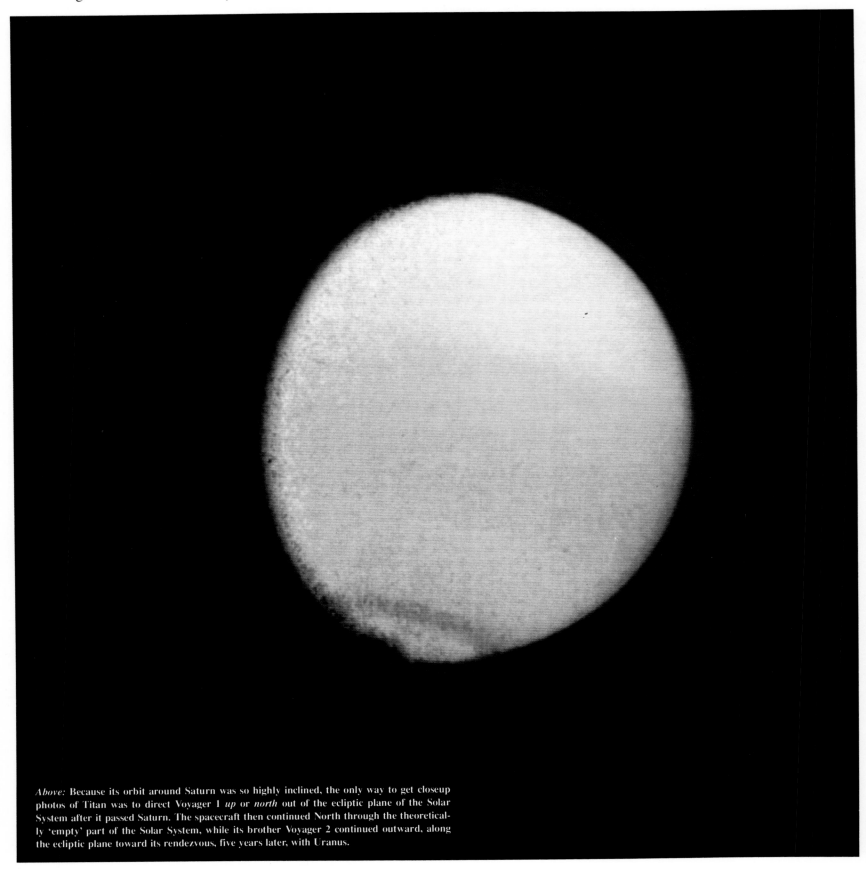

Above: Because its orbit around Saturn was so highly inclined, the only way to get closeup photos of Titan was to direct Voyager 1 *up* or *north* out of the ecliptic plane of the Solar System after it passed Saturn. The spacecraft then continued North through the theoretically 'empty' part of the Solar System, while its brother Voyager 2 continued outward, along the ecliptic plane toward its rendezvous, five years later, with Uranus.

Selection of the combination will be by onboard failure detection logic within the computer command subsystem (CCS), with ground command backup. The same arrangement of exciter-amplifier combinations makes up the X-band transmitting unit (*see pages 86–91*).

One S-band and both X-band amplifiers employ traveling wave tubes (TWT). The second S-band unit is a solid-state amplifier. The S-band transmitter is capable of operating at 9.4 watts or at 28.3 watts when switched to high power and can radiate from both antennas. X-band power output is 12 watts and 21.3 watts. X-band uses only the high-gain antenna. (S-band and X-band will never operate at high power simultaneously.)

When no uplink signal is being received, the transmitted S-band frequency of about 2295 MHz and X-band frequency of 8418 MHz originate in the S-band exciter's auxiliary oscillator or in a separate ultra stable oscillator (one-way tracking). With the receiver phase-locked to an uplink signal, the receiver provides the frequency source for both transmitters (two-way tracking). The radio system can also operate with the receiver locked to an uplink signal while the downlink carrier frequencies are determined by the onboard oscillators (two-way noncoherent tracking).

When Voyager was launched, only the 210-foot antenna stations of the Deep Space Network could receive the downlink X-band signal. Both these and the 85-foot antenna stations are capable of receiving at S-band.

Communications during launch, near-Earth and early cruise phase operations were confined to S-band and the low-gain antenna. An exception occurred during the first week of flight when the spacecraft, on inertial control, pointed the high-gain antenna toward Earth to support instrument calibration and an optical navigation high-rate telecommunications link test.

The high-gain antenna, with a 12 foot diameter parabolic reflector, provides a highly directional beam. The low-gain antenna provides essentially uniform coverage in the direction of Earth.

Under normal conditions after the first 80 days of the mission, all communications—both S-band and X-band—are via the high-gain antenna. X-band is turned off, however, and the S-band transmitter

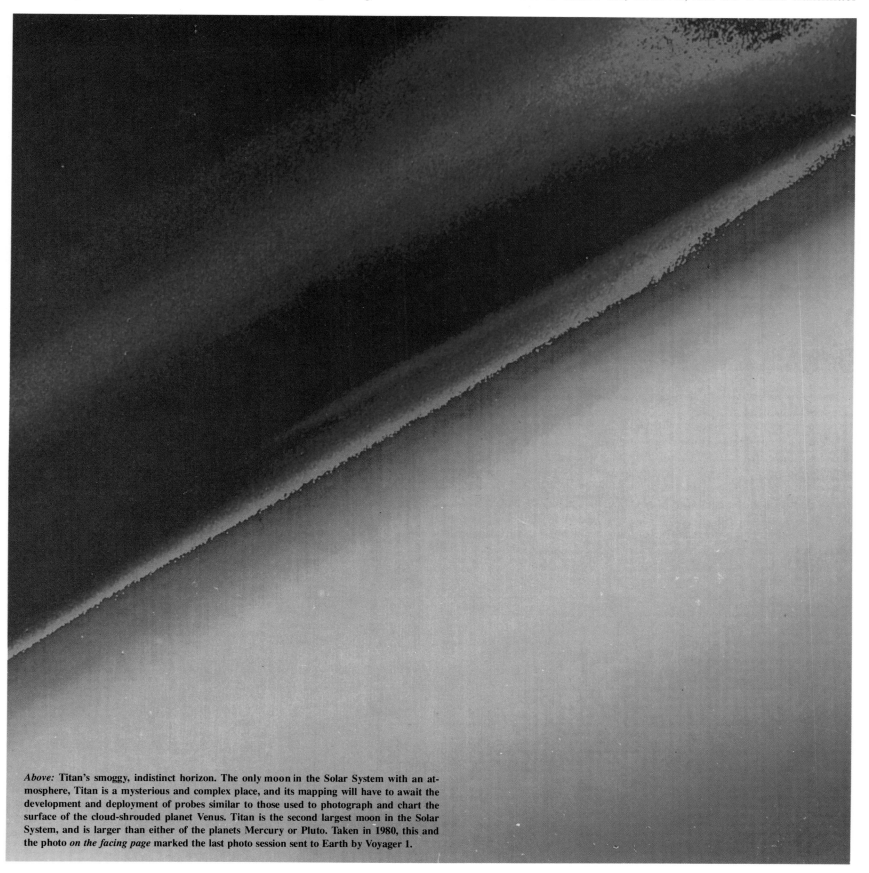

Above: Titan's smoggy, indistinct horizon. The only moon in the Solar System with an atmosphere, Titan is a mysterious and complex place, and its mapping will have to await the development and deployment of probes similar to those used to photograph and chart the surface of the cloud-shrouded planet Venus. Titan is the second largest moon in the Solar System, and is larger than either of the planets Mercury or Pluto. Taken in 1980, this and the photo *on the facing page* marked the last photo session sent to Earth by Voyager 1.

and receiver are switched to the low-gain antenna during periodic science maneuvers and trajectory correction maneuvers.

The S-band downlink is always on, operating at high power during maneuvers or during the cruise phase only when the DSN stations with 85 foot antennas are tracking low power whenever X-band is on. At Saturn, both S-band and X-band transmitters will be at low power when gyros and tape recorder are on simultaneously.

Uplink Telemetry

Ground commands are used to put into execution selected flight sequences or to cope with unexpected events. Commands can be issued in either a predetermined timed sequence via onboard program control or directly as received from the ground. Most commands will be issued by the spacecraft's computer command subsystem (CCS) in its role as 'sequencer of events' and by the flight data subsystem (FDS) as controller of the science instruments (*see page 32*).

All communications between spacecraft and Earth are in digital form. Command signals, transmitted at 16 bits per second (bps) to the spacecraft are detected in the flight command unit and routed to the CCS for further routing to their proper destination. Ground commands to the spacecraft fall into two major categories: discrete commands and coded commands.

A discrete command causes a single action on the spacecraft. For example, DC-2D switches the S-band amplifier to high high power; DC-2DR, S-band amplifier low power; DC-2E, S-band radiates from high-gain antenna; DC-2ER, S-band transmits low-gain. Coded commands are the transfer of digital data from the computer command system or from the ground via the CCS to user subsystems. Subsystems receiving coded commands are flight data, attitude and articulation control, modulation-demodulation, data storage and power.

Ground commands back up all critical spacecraft functions which, in a standard mission, are initiated automatically by onboard logic. Command modulation will be off during science maneuvers and trajectory correction maneuvers unless a spacecraft emergency arises.

Downlink Telemetry

Data telemetered from the spacecraft consists of engineering and science measurements prepared for transmission by the flight data subsystem, telemetry modulation unit and data storage subsystem. The encoded information indicates voltages, pressures, temperatures, television pictures and other values measured by the spacecraft telemetry sensors and science instruments.

Two telemetry channels—low rate and high rate—are provided for the transmission of spacecraft data. The low rate channel functions only at S-band at a single 40 bits per second data rate and contains real time engineering data exclusively. It is on only during planetary encounters when the high rate channel is operating at X-band.

The high rate channel which is on throughout the mission, operates at either S-band or X-band and contains the following types of data:

- ◆ Engineering only at 40 bps or 1200 bps (the rate usually occurs only during launch and trajectory correction maneuvers) transmitted at S-band only.
- ◆ Real-time cruise science and engineering at 2560, 1280, 640, 320, 160 and 80bps transmitted at S-band only.
- ◆ Real time encounter general science and engineering at 7.2 kilobits per second (a special 115.2 kbps rate was available for brief periods at Jupiter for the planetary radio astronomy and plasma wave instruments) transmitted at X-band only.
- ◆ Real time encounter general science, engineering and television at 115.2, 89.6, 67.2, 44.8, 29.9, and 19.2 kbps transmitted at X-band only.
- ◆ Real time encounter general science and engineering, plus tape recorder playback, at 67.2, 44.8 and 29.9 kbps transmitted at X-band only.
- ◆ Play back recorded data only at 21.6 and 7.2 kbps transmitted at X-band only.

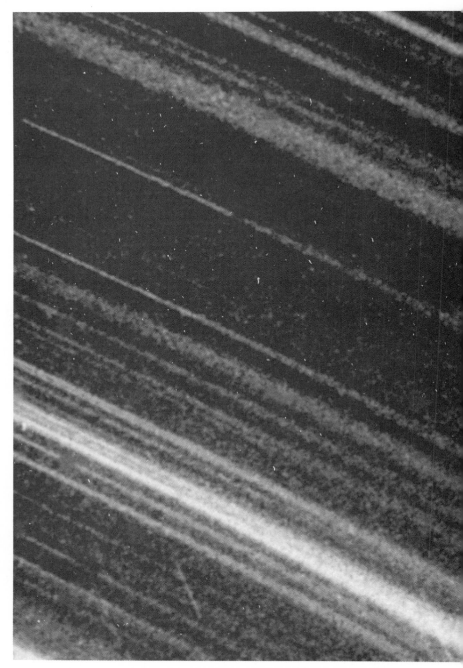

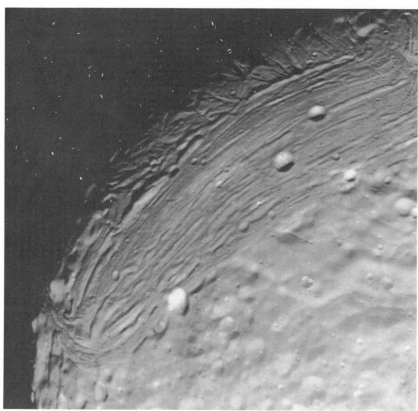

Voyager 2 was commanded to maneuver in such a way that the very dark Uranian rings were lit from behind by starlight (*at top*). Voyager 2's flight team devised a technique that allowed the spacecraft to drift and 'track' its camera target. The result was the astonishing high resolution photos of the Uranian moon Miranda seen *above, at right* and *at far right*. Voyager was maneuvered as near to Miranda as 18,730 miles for these views.

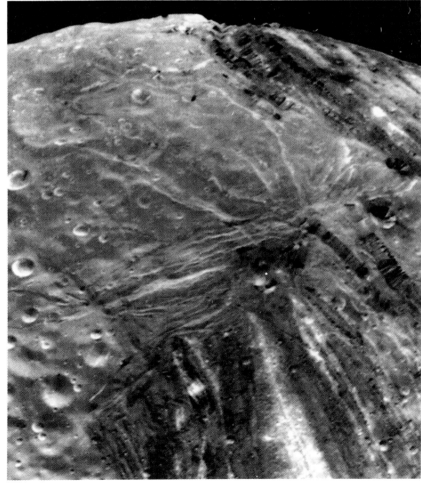

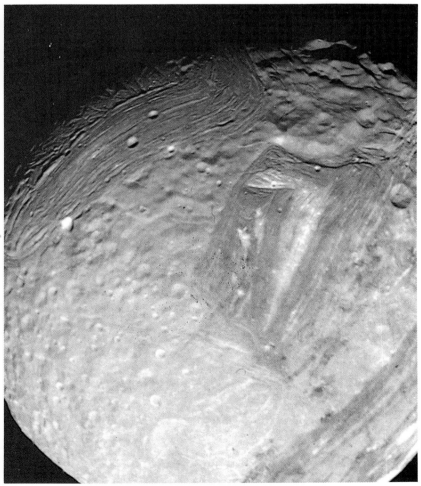

◆ Memory data stored in the three onboard computers—CCS, FDS and AACS—read out and played back at 40 or 1200 bps transmitted at either S-band or X-band (treated as engineering data).

The numerous data rates for each type of telemetered information are required by the changing length of the telecommunications link with Earth and the possible adverse effects of Earth weather upon reception of X-band radio signals. The S-band cruise science primary telemetry rate is 2.560 bps. Lesser rates result in reduced instrument sampling and will be used only when the telecommunications link cannot support the higher rate.

In order to allow real time transmission of video information at each encounter, the flight data subsystem handles the imaging data at six downlink rates from 115.2 to 19.2 kbps. The 115.2 kbps rate represents the standard full frame readout at 48 seconds per frame of the TV vidicon. Full frame, full resolution TV from Saturn was obtained by increasing the frame readout time to 144 seconds (3:1 slow scan) and transmitting the data at 44.8 kbps. A number of other slow scan and frame edit options are available to match the capability of the telecommunications link.

The data storage subsystem can record at two rates: TV pictures, general science and engineering at 115.2 kbps; general science and engineering only at 7.2 kbps (engineering is acquired at only 1200 bps, but is formatted with filler to match the recorder input rate).

The tape transport is belt driven. Its 1/2-inch magnetic tape is 1075 feet long and is divided into eight tracks which are recorded sequentially one track at a time. Total recyclable storage capacity is about 536 million bits—the equivalent of 100 TV pictures. Playback is at four speeds: 57.6, 33.6, 21.6 and 7.2 kbps.

Tracking the Spacecraft

To achieve the desired maneuver and flyby accuracies for a multiplanet/satellite encounter mission, very precise navigation is required.

To provide the standard Doppler tracking data, the S-band signal transmitted from Earth is received at the spacecraft, changed in frequency by a known ratio and retransmitted to Earth. It is possible to precisely determine the transmitted downlink frequency while measuring the Doppler shifted received signal, thereby measuring spacecraft velocity. This is called coherent two-way tracking. One-way tracking is when no uplink signal is received and the downlink carrier frequency is provided by an onboard oscillator. Noncoherent two-way tracking occurs when uplink and downlink carriers are operating independently (*see following section*).

C. The NASA Deep Space Network

Prepared by the NASA Jet Propulsion Laboratory

The NASA Deep Space Network is a worldwide system for navigating, tracking and communicating with spacecraft exploring the Solar System. The JPL-managed network of antennas is the link to distant spacecraft, transmitting instructions to them and receiving the data they return to Earth from deep space.

The DSN is a vital element in every space flight project. It is the communications link that ties the sophisticated instruments of the spacecraft to the scientific labs on Earth. The Jet Propulsion Laboratory of the California Institute of Technology pioneered the development of many of the critical elements of communications systems designed to function over the vast distances involved in planetary missions.

The DSN evolved from tracking and data recovery techniques which developed in JPL's missile work for the US Army during the 1950s. In 1958, the Laboratory established a three-station network of receiving stations to gather data from the first US satellite, Explorer 1.

The DSN uses large antennas, low-noise receivers and high-power transmitters at locations strategically located on three continents. It has grown to include 12 deep-space antenna stations in a global network. The three Deep Space Communications Complexes (DSCC's) are located at Goldstone in Southern California's Mojave Desert (DSCC 14); near Madrid, Spain (DSCC 63); and near Canberra, Australia (DSCC 43). The three locations are approximately 120 degrees apart in longitude so that as the Earth turns on its axis, a distant spacecraft is almost always in view of one of the stations. The Network Operations Control Center (NOCC) at JPL controls and monitors operations at the three complexes. The DSN Ground Communications Facility (GCF) provides the communications circuits that link the complexes and the NOCC together.

Below: A computer conception of Voyager 2's overflight of the Saturn ring system, which involved a planetary eclipse, blocking transmissions to Earth, and a 15-millisecond rocket burn—that set Voyager on its Uranus trajectory—which was programmed via directive from Earth. *Facing page:* conception of Voyager 2's closest Saturn approach.

For all of NASA's unmanned missions in deep space, the DSN provides the tracking information on course and direction of the flight, velocity and range from Earth. The DSN also assists other nations in tracking their unmanned scientific spacecraft. It receives engineering and science telemetry and sends commands for spacecraft navigation and scientific instrument operations. All data are forwarded to the appropriate mission control center, either at JPL or another location.

Each complex is equipped with a 210 foot diameter antenna station, soon to be improved in sensitivity by extending the diameter to 230 feet. In addition each complex has an 85 foot antenna and two 112 foot antennas. One of the 112 foot antennas at each of two of the complexes is a new high-efficiency antenna that provides improved telemetry performance needed for outer planet missions. The

complexes at Goldstone and Canberra have the new antennas and the third was completed at the Madrid facility in October 1987.

Different sized antennas have different communications capabilities. The 210 foot antennas, the most sensitive, support deep space missions; the 85 foot antennas support selected spacecraft in Earth orbit, and the 112 foot antennas are used to support both types of missions.

The 112 and 210 foot stations are remotely operated from a centralized signal processing center that houses the electronic subsystems that point and control the antennas, receive and process the telemetry, generate and transmit commands, and produce the spacecraft navigation data. The 85 foot stations have not yet been equipped for unattended operation. In addition to the giant antennas, each of the stations is equipped with transmitting, receiving, data handling and inter-station communications equipment.

The complexes can be teamed for scientific investigations with such techniques as very long baseline interferometry (VLBI), in which measurements made by two or more widely spaced antennas

Below: **This Tracking and Data Relay Satellite System (TDRSS) spacecraft is part of the complex and massive DSN network which has grown up around the world. Note that this TDRSS has two kinds of antennas, and two of each kind! These systems could be used to help relay telemetry from another craft in deep space.**

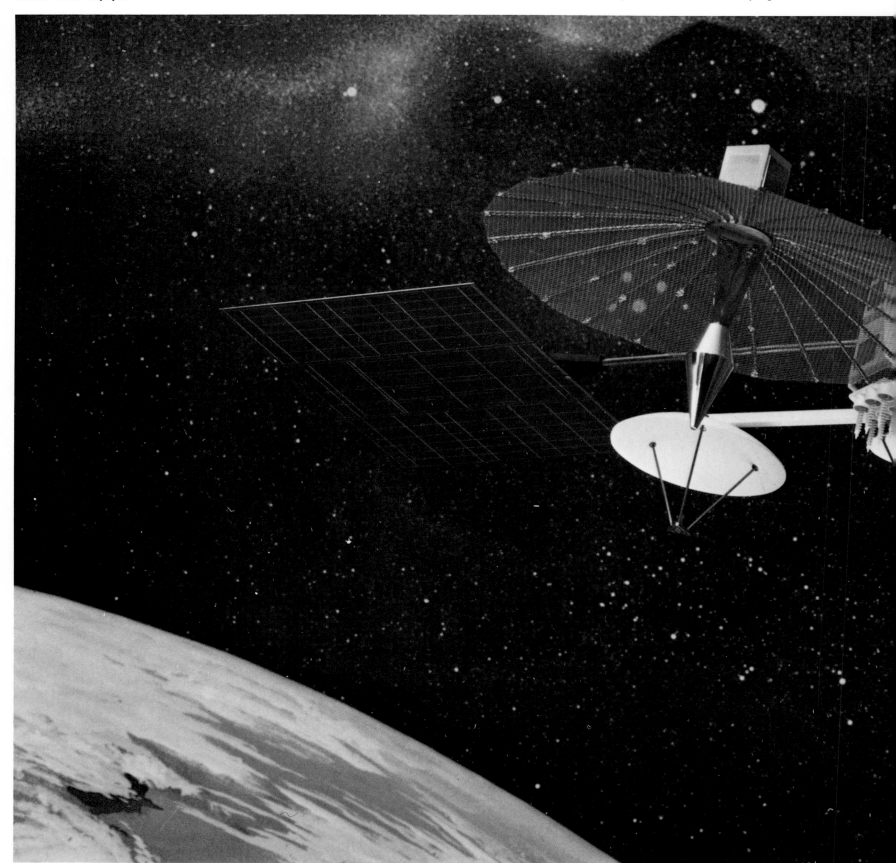

can be combined to obtain the resolving power of one giant antenna theoretically spanning the distance between them. Relatively new applications of the technique—such as mobile VLBI antennas for geodetic measurements and delta VLBI for measuring very slight advances in the Earth's crust—promise further advances.

Communication with spacecraft in deep space will always be DSN's primary focus, but the network also has assumed responsibility for all Earth-orbiting satellites that are not compatible with NASA's new Tracking and Data Relay Satellite System (TDRSS). In addition, DSN will provide launch and transfer orbit support to a variety of spacecraft bound for geosynchronous orbit, and emergency support for the tracking satellites themselves and for other spacecraft that would normally communicate through TDRSS.

The network also is a scientific instrument and has been used for many radio science experiments: probing natural radio sources—pulsars and quasars; planetary radar studies of planet surfaces and Saturn's rings; celestial mechanics experiments, some involving testing the theories of relativity; lunar gravity experiments; and Earth

physics experiments. One of the most dramatic of the non-flight experiments for the DSN is the Search for Extraterrestrial Intelligence.

The DSN Ground Communications Facility controls the circuits that link the three DSN complexes to the Network Operations Control Center at JPL, and to the flight project centers in the United States and overseas. The traffic between the various locations is sent via land lines, submarine cable, terrestrial microwave and communications satellites. The circuits are leased from common carriers and provided to the GCF as needed by the NASA Communications Network (NASCOM), which is located at the NASA Goddard Space Flight Center. Spacecraft data sent over the lines are automatically checked for transmission errors and outages by NASCOM error detecting and correcting techniques.

The Voyager 2 encounter with Uranus in early 1986 presented a serious challenge in deep space communications, as will the spacecraft's 1989 encounter with even more distant Neptune. During the Neptune encounter, Voyager 2's X-band radio signal will be less than one-tenth as strong as it was at Jupiter in 1979 and less than

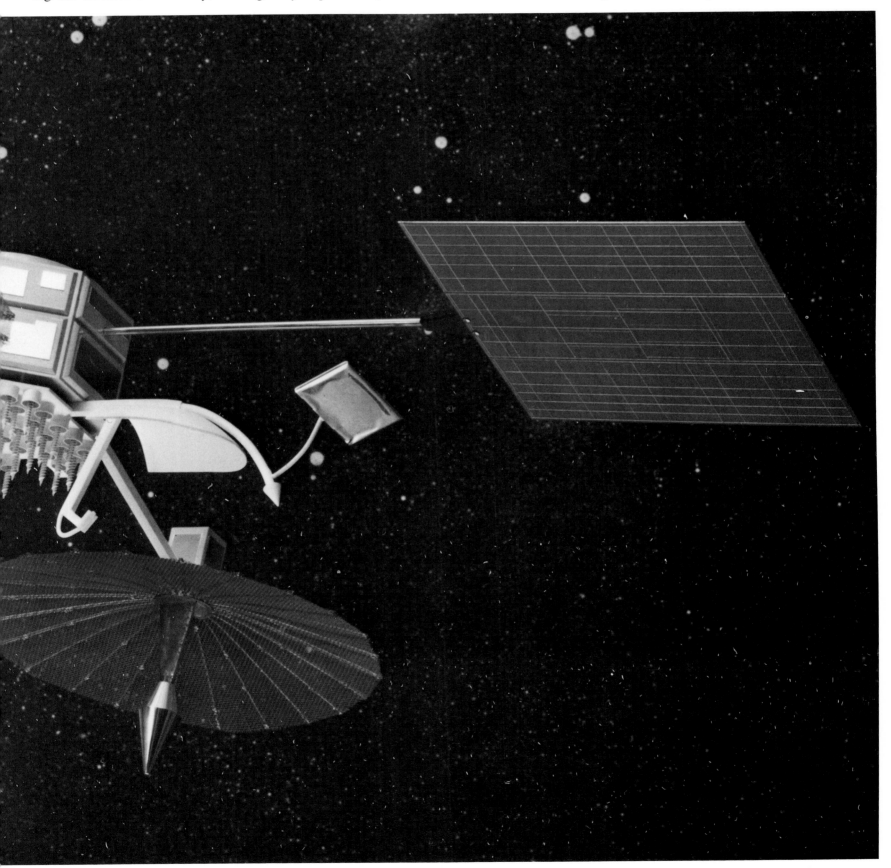

one-half as strong as it was at Uranus in 1986. The weaker signal strength required that data be sent at a lower rate from the spacecraft to be received clearly at the ground stations.

At Saturn, which is 10 times the distance from the Sun as is the Earth, or 10 AU (Astronomical Unit, the average distance of the Earth from the Sun, 93 million miles), the maximum data rate supportable by the signal-to-noise ratio was 44,000 bits per second. At Uranus, which is 19 AU distant, there was a reduction to only 21,600 bits per second because the arraying of several DSN tracking antennas, combined with the Australian government-owned Parkes radio astronomy 64 meter antenna, allowed scientists to arrest the natural fall of the signal to only half—instead of one-fourth—when Voyager 2 reached Uranus.

During the 1989 Neptune encounter, the DSN will again be joined by the Parkes Radio Telescope and by the National Radio Astronomy Observatory's Very Large Array (VLA) near Socorro, New Mexico.

Simultaneously with the routing to the control center of the spacecraft telemetry, distance and speed information are generated by the DSN and transmitted to the control center for spacecraft navigation.

Commands are sent from the control center to one of the DSN stations where they are loaded in a command processing computer, automatically verified for accuracy, and transmitted to the proper spacecraft.

The DSN has provided tracking and data acquisition support to the Ranger, Surveyor and Lunar Orbiter Moon exploration projects, the Mariner series of missions to Mars, Venus and Mercury; the pioneer Venus and Jupiter and Saturn flights; the joint US-West Germany Helios sun-orbiting probes, the second of which reached the end of its 10-year mission in early 1986; and supplementary support to the Manned Space Flight Network for the Apollo lunar landing program.

The network currently supports the sun-orbiting Pioneers 6 through 9; Pioneers 10 and 11 which are now beyond the orbit of Pluto; Voyager 1, which is seeking the outer boundary of the Sun's influence; Voyager 2 on a trajectory toward Neptune; the ICE spacecraft, which earlier explored the comet Giacobini-Zinner; Nimbus 7, a weather satellite used for oceanography and pollution monitoring; and ISEE 1 and 2, the International Sun-Earth Explorers that study the ways the Sun controls the Earth's immediate space environment.

The DSN also supported the international spacecraft armada to Halley's Comet in March 1986 that included two Vega spacecraft launched by the Soviet Union, two Japanese spacecraft and Giotto, launched by the European Space Agency.

After traveling across interplanetary space, the spacecraft signal that reaches a DSN antenna ranges in power from a billionth of a watt down to a billionth of one trillionth of a watt. New technology continually contributes to the DSN's ability to communicate with distant spacecraft.

In 1965, the DSN established a communications distance record of about 250 million miles with Mariner 4, America's first spacecraft to Mars (*see pages 14–15*). Pioneer 10, launched in 1972, was the first targeted beyond the orbit of Mars. It flew past Jupiter in December 1973, and departed the outer limits of the Sun's influence in 1987 (*see Figure 58*). It is anticipated that Voyager 1 and 2, with more powerful transmitters, X-band downlink and larger antennas, may be tracked beyond the limits of the Solar System. Should they continue to operate through the late 1980s, the Voyagers will be sending data across a range of 30 to 40 AU—2.8 billion to 3.7 billion miles (*see pages 86–91, 128*).

From the Australian Outback to the Outback of the Solar System. *Below:* **These Deep Space Network tracking antennas in rural Australia monitor the Voyagers in and beyond the Solar System—and search out deep space quasars; they are certainly able to monitor our Pluto mission. The Orion Nebula** *(at right)***, 215 light years from Earth, helps to illustrate what 'deep space' is: Voyager 2 will have spent 12 years reaching Neptune in 1989; it would have to travel for an additional *924,672* years to reach the Orion Nebula!**

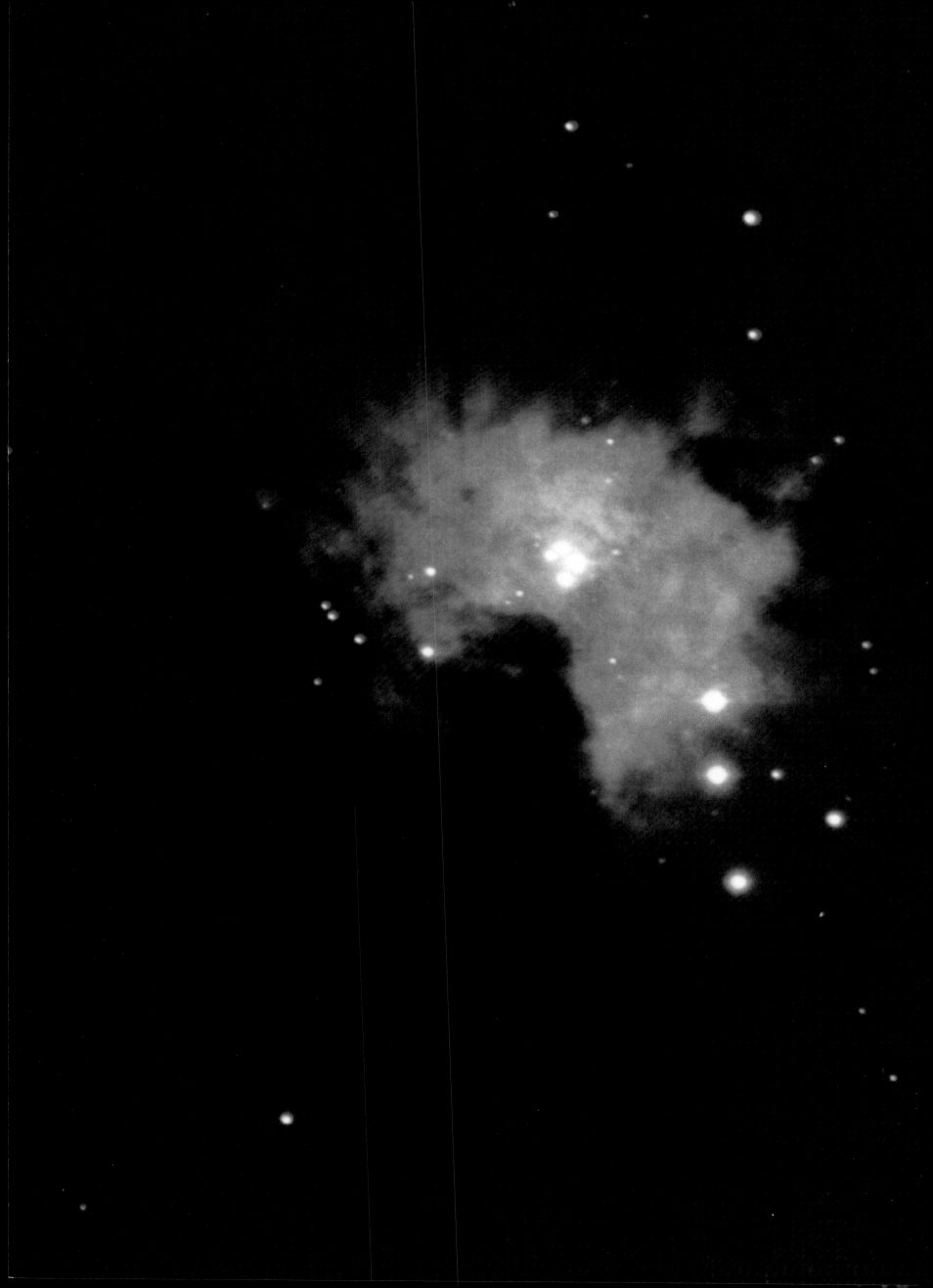

Index

Acronyms and Abbreviations

AACS – Attitude and Articulation Control Subsystem
AIMP – Anchored Interplanetary Monitoring
AT&T – American Telephone & Telegraph
AU – Astronomical Unit (= 93 million miles)
CCD – Charge Coupled Device
CCM – Continuous Channel Multipliers
CCS – Computer Command Subsystems
CRES – Cosmic Ray Energy Spectra
Delta V – see page 100
DSCC – Deep Space Communications Complexes
DSI – 94
DSN – Deep Space Network
DSS – Data Storage Subsystem
DSS – DSN Station (same as DSCC)
 DSS 14 – DSCC Goldstone, California
 DSS 43 – DSCC Canberra, Australia
 DSS 63 – DSCC Madrid, Spain
ERDA – US Energy Research & Development Administration
EST – Eastern Standard Time
eV – Electron Volts
FDS – Flight Data Subsystem
G/A – Gravity Assist
GCF – Ground Communications Facility
GTT – Geiger Tube Telescope
He – Helium
HYPACE – Hybrid Programmable Attitude
Hz – Hertz
 Control Electronics
IRIS – Infrared Spectroscopy and Radiometry Investigation
IRR – Infrared Radiometer
IRS – Infrared Spectrometer
ISEE – International Sun-Earth Explorers
ISI – Imaging Science Investigation
JPL – NASA's Jet Propulsion Laboratory (Pasadena, Ca)
JR – Jupiter Radii
JSP – Jupiter-Saturn-Pluto Mission
JUN – Jupiter-Uranus-Neptune Mission

Kbps – Kilobits per second
KeV – Thousand Electron Volts
kHz – Kilohertz
Kw – Kilowatt
LAN – Lithium anode thermal cell (*see page 78*)
LECP – Low Energy Charged Particle unit
LO_2, LOX – Liquid oxygen
MDS – Modulation Demodulation Subsystem
MeV – Million Electron Volts
MIRIS – Modified IRIS
MJS – Mariner-Jupiter-Saturn mission
MJU – Mariner-Jupiter-Uranus mission
MSFN – Manned Space Flight Network
N_2H_2 – Hydrazine (propellant)
N_2O_4 – Nitrogen tetroxide (oxydizer)
NASA – National Aeronautics & Space Administration
NASCOM – NASA Communications Network
nicad – nickel cadmium batteries
NOCC – Network Operations Control Center
NRAOVLA – National Radio Astronomy Observatory Very Large Array
PDSI – Particles and Dust in Space Investigation

PRA – Planetary Radio Astronomy
psi – Pounds per Square Inch
PTR – Planetary Trapped Radiation
PWS – Plasma-Wave Instrument
RDM – Remote Driver Module
RHU – Radioisotope Heating Units
RSI – Radio Science Investigation
RTG – Radioisotope Thermoelectric Generators
STAR – Self-Test-and-Repair Computer
TCM – Trajectory Correction Maneuvers

TDRSS – Tracking & Data Delay Satellite System
TMU – Telemetry Modulation Unit
TOPS – Thermoelectric Outer Planets Spacecraft
TRW – The Thompson Rado Woolridge Company
TWT – Traveling Wave Tubes
USAF – US Air Force
UV – Ultraviolet
VLA – Very Large Array
VLBI – Very Long Baseline Interferometry

Glossary

Cassegrainian telescope: A linear reflector type instrument set up in such a way that the eyepiece is situated behind the primary (large) mirror and a secondary (small) mirror is suspended face down, over the concave face of the primary. Light passes down the telescope tube, strikes the primary mirror, is reflected upward onto the secondary mirror, which then concentrates the light and focuses it down the hole in the primary to the eyepiece.

Doppler effect (also 'train whistle' effect): Refers to the phenomenon whereby one can tell if an object is getting nearer or farther away without actually seeing it by the use of waves, such as sound waves. For instance, when a train approaches a station, an observer out of sight of the station cannot see the train, but he knows it is approaching because its whistle becomes louder; as the whistle fades, the observer can surmise that the train is getting farther away.

geosynchronous: The type of artificial satellite which travels above the equator at the same speed as the earth rotates, so that the satellite seems to remain in the same place.

gyroscope: A wheel or disk mounted to spin rapidly about an axis, and is also free to rotate about one or both of two axes perpendicular to each other, *and* to the axis of spin. A rotation of one of the two mutually perpendicular axes results from application of torque to the other when the wheel is spinning, so that the entire apparatus offers considerable opposition depending on the angular momentum to any torque that would change the direction of the axis of spin.

Kapton: A trade name for polypyromellitimide (PPMI), a material (used in this case for a thermal blanket) with exceptional resistance to thermal degradation, great mechanical strength and stability at both very high and very low temperatures, and ductility even at cryogenic temperatures (*see page 80*).

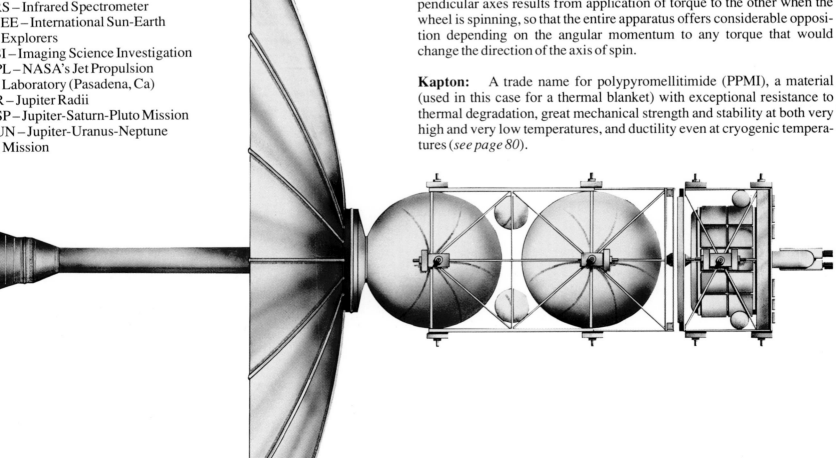

Shown here is a view of the Spiral 'Black-Eye' Galaxy in Coma Berenices, located the relatively short distance of 13 million light years from Earth (compare to 215 light years for the Orion Nebula pictured on page 125). A light year is equal to 10,752 AU, and an interplanetary spacecraft such as Voyager covers about 2.5 AU (232,500,000 miles) annually, so it is easy, albeit staggering, to ponder the vast difference between *interplanetary* and *interstellar* distances.

By 1996, Voyager will reach the edge of the Solar System—the heliopause—the magnetosphere-like dynamic boundary between the solar wind and the onrushing interstellar medium, a place and phenomena not currently fully understood. Fifty years, and more than 100 AU later, Voyager's faint transmissions will no longer be audible to the DSN as currently configured, although the spacecraft itself will continue to be capable of transmitting indefinitely. Stay tuned.